Integrated Approaches to Drug and Alcohol Problems

Action on Addiction

Edited by
Willm Mistral

Routledge
Taylor & Francis Group
LONDON AND NEW YORK

First published 2016
by Routledge
2 Park Square, Milton Park, Abingdon, Oxon OX14 4RN

and by Routledge
605 Third Avenue, New York, NY 10017

Routledge is an imprint of the Taylor & Francis Group, an informa business

British Library Cataloguing in Publication Data
A catalogue record for this book is available from the British Library

Library of Congress Cataloging in Publication Data
Names: Mistral, Willm, editor.
Title: Integrated approaches to drug and alcohol problems : action on addiction / edited by Willm Mistral.
Description: Abingdon, Oxon ; New York, NY : Routledge, 2016. | Includes bibliographical references.
Identifiers: LCCN 2015039177| ISBN 9781138854376 (hbk) | ISBN 9781138854383 (pbk) | ISBN 9781315714226 (ebk)
Subjects: | MESH: Substance-Related Disorders—psychology. | Substance-Related Disorders—therapy. | Behavior, Addictive. | Delivery of Health Care, Integrated—methods.
Classification: LCC RC564 | NLM WM 270 | DDC 616.86/0651—dc23
LC record available at http://lccn.loc.gov/2015039177

ISBN: 978-1-138-85437-6 (hbk)
ISBN: 978-1-138-85438-3 (pbk)
ISBN: 978-1-315-71422-6 (ebk)

Typeset in Times New Roman
by Swales & Willis Ltd, Exeter, Devon, UK

Contents

Figures

Contributors

Devin Ashwood

Programme leader and lecturer on the degree programme in addiction counselling for Action on Addiction and the University of Bath. Devin has worked therapeutically in a range of substance misuse settings, specialising in cognitive therapy, interpersonal group therapy and mindfulness, as well as training mindfulness-based teachers.

Nick Barton

Nick Barton MA was Chief Executive of Action on Addiction from 2008 to 2015. He has advised governments on treatment delivery, family support and workforce development. He co-founded the European Association for the Treatment of Addiction, which he chaired for eight years, and drafted some of the first treatment standards adopted in the UK. He is currently a trustee of the domestic abuse charity Safe Lives. In 2008 he was awarded an Honorary Doctorate of Health by the University of Bath for his contribution to the addiction field. He has written numerous articles on addiction related matters.

Brandon G Bergman

Dr Bergman is a research scientist at the Massachusetts General Hospital/Harvard Medical School (MGH/HMS) Recovery Research Institute, and a staff psychologist in the hospital's Addiction Recovery Management Service. He also serves nationally in the USA as the secretary for the American Psychological Association Society of Addiction Psychology. His work has been recognised by the National Institute on Drug Abuse (NIDA), and the Research Society on Alcoholism (RSA). For publications see https://www.researchgate.net/profile/Brandon_Bergman.

Patricia J Conrod

Research professor, Psychiatry department, Université de Montréal, Québec, Canada; Senior Lecturer and Consultant Clinical Psychologist, Department of

Psychological Medicine and Psychiatry, Institute of Psychiatry, King's College London UK; Clinical Psychologist, Ordre des Psychologues du Québec, Canada. Professor Conrod's research focuses on cognitive, personality and biological risk factors for the development and maintenance of drug misuse, and factors that mediate the co-occurrence of addictive behaviours with other mental disorders. For publications see https://www.researchgate.net/profile/Patricia_Conrod.

Ed Day

Dr Day is a Senior Lecturer at the National Addiction Centre, King's College London, and a Consultant in Addiction Psychiatry with Birmingham and Solihull Mental Health NHS Trust. His work is split between clinical research and teaching at King's and clinical practice in a drug treatment team in Solihull, England. Much of his research focuses on developing and testing medication or psychosocial interventions for tackling addiction. He is currently the Vice President of the Society for the Study of Addiction. For publications see https://www.researchgate.net/profile/Ed_Day.

Kirby Gregory

Kirby is Treatment and Care Director, Action on Addiction. He has worked in the addiction field since 1990, in first and second stage residential treatment centres, as a counsellor, supervisor, manager and director. He trained as a counsellor to Post Graduate Diploma level and is a Cognitive Analytic Psychotherapist and an Association of Cognitive Analytic Therapy Accredited Supervisor. He has contributed to expert groups for the UK National Treatment Agency.

Rhian Hills

Dr Hills is a Senior Policy Advisor for Substance Misuse within the Welsh Government, and national lead on the take-home naloxone project in Wales. Rhian holds an MSc in Child Protection and Substance Misuse, and a PhD in Criminology. She has worked in substance misuse since 1997 and has experience in community and prison work as well as commissioning. She currently also has responsibility for the development of other key areas in Wales, including harm reduction, overdose, recovery, over-the-counter and prescription-only medications, and the National Drug and Alcohol Helpline.

Kirsten Horsburgh

Kirsten Horsburgh is the National Naloxone Coordinator at Scottish Drugs Forum. She has a background in mental health nursing and is currently responsible for coordinating the Scottish Government's National Naloxone Programme which includes membership of several national groups: the National Forum on

Drug-Related Deaths; National Naloxone Advisory Group; Scottish Naloxone Network; National Prisoner Healthcare Network Expert Advisory Group for Medicines; and Scottish Needle Exchange Workers' Forum. She was also part of the WHO Guidelines Development Group for the Community Management of Opioid Overdose.

Carole Hunter

Dr Hunter is Lead Pharmacist and member of the management team for Addiction Services in NHS Greater Glasgow and Clyde. She has been in this post since 2003 and has previous experience in community pharmacy. She was a member of Scotland's Drug Strategy Delivery Commission and is a member of the National Forum on Drug-Related Deaths, Scottish Specialist Pharmacists in Substance Misuse group, and is Chair of the National Naloxone Advisory Group. For publications see https://www.researchgate.net/profile/Carole_Hunter2.

Mandip Jheeta

Dr Mandip Jheeta is a Specialist Registrar in General Psychiatry in Birmingham and Solihull, England. He has interests in substance misuse and forensic psychiatry, allergy recording on drug charts, knowledge of and attitudes to childhood vaccination in Asia and Africa. He is actively involved in medical education, volunteering and international psychiatry.

John F Kelly

Dr Kelly is Past President of the Society of Addiction Psychology, American Psychological Association; Elizabeth R Spallin Associate Professor of Psychiatry in Addiction Medicine at Harvard Medical School; Program Director of the Addiction Recovery Management Service and Director of the Recovery Research Institute at Massachusetts General Hospital. He is a licensed clinical psychologist specialising in treatment of alcohol and other drug addiction, and has served as a consultant to the White House Office of National Drug Control Policy and the Substance Abuse and Mental Health Services Administration (SAMHSA). For publications see https://www.researchgate.net/profile/John_Kelly15.

Tim Leighton

Tim is a UKCP registered Cognitive Analytic Psychotherapist, accredited trainer and supervisor. In 1988 he launched a further education diploma in Addictions Counselling, and then designed a postgraduate diploma for Guy's and St Thomas' hospitals, London. His long-term ambition to create a degree level course was realised in 2004 in partnership with the University of Bath, with the foundation degree and BSc (Hons) in Addictions Counselling. He was director of the

Centre for Addiction Treatment Studies, Warminster, England, 2008–2014, and is currently Director of Professional Education and Research at Action on Addiction.

Geri Lettle

Geri had a long history of addiction to both drugs and alcohol, which impacted disastrously on her own life and on those close to her. However, with the right motivation, and an integrated approach to treatment and aftercare, she is now in recovery and forging a career working with people who continue to have problems with addictive behaviours.

Andrew McAuley

Andrew McAuley is a Senior Epidemiologist in the Sexual Health and Blood Borne Virus Team at Health Protection Scotland, and an Honorary Senior Research Fellow within the School of Health and Life Sciences at Glasgow Caledonian University. He has worked in the NHS since 2001, specifically in the addictions research field since 2005. He is a member of the independent National Forum on Drug-Related Deaths and the National Naloxone Advisory Group. For publications see https://www.researchgate.net/profile/Andrew_Mcauley.

Rebecca McDonald

Rebecca McDonald is a PhD Student at the Addictions Department at King's College London, UK. Her doctoral research examines novel injection-free naloxone formulations. Her employer, King's College London, is registering intellectual property on a new product with which Rebecca is involved. Rebecca's academic background is in clinical psychology and neuroscience. She previously worked as Senior Research Assistant at the National Center on Addiction and Substance Abuse at Columbia University, USA. Rebecca served as consultant on the development of the WHO guidelines for the Community Management of Opioid Overdose. For publications see https://www.researchgate.net/profile/Rebecca_Mcdonald4.

Willm Mistral

For many years Dr Mistral managed a research team focused on alcohol, drug and mental health problems. He has been an honorary senior research fellow at the University of Bath, England, and link academic advisor for the University and Action on Addiction on their foundation and honours degree programmes in addiction counselling. He has authored numerous research papers and, as well as the present volume, has produced another edited book, Emerging Perspectives on Substance Misuse. For publications see https://www.researchgate.net/profile/Willm_Mistral.

Rosie Mundt-Leach

Qualified as a mental health nurse in 1994 and has worked in addictions since 2000. She is currently Head of Nursing for the South London and Maudsley NHS Foundation Trust Addictions Clinical Academic Group. Her interests include blood-borne virus prevention and treatment, sexual health, overdose prevention, clinical quality improvement work and the promotion of advanced nursing professional practice within addictions nursing.

Maeve O'Leary-Barrett

Clinical Psychology PhD candidate, Department of Psychology, McGill University, Montreal, Quebec, Canada. Ms O'Leary-Barrett is supported by an Aides à la Formation-Recherche (AFR) grant from the Fonds National de Recherche (FNR) du Luxembourg, and by a Lorne Trottier Accelerator Fellowship. For publications see https://www.researchgate.net/profile/Maeve_Oleary-Barrett.

Jane Rowley

Dr Rowley has worked across the homeless sector in both residential and community services since 1993, specialising in people experiencing difficulties with drugs and alcohol, whilst developing a career in the Further and Higher Education sector. Jane is a 2015 Clore Social Fellow sponsored by the Forces in Mind Trust, researching post traumatic growth and support for ex-forces personnel. She teaches Research Methods for the degrees in addiction counselling at Action on Addiction, and is a Senior Research Fellow on the RECOVEU project where she is developing her doctoral research into Addiction Recovery and Adult Education.

Sarah Small

Qualified as a nurse in 1994 and has specialised in critical care and resuscitation. She holds a BSc (Hons) in clinical leadership and is registered as a non-medical prescriber. In 2005, Sarah joined Clouds House where she is currently Head of Service/Registered Manager. Sarah recognises the benefits of providing take-home naloxone in preventing deaths from opiate overdose and is astonished that take-home naloxone is not routine practice.

John Strang

Professor Strang is Head of the Addictions Department at King's College London, and leader of the Addictions Clinical Academic Group within King's Health Partners. He has been a Consultant Psychiatrist in addictions for over 30 years, in a wide range of community and residential settings. For a fuller account see http://www.kcl.ac.uk/ioppn/depts/addictions/people/hod.aspx. Professor Strang is one of only six senior addictions researchers outside North America identified by the

Institute for Scientific Analysis as having a citation rate in the top half of one per cent of all publishing researchers in the last two decades. For publications see https://www.researchgate.net/profile/John_Strang2.

Lorna Templeton

Lorna Templeton is an independent Research Consultant. For over 15 years she has undertaken national and international research on addiction and the family. Lorna worked previously at the Mental Health R&D Unit (Avon and Wiltshire Mental Health Partnership and University of Bath) and the National Addiction Centre, London. She has authored over 50 peer reviewed articles, chapters and books. Lorna is a Trustee for Adfam, a UK umbrella organisation working specifically with families affected by drugs and alcohol, and of the Addiction and the Family International Network (AFINet). She is also on Alcohol Research UK's grants advisory panel.

William L White

Bill White is an Emeritus Senior Research Consultant at Chestnut Health Systems/ Lighthouse Institute. He has a Master's degree in Addiction Studies and has worked full time in the addictions field since 1969 as a streetworker, counsellor, clinical director, researcher, trainer and consultant. He has over 400 publications, and his book, *Slaying the Dragon: The History of Addiction Treatment and Recovery in America*, received the McGovern Family Foundation Award for the best book on addiction recovery. For publications see https://www.researchgate.net/profile/William_White22.

Foreword

At Action on Addiction we are only too aware of the devastating effect addiction has on individuals, families, and communities. In partnership with others, we work tirelessly to disarm addiction through research, professional education, policy campaigns, as well as through the direct delivery of services. This book makes an invaluable contribution to further developing effective ways forward in dealing with addiction. It appears at a time when it has never been more important to take an integrated approach to improving our understanding of addiction and finding ever more innovative and effective responses to what is the biggest preventable killer in the UK and elsewhere.

The book includes chapters from some of the most experienced and internationally recognised authors in the addictions field. The interventions they describe are at the leading edge of approaches to understanding the underlying causes of addictive behaviours, to treating and supporting those afflicted, and to enacting effective policies and practice to disarm the threat of addiction throughout society.

Graham Beech
Chief Executive, Action on Addiction
www.actiononaddiction.org.uk

Preface

Integrated approaches to drug and alcohol problems: Action on Addiction

The content and title of this volume are intended to convey several very clear messages.

All action on addiction should comprise **integrated approaches** which address not only the acute symptoms of addiction to drugs and alcohol but also, following treatment, provide the aftercare which is crucially important to reduce the likelihood of an individual returning to substance misuse. These integrated approaches must work towards each individual's full recovery and reintegration into society, an important aspect of which is to provide support where necessary for their partners and children, who may not be addicted but who suffer nonetheless. Integrated action must also include appropriate training for the addiction workforce, scientific investigations into the maintaining causes of addictive behaviours, preventive interventions and effective policies to reduce harm to the individual, families and wider society.

The integrated approaches described in this volume are very far removed from the concept of a 'war on drugs'. They represent quite the opposite. They seek to disarm, understand and build resistance to the physiological, psychological and societal drivers of addictive behaviours. The actions described are all scientifically based while at the same time being caring, considered and respectful of the *people* upon whom addiction impacts.

The subtitle, *Action on Addiction*, indicates the need to take action to eliminate or reduce the blight that addiction to drugs and alcohol inflicts on individuals, families, local communities and wider society. **Action on Addiction** is also the name of a UK charity which provides a wide range of treatment for individuals: support for families; training for the addiction workforce; preventive projects; and sponsorship of research. All authors in the present volume have contributed in some way to the work undertaken by this charity, and thus are representative of the integrated approaches it takes to drug and alcohol problems.

Acknowledgements

I am profoundly grateful to all those who contributed to this book. The authors are all very busy people, engaged in clinical interventions, research and training. That they have taken the time to write these chapters is a testimony to their commitment to furthering the dissemination of learning gleaned from many years of study, research and, especially, practical experience in the field of addiction to drugs and alcohol.

Willm Mistral

Part I

Routes to addiction

Chapter 1

From substance use to addiction

Willm Mistral

Introduction

We all use psychoactive substances which have the possibility of leading to addiction. We might take medication from a pharmacist or doctor to manage physical or mental illness; or drink coffee to keep us going through the day; or take a glass or two of wine, whisky, or beer to unwind; or smoke cigarettes; or share a marijuana joint; or snort cocaine; or inject heroin; or use other substances which have relatively minor or profound effects on our psychological or physiological state. The use of potentially addictive substances is commonplace. We are not, however, all addicted.

The *Diagnostic and Statistical Manual of Mental Disorders*, now in its Fifth Edition DSM-5 (American Psychiatric Association, 2013), is generally considered the gold standard text on the diagnostic features of every recognised mental illness, and this includes substance use disorders. DSM-5 recognises substance-related disorders from the use of a range of different drug classes including alcohol, caffeine, cannabis, hallucinogens, inhalants, opioids, sedatives, hypnotics, anxiolytics, stimulants (including amphetamine-type substances, cocaine and other stimulants), and tobacco.

DSM-5 lists 11 criteria from which a diagnosis of an addictive disorder may be made:

1. Taking the substance in larger amounts or for longer than you meant to.
2. Wanting to cut down or stop using the substance but not managing to.
3. Spending a lot of time getting, using, or recovering from use of the substance.
4. Experiencing cravings and urges to use the substance.
5. Not managing to do what you should at work, home, or school, because of use.
6. Continuing to use, even when it causes problems in relationships.
7. Giving up important social, occupational, or recreational activities because of use.
8. Using substances again and again, even when it puts you in danger.
9. Continuing to use, even when you know you have a physical or psychological problem that could have been caused or made worse by the substance.

10 Needing more of the substance to get the desired effect (tolerance).
11 Development of withdrawal symptoms which can be relieved by taking more of the substance.

DSM-5 bases the severity of an addictive disorder on the number of criteria met:

- 2–3 indicate a mild disorder
- 4–5 a moderate disorder
- 6 or more indicate a severe disorder.

So, standards have been established that allow substance use disorder, or addiction, to be diagnosed, and these are accepted by a large proportion of professionals working in the field of addiction. Now, this begs the question: how common is addiction?

Alcoholism is a common addictive disorder, particularly in the developed countries of the west. The *Global Status Report on Alcohol and Health* (World Health Organization, 2014) states that in the UK, 16.3 per cent of men and 6 per cent of women have an alcohol use disorder, while in the US these percentages are 10.7 per cent and 4.2 per cent respectively. Furthermore the same report states that, worldwide in 2012, 3.3 million deaths were attributable to harmful use of alcohol.

For obvious reasons, it is more difficult to come to firm conclusions about the use of, and problematic use of, illegal drugs. However, the World Health Organization (WHO) has estimated that in 2010 between 153 million and 300 million people aged 15–64 (3.4 per cent to 6.6 per cent of the world population in that age group) had used an illicit substance at least once in the previous year. And, in 2010, there were an estimated 15.5 million to 38.6 million problem drug users (almost 12 per cent of illicit drug users). It is also estimated that there were between 99,000 and 253,000 deaths globally as a result of illicit drug use (WHO, 2012).

In order to prevent or ameliorate problems deriving from substance use, it is useful to know why some people move from use to addiction, and how that process occurs within both body and mind. There has been a substantial amount of research seeking to identify risk factors for the development of addiction and, although these factors are often found to be inter-related, it can be helpful to consider them under different headings: Neurological, Genetic, Psychosocial, and Resilience.

Neurological factors

The DSM-5 (American Psychiatric Association, 2013) tells us that central to problems arising from psychoactive substance use is activation of the reward system in the brain. The reward system originally developed to promote survival by rewarding behaviour such as feeding, drinking, seeking shelter, and sexual reproduction. Many psychoactive drugs stimulate this same reward pathway. Although different types of drugs operate via different pharmacological mechanisms, all substances capable of leading to addiction have one thing in common, and that is that they increase the activity of the neurotransmitter dopamine in the reward pathway of the brain. Dopamine is produced when the brain receives a stimulus coupled with a reward, and will reinforce a behaviour because it produces a feeling of pleasure, and so is the driver of both intentional behaviours and desire. The reward pathway crosses the limbic region, or emotional centre, of the brain and connects with the orbito-frontal cortex or decision-making area. When drugs are used to excess, they may take over the normal functioning of the reward pathway. Drug molecules can merge with the brain's communication system and disrupt the way that nerve cells normally send, receive, and process information. New research has proposed that addictive behaviours are the product of an imbalance between separate, interacting neural systems which accounts for poor decision-making leading to increased risk of addiction and relapse (Noël, Brevers and Bechara, 2013).

Neuroadaptation or tolerance

Drugs such as heroin have a similar chemical structure to that of neurotransmitters naturally produced in the brain, and this similarity allows them to have a powerful effect. Other drugs, such as cocaine, ecstasy, or crystal methamphetamine, cause the release of large amounts of natural neurotransmitters, and can also block the process by which they are metabolised. This results in the brain becoming flooded with neurotransmitters. A number of biological responses attempt to restore the rate of neurotransmission to normal levels, and the mechanism of regulating neurotransmission is called homeostasis.

The term neuroadaptation, or tolerance, is used to describe this effort to maintain homeostasis. The concept of tolerance is important for understanding addictive behaviour, as a user has to keep increasing the dose to get that same effect. A long-term heroin user may need to inject four or five times a day, and use larger doses, to achieve the same effect compared with a less experienced user who may inject once or twice a day with relatively small doses. Over time, regular stimulation of the reward system by a psychoactive substance causes the brain to produce less dopamine and also to reduce activity within the dopamine receptors. In other words, the brain adapts to the presence of the drug and if the drug is stopped, the brain chemistry is no longer in balance and can take a considerable amount of time to re-adapt. The effects of this, once tolerance has developed and the drug effect starts to wear off, is that a person begins to experience a range of uncomfortable withdrawal symptoms such as nausea, depression, or aches and pains. These symptoms may last from a few hours to a few days but can be stopped immediately by re-taking the drug. This provides a strong motivation to keep on using.

Once tolerance is developed to one drug, it applies to all drugs in the same class. If tolerance is developed to heroin, for example, it will apply to other opiates such as morphine, codeine, and methadone. Without tolerance, reducing the amount of drugs used and gradually stopping use altogether would be considerably easier. However, tolerance does diminish during periods of abstinence and drug users become more susceptible to the effects of the drug. This accounts for the fact that, for drug users who return to use after release from prison, overdose rates peak and there is a high risk of drug-related death in the first few weeks (e.g. Merrall et al., 2010; Binswanger et al., 2012).

Genetic factors

The extent to which addiction may be influenced by heritable factors can be derived from genetically informative research designs, including family, adoption, and twin studies. Although family studies conclude that substance use disorders cluster in families, simply looking at familial similarity in behaviour cannot distinguish whether the influences on behaviour patterns are genetic or environmental (Agrawal and Lynskey, 2008). Well-designed adoption studies, however, can map any correlation between offspring behaviour with regard to problematic substance use, and the characteristics of both the biological and adoptive parents. Similarity between offspring and biological parents suggests genetic influences on that behaviour, while similarity between offspring and adoptive parents suggests environmental influences. One study in Sweden (Kendler et al., 2012) included a national sample of 18,115 adopted children born between 1950 and 1993; 78,079 biological parents and siblings; and 51,208 adoptive parents and siblings. Risk for addiction was found to be significantly increased in the adopted children of biological parents with addiction problems. But, liability to addiction was also affected by a range of environmental factors in the adoptive home including marital instability, psychopathology, and criminal behaviour. However, the adverse environmental effects on addictive behaviours were seen to be more pathogenic in individuals with high levels of genetic risk. The authors concluded that problematic substance use is an aetiologically complex syndrome strongly influenced by diverse genetic risk factors including a specific liability to addiction, and a general vulnerability to other criminal or psychiatric problems (Kendler et al., 2012). This study confirmed and extended previous studies (e.g. Kendler et al., 2000; Lynskey et al., 2002) showing a strong contribution of genetic factors to the aetiology of addictive problems.

Agrawal and Lynskey (2008) argue that twin studies have several advantages over both family and adoption designs for the study of addiction. For adoptive studies, neither biological nor adoptive parents may be representative of the population. This is because biological parents whose children are put up for adoption are more likely to have higher rates of disorders, including psychiatric problems and drug dependence, while conversely, adoptive parents are less likely to have recognised disorders, as well as, on average, being older and relatively socially advantaged.

The gold-standard twin study utilises identical (monozygotic or MZ) and fraternal (dizygotic or DZ) pairs of twins, each pair brought up together so as to nullify any confusion between the effects of genetic and environmental influences on any measured outcome. MZ twin pairs share, on average, 100 per cent of genetic influences while DZ twin pairs share 50 per cent of genetic influences. Shared environmental factors overlap 100 per cent between twin pairs raised together, presuming no one individual receives or perceives specifically different environmental input.

Following a review of a range of research evidence, including adoption, family and twin studies, Agrawal and Lynskey (2008) concluded that a convergence of findings provided compelling evidence that addiction to alcohol, nicotine, and illicit drugs is influenced by inheritance. Nonetheless, efforts to identify individual gene contributions to addictive disorders have been unsuccessful. It seems that multiple genes have a small, interactive and cumulative effect which shapes a liability to addictive behaviours.

It is important to remember, however, that there is nothing deterministic about this genetic influence, and findings vary considerably between different studies. Research has been cited indicating that between 48 per cent and 66 per cent of the variation in alcohol dependence is heritable (Agrawal et al., 2012); and large scale studies of opioid addiction show that, in men, between 23 per cent (Kendler et al., 2000) and 54 per cent (Tsuang et al., 1998) is attributable to genetic factors. This means that environmental, or psychosocial, factors may wield a considerable amount of influence. With rapid advances in gene technology there is likely to be an acceleration of discoveries which could identify specific genes conveying increased risks, or at least increase understanding of how genetic and environmental risks interact to shape liability to addiction.

Interaction of genes and environment

Different ways have been theorised in which genetic and environmental influences may be associated. One way is referred to as passive correlation. For example, children of parents who engage in problematic use of alcohol or other drugs may inherit genetic risk factors and, at the same time, be exposed to parental modelling of excessive use of alcohol or drugs, and have easy access to these substances, thus encouraging use. A second form of association is known as active correlation. This occurs when individuals with particular genetic propensities to alcohol or other drug use are moved to actively seek out corresponding environments. A third form of interplay is referred to as evocative correlation and occurs when genetically mediated traits in a child stimulate particular reactions in other people who then influence the child's environment (Lenroot and Giedd, 2011).

Of course, as well as applying to addictive or other pathological behaviours, these gene–environment interactions may equally influence more positive behaviours. For example, children who have a genetic tendency towards sport, music, or some other creative activity may either be raised in or seek out environments that encourage and support these activities. These positive interactions may encourage and support resilience and provide protection against addictive behaviours even if these children experience early-life environmental stressors. So, genetic and environmental factors may be correlated or interact in a range of different ways, both positive and negative. There is a growing literature demonstrating differences in gene expression as a function of environmental experience, and which shows the significant effects that the social world can exert on gene expression (Dick, 2011). We can safely say that the concept of nature versus nurture is obsolete, and there is little evidence that genes and environment act independently of each other (Moffitt, Caspi and Rutter, 2005; Agrawal and Lynskey, 2008).

However, in the light of research showing the powerful effects of environmental factors on substance misuse and addiction, an argument has been made from a public health standpoint that the benefits of genetic research in this area are relatively small. This is because genetic variants have relatively minor effect sizes, while environmental factors have a strong influence, are easier to identify, and are probably easier to modify (e.g., Merikangas and Risch, 2003). It is argued, therefore, that efforts to prevent exposure and use would be a far more effective intervention, even if gene-based treatment strategies should emerge. However, Agrawal et al. (2012) counter that the goal of genetic research is to provide a therapeutic alternative for people who remain addicted despite numerous repeated environmental interventions and treatment.

Psychosocial factors

Strong evidence related to psychosocial influences and an increased risk of addiction has come from longitudinal studies that follow individuals from an early age. Some research evidence suggests that variation in some genes may simply increase the risk of the development of addictive disorders in individuals who have experienced significant childhood stress (Heath and Nelson, 2003). A comprehensive evaluation of the influence of early-life stress has shown this to be a non-specific predictor of many forms of psychopathology and pathological behaviours, including early-onset drinking and adult addiction to alcohol and other drugs (Enoch, 2011). Nevertheless, of children exposed to severe maltreatment only 50 per cent or fewer go on to develop psychopathology, including addictive disorders, by early adulthood (DuMont, Widom and Czaja, 2007). This balance of risk and resilience with regard to vulnerability may result from a complex interaction between genetic and social-environmental influences (see Enoch, 2012, for a detailed discussion).

One UK study, involving a survey of over 5,700 school-students with an age range of 13–15 years, gathered robust information on a wide range of social influences on their levels of alcohol consumption (Bremner et al., 2011). It developed evidence of how different psychosocial influences work together, including demographic characteristics, individual behaviours, and family and local context, as well as media and celebrity influences. The study found that 70 per cent of younger students and 89 per cent of the older cohort had drunk alcohol, with regular drinking significantly more frequent amongst the older cohort. Overall the students were more likely to drink, to drink frequently, and to drink to excess if they:

- received less supervision from a parent or other close adult
- were exposed to a close family member, especially a parent, drinking or getting drunk
- had positive attitudes towards, and expectations of, alcohol
- had very easy access to alcohol, and
- spent more than two evenings a week with friends, or had friends who drank.

Although friends played an important role, close family had a strong direct and indirect influence. The parent or guardian had a particularly crucial influence. This ranged from the point at which alcohol was introduced, exposure to adult drinking and drunkenness, and the amount of supervision of their child's activities, such as knowing where their child was on a Saturday evening, or regulating how many evenings they spent with friends.

Other environmental factors, some of which appear quite distant from the individual, such as laws and societal norms, relative socioeconomic status, and inequality, can encourage or discourage substance use, if not addiction. Different psychosocial factors may also interact so that their effects on the risk of developing problematic substance use are accentuated in the presence of other risk factors, or risk may be increased only in a particular subsection of the population, perhaps with a genetic predisposition. In addition to societal or cultural factors, the strongest and most consistent effects are typically seen for age (Swendsen and Le Moal, 2011). Many studies have reported that the earlier the age of first drink the higher the later drinking levels and related problems (e.g. Dawson et al., 2008); Hingson and Zha, 2009). One of the largest studies, of 43,093 adults, showed that those who began drinking before the age of 14 years were 1.78 times more likely to develop alcohol dependence than those who reported starting to drink at age 21 years or later (Hingson, Heeren and Winter, 2006).

Researchers have presented a number of suggestions as to why an early age of first drink (taken to mean enough alcohol to have an effect, not just a sip) should impact on later problems. It has been proposed that an early experience of alcohol when the neural system is at a sensitive stage of development, coupled with a state of stress, may enhance the risk of later addiction because of a strong reinforcing effect of alcohol as a coping strategy (Buchmann et al., 2010; Blomeyer et al., 2011). It has also been suggested that early-age drinking could be a causal factor for binge drinking in adulthood in that it develops a higher tolerance to alcohol, or it could be a predictive factor mediating between peer or family influence and later binge drinking (Eliasen et al., 2009).

However, based on a sample of 44,801 alcohol-experienced 15-year-olds from 38 North American and European countries and regions, it has been argued that it is not early initiation into alcohol drinking per se, but early drunkenness that is a risk factor for problem behaviours such as smoking and cannabis use, as well as fights, and low academic performance (Kuntsche et al., 2013).

A recent systematic review of research focused on early age of drinking (Maimaris and McCambridge, 2014) found that many studies did not sufficiently control for a range of confounding psychosocial factors including socioeconomic status, family history of alcohol problems, other behavioural problems, or mental health issues. Only five studies met eligibility criteria for this review (Pedersen and Skrondal, 1998; Warner and White, 2003; Guttmannova et al., 2011; Guttmannova et al., 2012; Rossow and Kuntsche, 2013) and these showed only a weak or no association between early first drinking and later alcohol problems. They did provide some support, however, for the hypothesis that those who had an underlying vulnerability to alcohol problems may also be likely to start drinking early.

Vulnerability can arise from a range of situations and conditions. Using data from a nationally representative sample of the US population, spanning a 10-year period, Swendsen and colleagues (2010) examined the risk of pre-existing mental disorders for the initial onset of use and dependence on nicotine, alcohol, or illicit drugs. A strong association was observed for bipolar disorder, and five anxiety disorders (panic, specific and social phobia, PTSD, separation anxiety) were predictive of at least one form of substance dependence. Ystrom, Kendler and Reichborn-Kjennerud (2014), from a study of 208 monozygotic (MZ) and 113 dizygotic (DZ) pairs of male twins, 430 MZ and 255 DZ pairs of female twins, and 324 opposite-sex twin pairs, with an age range of 19 to 36 years, found that the association between an early age of initiation into alcohol and adult alcohol use disorders could best be accounted for by common underlying genetic factors.

Nevertheless, as stated above, there is nothing inevitable about developing addiction, even among those apparently most at risk. An increasing amount of research is now beginning to identify factors that may be associated with resilience to adverse life events and to addiction.

Resilience

Alim and colleagues (2012: 506) tell us that 'resilience can be defined as the absence of psychopathology despite exposure to high stress, and reflects a person's ability to cope successfully in the face of adversity, demonstrating adaptive psychological and physiological stress responses.'

As with a susceptibility to addiction, the neurological, genetic, or psychosocial influences underlying resilience are not as yet completely understood, but a developmental model of resilience wherein these three influences are combined has been suggested (Feder, Nestler and Charney, 2009). These authors propose that, as an individual develops, their genetic makeup, in interaction with the environment, shapes their neurological circuitry and neuro-chemical functioning, and this is expressed in a range of observable psychological strengths and behaviours.

Resilience has been associated with a number of psychological factors. Optimism has been linked with resilience to several stress-related disorders, including alcohol dependence (Alim et al., 2012). Being able to experience both positive and negative emotions at the same time in high-stress situations appears to increase flexibility of thinking and problem solving and protect a person from adverse consequences (Fredrickson, 2001; Southwick, Vythilingam and Charney, 2005); Ong et al., 2006). Low avoidance coping behaviours have been linked to stress resilience in general (e.g. Alim et al., 2012). Alim and colleagues (2012) report findings from several studies which suggest that a naturally higher availability of dopamine receptors in some individuals might promote resilience to alcohol use disorders, and to the reinforcing effects of stimulants.

Promoting resilience

The complexity of interactions between neural pathways is yet to be completely unravelled but there have been tentative suggestions as to ways of stimulating resilience by means of pharmacological agents affecting the dopamine delivery system (see Picciotto, 2013). Another way resilience may be enhanced is by use of psychological interventions such as cognitive behavioural therapy to reappraise traumatic events and increase optimism. Also, advances in functional magnetic resonance imaging (fMRI) have made real-time feedback on the activity of localised brain areas feasible and reliable. Studies using real-time neuro-feedback have shown that individuals can be trained to modify their own brain activity and attain control over emotionally relevant brain regions, which may in turn be able to increase resilience in a range of adverse circumstances (Weiskopf et al., 2004; Caria et al., 2007).

Public policy

Probably as far back as recorded history, governmental or religious authorities have tried to control the use of psychoactive substances, and this has been justified by a combination of economic, moral, criminal justice, and health arguments (Velleman, 2013). These controls have not always had a positive effect on the levels of substance use or the dangers of addiction. During the nineteenth century, Britain exercised economic control over the sale of opium, and fought two wars with China to force open its markets to the drug. It has been estimated that by 1906, 27 per cent of the male population of China were regular consumers of opium (McCoy, 2003), the sale of which generated vast profits for the UK government and private enterprise. However, as use spread across the western world, followed by development of other drugs, including heroin, increasingly moralistic attitudes emerged and legal controls were brought in with regard to many psychoactive substances. In the first quarter of the twentieth century a number of countries introduced major controls, including total prohibition, on the manufacture and sale of alcohol. Most of these laws were repealed after a few years as they proved difficult or impossible to police, encouraged organised criminal activity, and had massive unintended negative economic effects, in terms of the loss of jobs and tax income (Mistral, 2013). This failure to prevent use of alcohol or other substances did not impede the undertaking of a 'war on drugs' from the 1970s, and the introduction of draconian penalties for use or possession of a range of substances. However this 'war' has done nothing to reduce the demand for psychoactive substances, and vast criminal networks have developed to maintain supply. Recent years have seen a burgeoning market for an increasing number of synthetic psychoactive compounds. The availability of these 'designer drugs' or 'legal highs' which did not fall within the remit of existing laws has moved governments to legislate against possession of whole classes of chemical compounds. A number of prominent researchers regard this approach as ill-conceived and counterproductive, pushing users towards newer and perhaps more dangerous drugs, as well as impeding scientific research and development of treatments for different medical conditions (Nutt, 2013). The current justification for the illegality of many drugs is that they are harmful, and criminal sanctions are necessary to reduce use and consequent health hazards. However, this argument is difficult to justify while alcohol and tobacco, both of which are known to be addictive and to cause massive health problems, continue to be legally marketed.

Conclusion

People use psychoactive substances to alter their psychological state. This may be to increase social interaction and enjoyment, to escape physical pain or psychological distress, or to enhance religious or spiritual experience. Many people will, most probably, always do this, and it is not a problem as long as use is regulated so as to reduce the risk to the individual, their family, and wider society. The extent to which this regulation is imposed by the individual user, current social mores, or governing authorities, is and should be the result of ongoing debate. Addiction, on the other hand, is a problem which can and must be treated. However, the process of moving from substance use to addiction can be subtle, and can go unnoticed, explained away, or denied by the individual concerned and their friends and family. Increasing our knowledge and understanding of the neurological, genetic, and psychosocial factors involved in the addictive process, as well as the development of resilience, is crucially important in order that we may prevent or treat this disorder. These efforts need to be underpinned by enlightened public policies which seek to support the research and treatment facilities necessary to protect the individual, their family, and wider society.

References

Agrawal A and Lynskey MT (2008) Are there genetic influences on addiction? Evidence from family, adoption and twin studies. *Addiction* 103(7): 1069–1081.

Agrawal A, Verweij KJH, Gillespie NA, Heath AC, Lessov-Schlaggar CN, Martin NG, Nelson EC, Slutske WS, Whitfield JB and Lynskey MT (2012) The genetics of addiction – a translational perspective. *Translational Psychiatry* 2, e140. Available at: http://www.nature.com/tp/journal/v2/n7/full/tp201254a.html (accessed 02/04/2015).

Alim TN, Lawson WB, Feder A, Iacoviello BM, Saxena S, Bailey CR, Greene AM and Neumeister A (2012) Resilience to meet the challenge of addiction psychobiology and clinical considerations. *Alcohol Research* 34(4): 506–515.

American Psychiatric Association (2013) *Diagnostic and Statistical Manual of Mental Disorders (DSM-5)*. Arlington, VA: American Psychiatric Association.

Binswanger IA, Nowels C, Corsi KF, Glanz J, Long J, Booth RE and Steiner JF (2012) Return to drug use and overdose after release from prison: a qualitative study of risk and protective factors. *Addiction Science and Clinical Practice* 7(3). Available at: http://www.ascpjournal.org/content/7/1/3 (accessed 02/04/2015).

Blomeyer D, Buchmann AF, Schmid B, Jennen-Steinmetz C, Schmidt MH, Banaschewski T and Laucht M (2011) Age at first drink moderates the impact of current stressful life events on drinking behavior in young adults. *Alcohol Clinical and Experimental Research* 35(6): 1142–1148.

Bremner P, Burnett J, Nunney F, Ravat M and Mistral W (2011) *Young People, Alcohol and Influences: A Study of Young People and their Relationship with Alcohol*. York: Joseph Rowntree Foundation.

Buchmann AF, Schmid B, Blomeyer D, Zimmermann US, Jennen-Steinmetz C, Schmidt MH, Esser G, Banaschewski T, Mann K and Laucht M (2010) Drinking against unpleasant emotions: possible outcome of early onset of alcohol use? *Alcoholism: Clinical and Experimental Research* 34(6): 1052–1057.

Caria A, Veit R, Sitaram R, Lotze M, Weiskopf N, Grodd W and Birbaumer N (2007) Regulation of anterior insular cortex activity using real-time fMRI. *Neuroimage* 35(3): 1238–1246.

Dawson DA, Goldstein RB, Chou P, Ruan WJ and Grant BF (2008) Age of first drink and the first incidence of adult-onset DSM-IV alcohol use disorders. *Alcoholism: Clinical and Experimental Research* 31(12): 2149–2160.

Dick DM (2011) Gene–Environment interaction in psychological traits and disorders. *Annual Review of Clinical Psychology* 7: 383–409.

DuMont KA, Widom CS and Czaja SJ (2007) Predictors of resilience in abused and neglected children grown-up: the role of individual and neighborhood characteristics. *Child Abuse and Neglect* 31(3): 255–274.

Eliasen M, Kjær SK, Munk C, Nygard M, Sparen P, Tryggvadottir L, Liaw K-L and Grønbæk M (2009) The relationship between age at drinking onset and subsequent binge drinking among women. *European Journal of Public Health* 19(4): 378–382.

Enoch MA (2011) The role of early life stress as a predictor for alcohol and drug dependence. *Psychopharmacology* 214(1): 17–31.

Enoch MA (2012) The influence of gene–environment interactions on the development of alcoholism and drug dependence. *Current Psychiatry Reports* 14(2): 150–158.

Feder A, Nestler EJ and Charney DS (2009) Psychobiology and molecular genetics of resilience. *Nature, Reviews, Neuroscience* 10: 446–457.

Fredrickson BL (2001) The role of positive emotions in positive psychology: The broaden-and-build theory of positive emotions. *American Psychologist* 56(3): 218–226.

Guttmannova K, Bailey JA, Hill KG, Lee JO, Hawkins JD, Woods ML and Catalano RF (2011) Sensitive periods for adolescent alcohol use initiation: predicting the lifetime occurrence and chronicity of alcohol problems in adulthood. *Journal of Studies on Alcohol and Drugs* 72(2): 221–231.

Guttmannova K, Hill KG, Bailey JA, Lee JO, Hartigan LA, Hawkins JD and Catalano RF (2012) Examining explanatory mechanisms of the effects of early alcohol use on young adult alcohol dependence. *Journal of Studies on Alcohol and Drugs* 73(3): 379–390.

Heath AC and Nelson EC (2003) *Effects of the Interaction between Genotype and Environment: Research into the Genetic Epidemiology of Alcohol Dependence.*

National Institute on Alcohol Abuse and Alcoholism. Available at: http://pubs.niaaa.nih.gov/publications/arh26-3/193-201.htm (accessed 02/04/2015).

Hingson RW, Heeren T and Winter MR (2006) Age at drinking onset and alcohol dependence: age at onset, duration, and severity. *Archives of Pediatric and Adolescent Medicine* 160(7): 739–746.

Hingson RW and Zha W (2009) Age of drinking onset, alcohol use disorders, frequent heavy drinking, and unintentionally injuring oneself and others after drinking. *Pediatrics* 123(6): 1477–1484.

Kendler KS, Karkowski LM, Neale MC and Prescott CA (2000) Illicit psychoactive substance use, heavy use, abuse, and dependence in a US population-based sample of male twins. *Archives of General Psychiatry* 57(3): 261–269.

Kendler KS, Sundquist K, Ohlsson H, Palmer K, Maes H, Winkleby MA and Sundquist J (2012) Genetic and familial environmental influences on the risk for drug abuse. A national Swedish adoption study. *Archives of General Psychiatry* 69(7): 690–697.

Kuntsche E, Rossow I, Simons-Morton B, Ter Bogt T, Kokkevi A and Godeau E (2013) Not early drinking but early drunkenness is a risk factor for problem behaviors among adolescents from 38 European and North American countries. *Alcoholism: Clinical and Experimental Research* 37(2): 308–314.

Lenroot RK and Giedd JN (2011) Annual research review: developmental considerations of gene by environment interactions. *Journal of Child Psychology and Psychiatry, and Allied Disciplines* 52(4): 429–441.

Lynskey MT, Heath AC, Nelson EC, Bucholz KK, Madden PA, Slutske WS, Statham DJ and Martin NG (2002) Genetic and environmental contributions to cannabis dependence in a national young adult twin sample. *Psychological Medicine* 32(2): 195–207.

McCoy AW (2003) *The Politics of Heroin: CIA Complicity in the Global Drug Trade: Afghanistan, Southeast Asia, Central America, Colombia*. Chicago, IL: Lawrence Hill Books.

Maimaris W and McCambridge J (2014) Age of first drinking and adult alcohol problems: systematic review of prospective cohort studies. *Journal of Epidemiology and Community Health*. Available at: http://jech.bmj.com/content/early/2013/11/18/jech-2013-203402.full (accessed 02/04/2015).

Merikangas KR and Risch N (2003) Genomic priorities and public health. *Science* 302(5645): 599–601.

Merrall ELC, Kariminia A, Binswanger IA, Hobbs MS, Farrell M, Marsden J, Hutchinson SJ and Bird SM (2010) Meta-analysis of drug-related deaths soon after release from prison. *Addiction* 105(9): 1545–1554.

Mistral W (2013) Binge drinking: consumption, consequences, causes and control. In: Mistral W (ed.) *Emerging Perspectives on Substance Misuse*. Chichester: Wiley Blackwell.

Moffitt TE, Caspi A and Rutter M (2005) Strategy for investigating interactions between measured genes and measured environments. *Archives of General Psychiatry* 62(5): 473–481.

Noël X, Brevers D and Bechara A (2013) A neurocognitive approach to understanding the neurobiology of addiction. *Current Opinion in Neurobiology* 23(4): 632–638.

Nutt D (2013) How current drug laws impede research and clinical treatments. In: Mistral W (ed.) *Emerging Perspectives on Substance Misuse*. Chichester: Wiley Blackwell.

Ong AD, Bergeman CS, Bisconti TL and Wallace KA (2006) Psychological resilience, positive emotions, and successful adaptation to stress in later life. *Journal of Personality and Social Psychology* 91(4): 730–749.

Pedersen W and Skrondal A (1998) Alcohol consumption debut: predictors and consequences. *Journal of Studies on Alcohol* 59(1): 32–42.

Picciotto MR (2013) An indirect resilience to addiction. *Nature Neuroscience* 16: 521–523.

Rossow I and Kuntsche E (2013) Early onset of drinking and risk of heavy drinking in young adulthood – a 13-year prospective study. *Alcoholism: Clinical and Experimental Research* 37(Suppl 1): E297–E304.

Southwick SM, Vythilingam M and Charney DS (2005) The psychobiology of depression and resilience to stress: implications for prevention and treatment. *Annual Review of Clinical Psychology* 1: 255–291.

Swendsen J and Le Moal M (2011) Individual vulnerability to addiction. *Annals of the New York Academy of Sciences, Addiction Reviews* 1216: 73–85.

Swendsen J, Conway KP, Degenhardt L, Glantz M, Jin R, Merikangas KR, Sampson N and Kessler RC (2010) Mental disorders as risk factors for substance use, abuse and dependence: results from the 10-year follow-up of the National Comorbidity Survey. *Addiction* 105(6): 1117–1128.

Tsuang MT, Lyons MJ, Meyer JM, Doyle T, Eisen SA, Goldberg J, True W, Lin N, Toomey R and Eaves L (1998) Co-occurrence of abuse of different drugs in men: the role of drug-specific and shared vulnerabilities. *Archives of General Psychiatry* 55(11): 967–972.

Velleman R (2013) Changing perspectives on problematic drug use. In: Mistral W. (ed.) *Emerging Perspectives on Substance Misuse*. Chichester: Wiley Blackwell.

Warner LA and White HR (2003) Longitudinal effects of age at onset and first drinking situations on problem drinking. *Substance Use and Misuse* 38(14): 1983–2016.

Weiskopf N, Scharnowski F, Veit R, Goebel R, Birbaumer N and Mathiak K (2004) Self-regulation of local brain activity using real-time functional magnetic resonance imaging (fMRI). *Journal of Physiology-Paris* 98(4–6): 357–373.

World Health Organization (WHO) (2012) *World Drug Report 2012*. Geneva: World Health Organization.

World Health Organization (WHO) (2014) *The Global Status Report on Alcohol and Health 2014*. Geneva: World Health Organization.

Ystrom E, Kendler KS and Reichborn-Kjennerud T (2014) Early age of alcohol initiation is not the cause of alcohol use disorders in adulthood, but is a major indicator of genetic risk. A population-based twin study. *Addiction* 109(11): 1824–1832.

Chapter 2

My story of addiction and recovery

Geri Lettle

My life started in South Africa in 1978. My childhood was probably as 'normal' as anyone's but somehow I felt very different from everyone else. My mum and dad brought me up and we moved from Johannesburg to Cape Town when I was around 3-years-old with my sister who is 3 years older than me. I remember being a very shy and timid child and I was quite socially anxious. When I reached primary school age I became the target of boys. I was bullied physically and emotionally which made me retreat into myself and at times I remember teachers and my parents saying I was 'different'. My parents would often say that I didn't like physical attention but in fact, I think I craved this the most but didn't know how to ask for it or show it. I struggled through primary school and tried to be a wallflower and hoped that no-one would see me. My greatest love was horse riding. I owned a horse and would escape to the stables every day after school and found that I was happiest being isolated and on my own with my horse.

When I moved on to high school I remember that my parents were starting a new business and were preoccupied a lot. I don't know what happened to me but I started rebelling at quite a rapid pace. I think that I put on a tough mask to avoid being bullied again. I tended to gravitate towards the older children and around 13/14-years-old I started smoking cigarettes, drinking and getting into trouble. I would sneak out at night and go to the clubs and drink myself into oblivion; this is when I probably formed the idea that drink was a solution to my shyness. I started to bunk off to smoke and drink with some other classmates and my schoolwork began to deteriorate. Around this time I started smoking weed and would also sell it to my friends. I liked being accepted and became the life and soul of the party. I felt like one of the 'in-crowd' and enjoyed being the centre of attention and the rebel. I started going to rave clubs and taking acid and ecstasy, and at the age of 15 got free entry to some of the popular clubs because I was mates with the dealers and older guys. Warnings were flagged up by the school but I carried on my destructive path and eventually got expelled.

My parents became wise to the idea that I was using when they got a call to say that I had OD'd at a friend's house and they had to collect me foaming at the mouth. I remember telling my dad I was on drugs. The shock on his face said it all and the disappointment he felt was palpable. From there on I was moved to a different school and taken to psychiatrists to see 'what was wrong with me'. I kept on rebelling so I eventually was taken out of school when I was 14-years-old and my parents contacted social services because they didn't know what to do with me any more. I was running away from home on a regular basis and eventually they sent me to a school for delinquent children with psychiatric issues. The children there were vulnerable and when I look back, things happened there that shouldn't have. This is where I met Lee who introduced me to the 'other side of the tracks'. She was involved with gangsters and I was drawn to this lifestyle. I wanted to feel a part of something, a sense of belonging, and this glove seemed to fit. I was introduced to gang members, got involved in drug dealing and witnessed a lot of violence. My parents were at their wits' end and enrolled me into college which I attended sporadically. Throughout college I was still getting 'off my head' on various drugs, and dealing to support my habit.

Through my clubbing I met my soul mate and best friend, Chad, and we just connected. He was older than me, in with the drug scene, and a dealer. It was much more than a friendship, he seemed to 'get me'. My parents didn't approve but I didn't care and used to bunk off college and go and spend time with him. Nevertheless I did leave college with a Diploma in Paralegal Business Studies. At age 17 my parents were very worried about me and together we thought that I should go to London. They were thinking it would be safer for me in the long term but it was only the start of my decline. At age 18 I set off on my travels across the world, thinking that life would be great. It wasn't. I was naïve and, not having any life experience of how to live and pay bills, things got quite scary. I got a job but would spend all my money on cocaine and not think about how I would pay my way. After six months there I was scared and alone and called my parents to say I wanted to come home. To my shock, they said that I didn't have a home to come to. I think they were trying a bit of 'tough love' but I felt rejected and abandoned with no-one to turn to.

I got on with things, got jobs and supported myself as best I could, sofa surfing, flat sharing with other South Africans and Australians. Because I was earning, I was partying a lot and, because I thought no-one cared, I got myself into some scary situations whilst drinking and using. I would wake up not knowing where I was, ended up in hospital and police cells a few times. In 1998 my sister woke me up at 2 a.m. to inform me that Chad had been shot and was on life support. I called my work, took compassionate leave and flew back to South Africa. By the time I got there, he had died. I had no support from my family and I felt like dying myself. I felt that he was the only person that 'got me' and now he too had abandoned me. I started using crack and mandrax for the first time, got absolutely smashed for two weeks then flew back to London. I felt like my world had ended and I had no-one to turn to, so to take away my pain, I used, worked and used more. My friend Lee said she knew who murdered Chad and I held on to the thought that one day I would go back and kill him.

In London at that time I got a job I really enjoyed, working as a PA for the Director of Building services for the Saudi Royal Family. However, I was still drinking heavily on weekends and taking a lot of time off sick and after about two years my boss called me in and I decided to resign before being fired. This is when I thought that I would try get off the drugs by going back to South Africa and starting afresh. I moved back without my parents' blessing, got a flat and looked for a job. This was short lived as I got back in contact with Lee who was married to one of the Moroccans who were 'controlling' parts of the Cape Town nightclub scene including racketeering, prostitution and drug dealing. One day Lee told me that the person who had killed Chad was sitting in her flat. I raced over there and wanted to confront him but was invited in and given drugs. However wrong this may seem, I became friends with this guy. He was exciting, involved in gangs, violence and was well known in the Cape Town underworld. This is where my problems really started and after months of getting more and more involved in this lifestyle my life became at risk because of various things including my car being linked to a murder when this guy had used it. I was pulled in by the Scorpions (police unit dealing with gangs) and told that some of the people I was with were linked to terrorism, murder and rape and that my life and my family were at risk, and they wanted information. Even though I had been so high on drugs, I had seen a lot and heard a lot of what these gangs were doing so I was seen as a liability. Because of corruption within the police force my parents believed that something really bad would happen to me, and within 24 hours they got me a one way ticket back to London and I was gone. They told me not to contact them again and my dad said 'If anything happens to your mother or me, let it be on your head'. For months after I left my parents were frightened for their lives, slept with a gun under their bed and felt like they were being followed.

Back in London I stayed with a guy that I had known for a few years, Zak, and my using and drinking escalated. I was smoking a lot of crack, and one evening I got into a fight in a crack house with two blokes and they jumped on me and ended up breaking my femur bone. I was taken into hospital where they operated on my leg and put in a plate. After less than a week in hospital I got Zak to bring me alcohol and I left drunk and on crutches. On my way home I stopped at the same crack house where the fight had happened and scored again.

At this time I started going to various drug treatment agencies and day programmes but couldn't stay clean. I became so manipulative and evil that Zak ended up trying to commit suicide and while he was taken to hospital, I sold all his belongings and maxed out his card. Then, whilst doing the rounds of crack houses in West London, I met my first 'proper' boyfriend. He had just been released from prison; we ended up robbing someone, and our relationship 'blossomed' from there. Eventually we were doing house burglaries together, stealing car keys and selling the cars for money to smoke crack. This relationship was extremely volatile and violent and I ended up in hospital a few times. After being arrested in a stolen car he was remanded and I was bailed. I was at my lowest point, I hated being alone and felt I couldn't cope. I wanted my pain to go away and developed bulimia. I had no money so I would go shoplifting for alcohol and food, eat it all and then purge. I wanted to punish myself more and more and started cutting myself on numerous occasions to see if it would take the pain and hatred of myself away. After some time I accessed a drug service which referred me to a psychiatrist. I was diagnosed with personality disorder, along with a string of other labels, and was prescribed a large dose of anti-psychotic medication, Valium and Temazapine. Because I lived in an area where it was difficult to access drugs, I was drinking and taking large amounts of prescription drugs. I would regularly overdose and after the third time in an intensive care unit they sectioned me. I was referred to the mental health services but, when released from section, carried on drinking. There were many times when I woke to find the police and ambulance service in my front room doing a welfare check on me.

At this time I really believed there was something wrong with me. I was depressed, hated being me and wanted to die. I would fantasise about being someone else, somewhere else in the world, or about dying, and wondering if anyone would turn up to my funeral. My parents had banned me from the house after I had attacked my dad and I could only access my stuff with police presence. I wanted to punish my family because I didn't know why I was the way I was and hadn't yet figured out that I was an addict. I didn't know how to stop the pain inside me and thought that drink and drugs were my solution. I would go into the church absolutely drunk and ask the vicar to help me. She was a support for me and came to the court case with me and my partner. The police were aware of my partner's violence and tried to get me to leave him. In 2002 I was charged with a few criminal convictions and my partner got three years. My sister fought hard for me and tried to get me into treatment. At this time there was only one treatment bed available in Surrey and the waiting list was huge. My family rallied around and eventually went to see the local MP who helped get me into my first detox and treatment centre. I completed a 31-day detox in South London and was then transferred to a therapeutic community in Forest Gate.

Whilst in treatment I met Brian who I got very close to. He was discharged from treatment and I eventually left treatment to be with him. I broke up with my partner in prison and thought that this new relationship was going to be different. I was very wrong, and the second day out of treatment we had an argument and he punched me in the face and I blacked out. This set the tone for our relationship. We lived in a flat in East London and he introduced me to heroin, and crime became a daily occurrence. We used to drive out to little towns and do commercial burglaries, and cheque and card fraud. I didn't like using heroin and every time he got arrested and went to prison I would try and sort myself out, get a job and stop using. Again it was a vicious cycle where I would work, get money and use crack at night. I justified it by saying 'at least I stopped using heroin'. I would sometimes be up for three days, working during the day and smoking crack at night. When Brian was released from prison, anything that I had bought for the flat or myself he would sell or smash up and deliberately give me a black eye so I couldn't go into work. He didn't like me being independent and sabotaged everything. With the heroin, domestic violence and emotional abuse I sunk deeper into myself and let the drugs numb me.

Because I wasn't close with my family I had no-one to turn to. My world became very small and every day I wanted to take my life. My partner went into prison once again, I hated being on my own and the only way for me to get out of a relationship was to find a new one. This is when I met Dave who was a crack user and a criminal but wasn't violent, and we got on well. My crack and heroin use picked up momentum. We would stay up four days committing crime, smoking and then passing out for 48 hours. This went on for two years until in 2003 I became pregnant. I really thought that this would make me stop. I was getting more and more frustrated with being me and feeling 'weak'. I didn't want to carry on using and hurt my baby, but I just couldn't stop. I used to sit smoking crack and cry because I wanted to stop but every time I tried, I failed. I had always wanted someone to love and now I was pregnant I thought that this would end my using and I would become a great mum and live happily ever after.

Social services got involved in my case and advised me to seek help. I accessed a day programme in West London but didn't turn up half the time. I got on a script and tried to cut my using down but would just use on top. After trying and trying, I think I reasoned that I wasn't pregnant so I could carry on using. I had no support around me as my baby's dad was still using and when I told him I was pregnant he did a runner. My parents decided to go to South Africa so I was left in my flat on my own with my addiction and pregnancy. In my mind I never thought that there would be a possibility that my baby could be taken from me as I would go to all the scans and midwife appointments. This kind of thing didn't happen to someone like me. I went to a scan one day and the midwife stated that I needed to be admitted to hospital immediately as they thought I had pre-eclampsia. I said that I would go to the ward but disappeared to go and score. The police were sent to my house as I was in a high risk situation. I didn't realise at the time how risky it was to me and my baby and that we could have died. I eventually turned up at the hospital four hours later with everyone in a panic. I was kept in, and a week later I was induced and my daughter was born 4 pound 1 ounce, premature and withdrawing.

This is when momentum kicked in with social services and I wasn't allowed to remove my daughter from the hospital. I was told I needed to get a solicitor as they were planning to remove her from me at the hospital. My parents had flown in from South Africa and they agreed that in order for us to take my daughter home they would put themselves forward to be her carer. This was a nightmare as they stayed at my flat and I was still using and periodically looking after her. I felt that my parents were in control, that they were using her against me, and I rebelled against it. The case went to court, and social services wanted my daughter to go up for adoption. I tried to get clean and went into a detox but after ten days was discharged for aggressive behaviour. By this time my parents had taken my daughter back to their house and had full custody of her. I was only allowed supervised contact and felt that I was useless, I couldn't even look after my child and felt my life wasn't worth living.

After attending yet another drug service I got the chance to attend Clouds, for a six week 12 Step residential treatment programme. By the time I got in there I weighed around 6 stone and was beaten by the drugs. I put my all into the programme, came to understand why I was the way I was and that I was powerless over drugs. During the programme I received a letter from my solicitor stating that my cousin in Scotland was putting herself forward to adopt my daughter. I felt that this was a punch in the face when I was trying to get myself right, and they were still planning to take my daughter away. I finished the programme armed with information and the drive to be a mum. I went to Stapleford Clinic straight after leaving treatment and got a Naltrexone implant just to be sure I wouldn't use, but I went back to East London and used anyway, to reward myself for completing treatment. I used for two days and then went to the gym to sweat it out of my system so I could test negative for my upcoming RAPT day programme (the Rehabilitation for Addicted Prisoners Trust). I completed this and fought to get my daughter back. When social services asked me to jump, I only asked how high.

I moved from my flat to another house out of the area and felt that I was doing well. The court eventually came around to making an order for the planned and structured return of my daughter to me, and I gained custody in 2007. I thought that having a child and living in a new house would be the answer and I would be fine. Though I had no support around me, all was fine for a while and I ended up getting a part time job in a hospital and started earning money. I was coping and thought my life was balanced, and didn't think that having a use-up every weekend would affect me. Then the using got more and more frequent until it was every day and even at work. I became very calculating and would get my clean friend to do my drug test for me so I could deceive social services. I was there physically for my daughter but not emotionally. My parents had an inkling that I was using and paid for me to see a hypnotherapist in Harley Street. This was a waste of time because I would go into the toilet beforehand and smoke crack. I would leave my daughter alone sleeping during the night and go out in my car to score. I would take my daughter shoplifting and grafting and because my car had a police marker for 'possible drugs car' I got stopped on numerous occasions. My nights would become day and my days would become night and my daughter suffered emotionally.

I did just enough so that social services wouldn't be alerted to my drug taking. I would take my daughter to nursery, turn up for meetings and attend psychotherapy sessions regularly. I eventually got back on a script as things were getting out of hand. My parents were moving back to South Africa permanently and suggested that I go to rehab and then we all fly out and start a new life. At the time this seemed like a great idea in my cloud of misjudgement on crack and heroin. I got funding again to enter Clouds but this time I really didn't want to be there. Again I controlled my treatment plan and decided to leave after four weeks and get the Naltrexone implant again. I spent the next two weeks before flying out to South Africa using crack and benzos. In those two weeks things got really out of control and my using picked up momentum because I thought that this could be the 'last use-up' before starting my new life in South Africa.

I gave my keys to my house back to the housing association and flew back to South Africa, doing a geographical thinking that everything would be fine. I lasted two weeks, and one day picked my daughter up from nursery in my mum's car and disappeared into Brooklyn, which is a deprived gangland area. I stayed with a friend, turned my phone off and smoked crystal meth and crack. I didn't sleep for six days and my behaviour became so erratic that I bought a knife, thinking someone was going to kill me. My daughter and I ended up sleeping in a flat where there were violent criminals and prostitutes. My daughter was scared and she really suffered emotionally having to witness me using crack, having physical fights and behaving erratically.

I eventually ran out of money and in my deluded thinking phoned my family to give me money. They turned up and when I got in the car they locked the doors so I couldn't get out. Then the police cars arrived and they were screaming at me 'where is your kid' to which I replied 'I don't have one'. They started to reason with me, saying that my child was not safe in a place like this, and I eventually took them to this run-down flat. They marched me up the stairs in handcuffs and rescued my daughter who was absolutely distraught. They then arrested me for theft of a vehicle and kept me in the police cells for two days before I appeared in court. I was remanded and was taken to Pollsmoor Prison. This prison was absolutely awful, there were at least 70 women in the cell and the calibre of the criminals varied from petty thieves to arsonists and murderers. The food was inedible and thefts and beatings were a daily occurrence. I was in there for ten days before being taken to court again where they dropped the charge. I thought I would be released but I was re-arrested and taken to the Family Courts. Once there I was sectioned under the Prevention and Treatment of Drug Dependency Act, 1992. I was ordered to be sent to Family Outreach Ministries, which is a Christian rehab, for at least six months.

This treatment centre was in the middle of nowhere, ten hours out of Cape Town, and one of the worst rehabs I have ever experienced. We were locked in huts and there was an electric fence around the property. There was one road going in and out so escaping was difficult. They would punish people if they tried to run away by handcuffing them to the beds and leaving a bucket as a toilet for them. They would make people walk around for days with a piece of railway track handcuffed to their arm. They played psychological games with us including withholding detox and mental health medication and confiscating cigarettes for days. Women were separated from the men and told not to have eye contact with them. My mental health was deteriorating and I was taken to see a psychiatrist in the town centre. He diagnosed me with bi-polar disorder and wanted to section me. Eventually I escaped through the electric fence and made my way back to Cape Town where I continued to use. Through this my addiction was so all-consuming that I didn't have a thought for my daughter or my family. I was only concerned with how I would get money for my next fix.

My parents got me a one way ticket back to London and I left with a suitcase and without my daughter. I arrived back in London and was homeless. My using went to another level after leaving South Africa. I had lost everything, my daughter, my family, my home and my sanity. I picked up with Dave who was clean at the time, but not for long after I got back. I sofa surfed and lived where I could, sometimes in stairwells or electricity cupboards that I broke into for warmth. I was shoplifting during the day and with my partner doing commercial burglaries at night and selling paracetamol as cocaine in Shoreditch. I was sent to Holloway Prison numerous times and came out and did the same thing, using and committing crime. Many times I would be released only to go back in again after seven days. Finally, before being released, I was asked to go to the police station as I had been identified as a PPO (prolific and other priority offender).

I met my PPO officer and he managed to get me to the Housing Team and I eventually got placed in a women's hostel in Aldgate. However, my drug use had got out of control and my world revolved around using. Every minute of every day was consumed by using and finding more money to use. Dave and I got arrested yet again for burglary and I found out in the police station that I was pregnant. I was fearful and told my probation officer. Social services were alerted and I avoided having to see them. My saving grace was my PPO officer who stated that I would lose my child if I didn't get clean. He encouraged me to go into treatment and went for funding. Every other person involved in my case thought I was a lost cause and opposed me detoxing whilst pregnant. My PPO officer went against them and got me a place at Broadway Lodge, a residential addiction treatment services in the west of England.

The route to recovery

If it wasn't for my PPO officer things would have turned out very differently. I entered treatment four and a half months pregnant but with a flat stomach. I hadn't been eating and weighed 7 stone. I think with all my previous treatments I had gained a lot of knowledge about my addiction and knew where it would take me. However, the love and care that I received while in treatment was difficult for me to embrace as I had become so very hard and angry. My previous experience of losing a child weighed heavily on my mind and for the first time in my life I became willing to listen to others and not do things my way. It took six weeks to detox me and I was moved down to secondary care after the detox. Whilst in treatment my social worker told me that they were planning to take my child at birth. This only made me more determined not to let this happen and I decided not to go back to London. The problem was that I was homeless and had no link to the area. Steph, who was the Medical Manager, was looking after my case and she was so supportive of me I finally felt that someone was on my side and that people actually cared about me, even if I didn't care about myself.

With a housing crisis looming and my determination to keep my baby they offered to pay for a deposit on a flat. Whilst still in treatment I got a flat in Bristol, and Broadway Lodge helped me with baby clothes and other items for the baby. Steph made sure that I had the basics to live and I organised furniture. On 28 August 2012 I left Broadway Lodge and moved into my flat with the help of support workers. Social services tried to get a planned placement for my baby so they could 'test me in the community' but I fought against this and a child protection case was ordered. I was admitted into hospital due to fears that I was developing pre-eclampsia. I had my son on 10 September 2012 but he stopped breathing and was taken into a specialist unit. They thought I had used and took a urine sample from my son. I was put on an observation ward and was monitored, with social services coming in every day. Finally the test results came back and it was all negative and my son came back up to the ward. I left hospital ten days later in a taxi back to my flat. I was on my own with my baby in an unfamiliar area and with no-one around me. This was the toughest part of my recovery, I was just out of treatment, no support apart from social services and with a new baby to care for. I was petrified and alone but I was determined to get through it. I accessed support from a local drug agency and social services sent around a support worker once a week.

When my son was ten months I decided to tell my mum and dad. I had been in letter communication with my daughter since going into treatment and spoke to my parents once a month so it was a shock to them to hear that I had been pregnant. Then, when I was offered some childcare through the local authority I took it in order to go to college to educate myself. I started volunteering in a homeless centre and eventually worked myself up to a volunteering position as a Prison Outreach Worker. I felt that I was getting on with my life and enjoyed working with people, it made me feel good giving something back. My parents came over for a brief visit and gave me an inkling that if I stayed clean maybe one day I could go back to South Africa to be with my daughter. This prompted me to look for a qualification so I would be able to get a career and support my children. I was so happy when I found the Foundation Degree in Addiction Counselling at Action on Addiction. This degree course accepted people who might not meet the normal academic criteria but could be considered on an accreditation of prior experiential learning (APEL) application. All the courses I had done, along with my volunteering work, gained me an invitation to the selection process.

Following an interview I was selected and started my degree studies in September 2014. I have now passed the first year and am currently on placement at Broadway Lodge. Never in my wildest dreams did I think that I would one day be on the other side and be training to be a counsellor. I had always wished that my life would change but never believed that it could. It shows that with the right conditions people can recover, and anything is attainable in recovery. I am now in phone contact with my daughter on a weekly basis, social services are now out of my life and I have a healthy and happy son living with me. I am planning on moving back to South Africa when I finish my degree to be with my daughter and family.

Part II

Action for individuals

Chapter 3

SHARP intensive day treatment

Tim Leighton

This chapter will trace the development of Action on Addiction's intensive day treatment model, known as SHARP (Self-Help Addiction Recovery Programme). It is currently implemented in several locations in England, and is deliberately designed to take on local characteristics while retaining core underlying concepts and practices. Before describing the underlying principles and practice of SHARP it is worth tracing the history of the model.

Origins of SHARP

SHARP developed from the Minnesota Model, which began in the US state of that name around 1950 and over subsequent decades became enormously influential, not to say dominant, in the alcoholism and substance dependence treatment field in the US. While well known, it is not well understood in terms of its foundational ideas. It is usually identified with '12 Step' treatment (for more detail see chapter by John F. Kelly in this volume), that is to say treatment whose primary aim is to foster engagement with the 12 Step organisations of Alcoholics Anonymous (AA), Narcotics Anonymous (NA), Cocaine Anonymous (CA) and others. However, while it is true that facilitation of 12 Step recovery is an important feature of the model, it includes a pragmatic and flexible attitude, typically characterised by a thorough ongoing assessment of all aspects of the client and of multimodal therapeutic approaches.

The simple underpinning ideas, listed by Spicer (1993), which are still relevant to the work of our charity, Action on Addiction, today are: 'treat people with chemical dependency', 'treat them with dignity' and 'treat them as whole persons – mind, body and spirit'. The concept of chemical dependency was formulated when clinicians working with the Minnesota Model noticed that people with alcohol dependence often had concomitant or substitute dependence on other drugs, and that the treatment was equally useful for those whose main dependence was on a drug or drugs other than alcohol. Chemical dependency was once again a pragmatic, practice-derived concept, designed to facilitate the identification of patients with different chemical preferences but similar patterns of behaviour in relationship to chemical use. It de-emphasised the primary substance, the 'drug of choice', recognising instead a dependency on altering mood with psychoactive chemicals. This raised the possibility of 'cross-addiction' and provided a rationale for a treatment goal of complete abstinence from all drugs.

This concept is still relevant for many of our clients today who seek admission to our abstinence-based programmes, including SHARP. Most have patterns of problematic or dependent use of more than one drug, often many. Most do not have much difficulty accepting that the chances of recovery will be much enhanced if complete abstinence is established, and what is seen in some quarters as a very rigorous treatment goal does not seem a stumbling block in most cases. The term 'chemical dependency' is not so much used currently, and indeed the idea of addiction as a disease (a conception commonly considered central to the 12 Step philosophy) is less insisted upon than in previous times, but the function of these concepts is still actively inherent in the practices of the programme, as described below. Inasmuch as the disease concept of addiction is useful, it is so only if used to foster responsibility for health and recovery, and at the same time offering a less stigmatising and shame-producing alternative to moral weakness, recalcitrance or stupidity as an explanation for continued destructive drug use. In short if the disease concept is not empowering, it is of no use. The SHARP programme is designed to foster mutual respect, solidarity and responsibility, and as a community-based day programme it does so, as we shall see, in reciprocal relationship with the local 'recovering community' (see below).

The move from residential to day programmes

During the 1980s in the US, the treatment centres providing programmes in the tradition of the Minnesota Model, usually in a residential or in-patient setting, began offering programmes with similar components on a day attendance basis. This was primarily done to offer more convenient treatment to those who did not wish or need to move to a residential setting, often those who had a good local support system including stable and safe accommodation. For those who had jobs, evening programmes became available to enable them to continue with employment while receiving treatment. The programmes consisted of group therapy, individual counselling, educational lectures, exploration of and encouragement to attend the 12 Step mutual aid resource (usually AA), and recovery planning. Family involvement was also common in the form of couples counselling, education and information about support.

A number of research studies at the time found that out-patient (day programme) outcomes were not inferior to the more expensive in-patient (residential) outcomes (see Miller and Hester, 1986). The move towards day programmes received enormous impetus when Managed Care systems were introduced in the US in order to reduce the cost and improve the quality of care commissioned by health funders, both public and private. This resulted in aggressive gatekeeping processes which reduced admissions to in-patient addiction treatment in the US (White, 2014: 400).

SHARP London (1992–2011)

The establishment of the first SHARP day care programme in West London in 1992 was not driven by concerns about reimbursement. The Chemical Dependency Centre (a charity which became part of the merged Action on Addiction) opened SHARP as a Minnesota Model-type day programme because the founders and board of the charity, in particular Dr Brian Wells, believed that such a programme would benefit many who were unable to or perhaps did not need to go to a residential treatment centre. In order to get the programme up and running, the charity raised donations to meet start-up and two years' running costs, including restoring and refitting the premises. The funding of treatment through the National Health Service and Community Care Act 1990 had just become possible, and almost all of SHARP London's clients in the early years were paid for in this way. SHARP deliberately offered its services to people throughout London, and a number of Community Care assessors in various London boroughs saw the value in the programme and supported the funding of suitable clients. The programme itself was closely based on a typical contemporary residential Minnesota Model centre such as Clouds House (for details see chapter by Kirby Gregory in the present volume), and was delivered over 12 weeks with clients attending five days a week. Clients would receive guidance in exploring the 12 Steps, and were expected to attend meetings of AA or NA several times a week while on the programme. An obvious difference from a residential setting was that participants returned home in the evening and had to manage the weekends without treatment activities. This produced a different kind of material for the group therapy sessions as the members were exposed to everyday issues and potential relapse risks such as relationship conflict or environmental triggers, from which they would have had some protection in a residential centre. This might have raised the risk of a lapse for some, but there was the significant advantage of being able to address such issues as they arose on a daily basis. The day programme format also fostered reliance on local mutual aid and allowed clients to experience more immediately the support of AA and NA meetings. For several years SHARP London was successful in attracting clients from across the metropolitan area. However by 2010 a growing emphasis on localism made commissioners less likely to support services out of their own borough, and it was not possible to secure enough referrals from across the city to sustain the service. In 2011 the decision was made reluctantly to close the programme down. But the SHARP model had already taken root elsewhere.

Liverpool

Liverpool, on the north-west coast of England, was under-served until the twenty-first century in terms of resources for abstinent recovery for drug users. Although at the turn of the century there were a large number of Alcoholics Anonymous meetings in the city there were very few Narcotics Anonymous meetings and no Cocaine Anonymous or SMART Recovery meetings. SMART Recovery ® is a network of cognitive behaviour-based mutual aid meetings, created as an alternative to 12 Step mutual aid.

Having experienced a heroin 'epidemic' in the 1980s Liverpool had been in the forefront of the Harm Reduction movement but resources for abstinent recovery, both mutual aid and treatment services other than opioid substitute prescribing, had found it hard to get established. However by 2006 there were 10 weekly NA meetings in the area, and currently (2016) there are at least 35 NA meetings weekly. SMART Recovery has 7 meetings in the area, and CA has 12 meetings. This is amongst the highest density of addiction recovery mutual aid in the country. In 2009 Liverpool was the venue for the first annual UK Recovery Walk attracting almost 1000 walkers (for details of similar events in the US see chapter by William White in the present volume). This remarkable rise in visible recovery is a very important part of the history of SHARP, as the reciprocal and reinforcing relationship between the SHARP programme and the local recovering community is key to understanding its success in its current sites and its potential in future locations. SHARP is not solely responsible for this growth in abstinent recovery as a residential facility, Park View, with a treatment philosophy closely aligned with the 12 Step programme, had opened in 2003, and many of its alumni were and are active in the local recovery scene. Also, several people from Liverpool who had been to residential rehabilitation and started their recoveries elsewhere in the country returned to their home area in the early 2000s, strengthened the local meetings and helped to start new ones.

So when the Chemical Dependency Centre opened SHARP in Liverpool in January 2005, change was already beginning and the programme was well placed to play its part in the development of a burgeoning recovering community. SHARP Liverpool began with a programme very similar to that at SHARP London. The premises, a Georgian town house with a courtyard behind, was conducive to a sense of community, and a small team of counsellors and admissions staff managed a programme that offered structure and quite demanding expectations. Clients were asked to arrive promptly at 8.30 a.m. and, each day from Monday morning until Friday lunchtime, there were scheduled activities from 9 a.m. to 4.30 p.m. which all participants were expected to attend. An atmosphere of welcome and acceptance was actively maintained, something which many clients appreciated and to which they frequently attributed their success on the programme. There was a clear endorsement of the 12 Step philosophy. Clients were introduced to the 12 Steps and helped to explore how they could be used to support recovery, they were expected to attend meetings, and the house very soon began to host Narcotics Anonymous meetings, bringing local recovering people into contact with the agency.

Over time, the development of SHARP produced new recovery practices, both originating in the SHARP programme and from links with other projects in Liverpool. Examples include a 'recovery choir', the Raucous Caucus Recovery Chorus, whose members include staff and graduates of SHARP; creative workshops at Genie in the Gutter and the Spider Project (now Art and Soul); as well as volunteering opportunities at SHARP and at the Brink, a 'dry bar' opened in 2011 in a neighbouring street. The relationship between these activities and SHARP works reciprocally to enhance the recovery system in Liverpool, as well as the positive experience of individual clients.

Bournemouth

Bournemouth, along with several other seaside towns in England, has for some time contained a flourishing community of recovering people. This is because in the 1970s and 1980s some of the first Minnesota Model centres opened in these towns. Agencies such as Streetscene opened recovery houses there, and a person who had received treatment at Clouds and who ran a carpentry business opened a project to train people in early recovery in woodwork and cabinet-making, under the name Working Recovery. A result of this activity was the settlement in Bournemouth of a significant number of people who had been through abstinence-based treatment, and this led to a strong presence of Narcotics Anonymous, Cocaine Anonymous and, now, SMART recovery meetings in the town.

In 1998 the charity Clouds extended its treatment activity beyond the residential centre at Clouds House (see chapter by Kirby Gregory in present volume) by opening an intensive day programme in Bournemouth. By the time it became known as SHARP it had been running for almost ten years. The strong recovering community in the area when the programme opened, ensured a level of local support for clients attending and graduating from the SHARP programme.

The SHARP model

The charities running the day programmes in the above locations merged in 2007 to form Action on Addiction, and the leadership team considered that intensive day programmes were more amenable to replication than residential ones, and had the potential in due course to help a larger number of people. The placing of treatment programmes on a day attendance basis within the community produces a situation in marked contrast to the traditional rehabilitation model, located perhaps in a country house and to a great extent insulated from everyday society. For those who are unable to maintain abstinence without such insulation, or whose physical or psychological issues require more intensive care, residential treatment will be the right choice. But for many others the advantages of intensive psychosocial treatment in the community may well be considerable.

The three SHARP programmes shared most of their therapeutic components but had evolved in different settings in different communities with different staff teams. This had led to some interesting differences in practices, and when the leadership team began the task of specifying an integrated treatment model that could be used to benchmark current programmes and provide a framework for future ones, these local differences were one aspect that needed to be analysed. Consideration was given to whether local variation could be tolerated as long as the core components were well specified, or whether this variation was an integral part of the model itself, an indispensible feature of a community-based programme that provided it with local congruence (Leighton, 2013: 178).

The SHARP programme is conceived primarily as an integrated or holistic experience consisting of participation in a treatment community. Although there are nowadays some elective activities, treatment is generally undertaken conjointly with other clients. Treatment activities are shared, and therapeutic mechanisms are assumed to be activated by developing a sense of belonging and acceptance, and by facilitating interpersonal learning through respectful mutual feedback and shared experience of change. The individual components each play their part in the change process, and it is assumed that individual coping can be enhanced by learning and practising skills in thinking, problem solving and behavioural choice. The cognitive-behavioural aspect of the programme is manifest in a series of weekly relapse prevention and recovery skills workshops attended by all clients, which work to identify and challenge thoughts and assumptions that might tend to perpetuate substance use or sabotage recovery. However as research has shown (Morgenstern and Longabaugh, 2000; Westen, Novotny and Thompson-Brenner, 2004) the relationship between the theoretical mechanisms of cognitive-behavioural skills training and outcomes is far from simple. Often there is little evidence that skills acquisition alone mediates the improved drug or alcohol use outcomes produced by such interventions.

The assumption at SHARP (as revealed in interviews with counselling staff and programme participants) is that although the skills learned in treatment are often of real practical use, another important value of participating is that the workshop and counselling sessions are *felt* to be relevant and engaging, and that the systematic and structured aspect enhances the *meaning* of the activities to the participant ('this is high quality, professional treatment that makes sense to me and is relevant to my concerns and those of my peer group'). The feeling of quality and professionalism is intended to enhance participants' experience of being valued, as demonstrated by independent qualitative and quantitative evaluations of the service (below).

A central treatment activity in SHARP day care, as with the residential centre, is interpersonal group therapy (Yalom, 1995; Leighton, 2004; Flores, 2013). There is a double rationale for this. First, by learning to make more satisfying relationships, clients will form a social network which is mutually supportive, with some friendships developed in treatment continuing and enhancing recovery; and second, the problem of managing relationships without drug and alcohol use is addressed. This perspective on addiction stresses the relational aspects: not only is there usually a powerful, conflicted and disruptive emotional attachment to the addictive substance or behaviour itself, but relationships with others and with oneself are managed by using substances. Emotional closeness and distance, reward and punishment of self and others and many other aspects of relationship are mediated by the use of substances. Without the addictive behaviour a person has to relearn different ways of relating, and interpersonal group therapy offers what Yalom (1995) has called a 'laboratory for change' where new understandings of the impact and meaning of interpersonal interactions can be learned and new ways of improving relationship can be tried out. At the start, group therapy can seem an intimidating prospect but in most cases it comes to be experienced as perhaps the most important and helpful activity in treatment. In end-of-treatment client satisfaction questionnaires it is consistently rated the highest.

Each client is also assigned a personal counsellor with whom they meet regularly to create an individual treatment plan and to discuss issues that arise. The individual counselling is intended primarily as a process of escorting the client through the group-based treatment experience, but it also offers a private space to develop a therapeutic relationship, to disclose sensitive material which the client might not yet be ready to talk about in a group, and to have certain kinds of therapeutic conversation. These are usually of a motivational or supportive kind, or they involve the agreeing, explaining and processing of treatment tasks, such as cognitive behavioural worksheets and behavioural experiments, or exploring programmes of mutual aid.

Family involvement

The personal counsellor will also arrange and facilitate family meetings. These meetings usually involve one or two family members (perhaps a spouse or partner, a sibling or a parent) and the client, and are provided so that the participants can talk about the impact of the addiction in a safe space, to learn about supportive resources (such as mutual aid groups for family members), to discuss issues of responsibility (for example about family finances or childcare) and to plan for the immediate future. It is of course up to the client to consent to the involvement of their family members, but when it does occur it is almost always found to be helpful, and in evaluations family involvement is associated with a range of good outcomes. Therefore the possibility of family visits is always explored and encouraged where appropriate. The placing of the treatment programme in the community generally makes family involvement easier as they are more likely to live locally. Family members are frequently invited to client graduation ceremonies at SHARP, and their presence can make these events even more moving. The involvement of family members with children also facilitates referrals to the M-PACT programme (described by Lorna Templeton elsewhere in this book) which is offered several times a year in all the localities where SHARP is currently running.

The physical and social environment

The activities described above are examples of formal interactions, but these take place in a context that includes the physical environment, the personalities of the staff encountered by the clients, the ethos as exemplified in simple practices such as smiling and greeting each other, making each other cups of coffee, or in traditions such a weekly communal lunch with food and beverages contributed by clients (longstanding in Liverpool on Fridays, about to be introduced in Bournemouth). Meeting each other informally out of programme hours, for friendly interaction or for support and encouragement also plays a part in maintaining the therapeutic power of the programme. As we shall see even shared transport arrangements can enhance the client experience. When a client rings the door bell in the morning, signs in with a friendly bit of banter in reception and moves into the kitchen to join others making refreshments before the day starts, chatting and laughing, perhaps going out to the courtyard for a cigarette, they are clearly being invited to belong. The responsibility for washing up and keeping the place tidy is also partly that of the client group, and it is plain to any visitor that they take this seriously. An attractive, clean and comfortable environment is an important message about the value and dignity of their clients that programme providers wish to underline.

Nevertheless, the process of a client coming to feel that he or she is 'in the right place', to feel accepted and part of the group, is not always straightforward. Clients often enter the programme with significant problems in a range of life domains. Most are vulnerable, not least because they have only recently become alcohol and drug free, and during the programme they may well experience setbacks, disappointments or personal problems. A common sight in the morning gathering just described is that of one or two clients talking encouragingly with another who seems forlorn or distressed. At the same time the counselling team is meeting upstairs, taking note of which clients are struggling, and making plans to try to support them during the day. This might range from a counsellor having a brief check-in with a client, to accompanying them to a family hearing or social services conference about child custody. On some mornings the team may become aware that a client has not arrived for the programme, perhaps because they are distressed, on the verge of dropping out or preoccupied with some life problem. Attempts will be made to contact the person and encourage them back to SHARP as soon as possible. Arrangements are in place (varying in each location in accordance with treatment system procedures) to maintain contact if the client has lapsed to alcohol or drug use and to readmit them at an appropriate point, when they are again drug free and ready to address the reasons for their lapse.

This atmosphere of caring concern for individual clients and for the client group as a whole does not simply reflect the humane ethics of the staff, it is regarded as essential to the therapeutic power of the programme. It is only by fostering this kind of mutual respect and valuing that clients can be expected to immerse themselves in the treatment community, to become committed to it (of course to varying degrees and in individual ways) and to embark, to a greater or lesser extent, on a project of identity change or renewal. The feeling of acceptance makes it possible to engage with the demands and challenges of treatment, as well as the emotional re-awakening, often painful but often exhilarating, that accompanies the emergence of care and concern for self and others. The experience of the programme is tough not because it is oppositional or confrontational, but because it invites one to care, to experience emotional intimacy through trust and openness. It is likely that disrespectful, self-defeating behaviours and attitudes will be pointed out by fellow clients or staff, but not in a disparaging or humiliating way, and this kind of honesty is regarded as a mutual responsibility. Simultaneously there are opportunities to enact responsible, caring and creative behaviours, to give as well as to take, and thus to start the process of regaining a feeling of value and participation. For someone whose substance dependence has progressed to the point where their self-respect has eroded away, and where one of the functions of the substance use has been to blanket difficult feelings and problems and avoid responsibility, which is the case with almost all of SHARP's clients, a programme of this kind can seem frightening or overwhelming. But it is also clear to most that if they are able to engage, it offers an exciting glimpse of hope. The connection with people who are further on in their recovery journeys, for example by meeting volunteers working at the project, or people at mutual aid meetings, adds to the feeling that significant and sustained change might be possible.

Another important aspect of the treatment experience consists of the social activities and opportunities for recreation and fun. So in Liverpool, the Brink, an alcohol and drug free bar and social space run by Action on Addiction, offers a place for people to meet after the day's programme before going home or attending a mutual aid meeting. Evening events, such as film screenings and music performances, are also held here and can be attended by those on the day programme. The bar is also a resource for people before they embark on the SHARP programme: they can come along and informally meet others in recovery who can share their experience of treatment and encourage them, or they may access a confidential and discreet counselling service, known as the Brink of Change, which can support, motivate and inform a prospective SHARP participant. Many SHARP clients attribute the courage to start and persist with the SHARP programme to this preparatory experience.

During the programme, the team may take occasional opportunities to offer activities which provide an experience of fun, laughter and spontaneity without alcohol or drugs. A recent example was that clients of SHARP together with some of the counsellors organised an afternoon game of rounders in a local park. Some passers-by were so taken with the impression of exuberant enjoyment this produced that they struck up a conversation, and wanted to know where the group were from. The clients were unabashedly open about being in treatment and the enquirers were astonished and edified. This example of interaction with the local community could not be reproduced in a residential treatment centre.

Exploring mutual aid

The SHARP programmes have as one of their core elements the exploration of mutual aid. The tradition of the Minnesota Model is to focus exclusively on the 12 Step versions of mutual aid, and the original SHARP programme followed this tradition. Participants are expected to attend several 12 Step meetings a week, several other group sessions, as well as individual assignments exploring the 12 Step programme itself, perhaps by studying one or more of the steps and understanding their application. This element is still available, and there are 12 Step meetings available in Bournemouth and Liverpool, and formal treatment sessions examining the 12 Steps are still part of the weekly schedule. However, for some time now these activities have become elective: it is possible for all clients to choose a non-12 Step pathway through the programme, where alternative recovery skills workshops are provided and meeting attendance is optional. All clients are also encouraged to consider alternatives to 12 Step mutual aid, such as SMART Recovery meetings.

Evaluation

In 2013, a new SHARP programme was rolled out in Braintree, in the east of England. This was commissioned by the local Drug and Alcohol Partnership, which asked for certain variations in the programme. First, the programme was to run in cohorts, rather than as a rolling programme, and the treatment was to be of eight weeks' duration rather than twelve. Clients could be referred there from other local towns from where transport would be provided. This project was a pilot, and subject to an independent evaluation. Local academics produced quantitative and qualitative evaluation reports (Elwell-Sutton, 2014; Senker, 2015) which assessed the value of the programme to participants as well as quantifying certain change indicators during the period of treatment.

Partly as a result of this pilot study, a new therapeutic framework (described in more detail in Leighton, 2013) was devised for SHARP which mapped the various components on to a treatment process model, of overlapping stages of motivation-engagement, psychosocial change, building recovery capital, and reintegration-recovery. Of these the conceptual centre of the model was building recovery capital (Cloud and Granfield, 2008) and it was decided to evaluate and rationalise the components of the programme in terms of the potential to increase recovery capital, in particular what is referred to as human, social and cultural capital.

The domains of recovery capital in our framework derive from an instrument called 'Assessment of Recovery Capital' or ARC (Groshkova, Best and White, 2013). These are Substance use and sobriety, Global psychological health, Global physical health, Citizenship, Social support, Meaningful activities, Housing and safety, Risk-taking, Coping and life functioning, and Recovery experience. The framework for SHARP is designed so that the core and optional activities each contribute to building these domains (in our framework 'citizenship' has been renamed 'community involvement'). We asked that the ARC be included as part of the above evaluations. The use of this instrument has been extended to all our treatment services in a form that produces a coloured bar chart, which is shared with and explained to each client at each assessment point, so that they receive a visual representation of this aspect of their change process.

In the case of Elwell-Sutton's evaluation of the first two SHARP Essex cohorts, he was able to show that the ARC strengths scores for these cohorts increased significantly over the period spent in treatment, even for those who did not complete the programme. The finding of benefits for those who did not complete the full eight weeks was supported by statements from the qualitative interviews. These interviews, conducted by Sarah Senker, were later augmented with further interviews and focus groups from the fifth and sixth cohorts to produce a rich picture of clients' experiences of the programme. One client, who had been asked to leave the programme shortly before he was due to complete, for breaching the abstinence requirement, was also interviewed. Senker included family members of a client in a small focus group session and interviewed members of the counselling team. Despite an excellent research method that did not inhibit criticisms or negative views, Senker's analysis of these later interviews produced such a weight of positive statements from clients and so few critical ones, even from deselected clients, that she felt obliged to comment on this in her discussion.

A variety of themes emerged from Senker's study. Strikingly, several clients had entered the programme with some scepticism, but had become positive about the advantages of being situated in the community. Several were worried about speaking out in group therapy, and one continued to find groups uncomfortable, but had committed to attending all groups and offered specific examples of what he had gained. Overall, clients found group therapy of significant benefit, and it seems to have played a key part in developing a sense of community which was also particularly valued. One client said that as a result of group therapy she had developed a mutually supportive friendship with someone she would not normally have spent time with. The programme particularly emphasises peer support, the opportunity to offer help and companionship to others, and not just to receive a service. Many comments were made about the value and importance of this mutuality. Some explicitly stated that this was the most important aspect of what they had gained, and there was a general appreciation that these benefits would endure past the end of the formal programme and form part of the support structure for their recoveries.

Counsellors were highly regarded by those interviewed, with clients not only valuing the opportunity to have a confidential space to talk to their assigned counsellor, but also appreciating the counselling team's competence and accessibility, and their ability to inspire hope and encourage persistence when a client felt like leaving. Since most of the team were new to this type of programme when SHARP began, this high regard on the part of the client group might be seen to reflect not only their professional and human qualities, but also the robustness of the treatment model itself, with its clear structure and coherent therapeutic approach. Furthermore, the ability of the programme to be flexible and to attend to the needs of both individuals and the group as a whole was noted and appreciated by the interviewees.

Even the logistical arrangements required to enable clients to travel to SHARP, such as shared taxis, were seen as contributing to the sense of community. Spending time travelling with peers on the same programme, or with volunteers who had completed a previous one, 'consolidated friendship' as one client put it. The programme was seen as responsible for rebuilding morale and confidence in people who, before entering SHARP, had been in a very low state, generally demoralised, withdrawn and isolated, depressed and even suicidal. It was seen by those who completed it as a chance at a new life which was already beginning to be actualised. Senker's interview sample was small, and the participants volunteered to be interviewed, so not everyone's views were included. It would certainly be of value to hear from more of those who did not complete the programme, as it is not conceivable that every client will benefit to the same extent as those interviewed. However the themes that emerge from both the earlier and later interviews are unusually clear.

As the SHARP programme in the east of England has proceeded through several cohorts, the completion rates have increased, and this is probably partly to do with 'bedding in', but it is also likely that more appropriate referrals are being made of clients who are 'ready, willing and able'. Appropriate referral is critical to the success of SHARP because, as has been made clear, it places expectations on clients to make very significant changes in their lives. The best candidates are those whose predicament has created a real desire for change, or those in whom hope and motivation could be instilled by exposure to the programme. Self-selection is of great importance here, but the encouragement of knowledgeable drug or alcohol service staff may also be crucial. A person cannot choose what they do not know or have minimal understanding of, and this applies to both programmes like SHARP and addiction recovery generally.

Conclusion

There is a gap between mainstream community drug services and residential rehabilitation in the United Kingdom. Although there is still a place for residential services, and for some clients they may be essential, evidence is emerging that equivalent outcomes can be produced from structured treatment programmes such as SHARP, based in the community. As we have seen, such programmes have some advantages over residential in terms of their relationship to local recovery resources and the recovering community. Programmes like SHARP are still rather rare, as the model has not yet properly entered the consciousness of the addiction treatment field. Day programmes of a much less structured kind are sometimes offered, but these do not usually resemble the structured intensive experience of SHARP, which is designed to provide a cohesive and involving therapeutic milieu equivalent to that offered in the best residential programmes. The number of people that can be referred to residential is currently limited and is likely to remain so, for various reasons including cost and accessibility. Many more could benefit from community-based treatment if it were available more widely. It will be important for its replication that the programme continues to receive evaluation and that its cost effectiveness is demonstrated, as it has the potential both to be the entry point into recovery for many more people, and also to strengthen local recovery wherever the programme takes root.

References

Cloud W and Granfield R (2008) Conceptualizing recovery capital: expansion of a theoretical construct. *Substance Use and Misuse* 43(12–13): 1971–1986.

Elwell-Sutton T (2014) *Community-based Drug Rehabilitation Pilot – Interim Evaluation*. Unpublished report available from: Tim.Leighton@actiononaddiction.org.uk

Flores PJ (2013) *Group Psychotherapy with Addicted Populations: An Integration of Twelve-Step and Psychodynamic Theory*. London: Routledge.

Groshkova T, Best D and White W (2013) The assessment of recovery capital: properties and psychometrics of a measure of addiction recovery strengths. *Drug and Alcohol Review* 32(2): 187–194.

Leighton T (2004) Interpersonal group therapy in intensive treatment. In: Reading B and Weegmann M (eds.) *Group Psychotherapy and Addiction*. London: Whurr.

Leighton T (2013) Counselling in structured day treatment: the co-production of recovery. In: Mistral W (ed.) *Emerging Perspectives on Substance Misuse*. Chichester: Wiley Blackwell.

Miller WR and Hester RK (1986). The effectiveness of alcoholism treatment. In: Miller WR and Heather N (eds.) *Treating Addictive Behaviors*. New York: Springer, 121–174.

Morgenstern J and Longabaugh R (2000) Cognitive-behavioral treatment for alcohol dependence: a review of evidence for its hypothesized mechanisms of action. *Addiction* 95(10): 1475–1490.

Senker S (2015) *A Qualitative Evaluation of SHARP Community Rehabilitation Programme*. Unpublished report available from: Tim.Leighton@actiononaddiction.org.uk

Spicer J (1993) *The Minnesota Model*. Center City, MN: Hazelden Foundation.

Westen D, Novotny CM and Thompson-Brenner H (2004) The empirical status of empirically supported psychotherapies: assumptions, findings, and reporting in controlled clinical trials. *Psychological Bulletin* 130(4): 631.

White WL (2014) *Slaying the Dragon: The History of Addiction Treatment and Recovery in America* (2nd ed.). Bloomington, IL: Chestnut Health Systems/Lighthouse Institute.

Yalom ID (1995) *The Theory and Practice of Group Psychotherapy*. New York: Basic Books.

Chapter 4

Residential treatment

Countering the chaos of addiction

Kirby Gregory

Introduction

Residential rehabilitation facilities for addiction in England (and the programmes they offer) differ according to their aims, client group and length of stay. They can be either rehabilitative or supportive, long stay or short stay. Rehabilitative short stay programmes usually last less than 12 weeks. These can be divided into intensive programmes (providing medical and therapeutic interventions for clients with complex medical needs) and lower intensity programmes for clients with shorter drug and alcohol misuse histories and who are more likely to be able to return to employment and housing with community or family support. Rehabilitative long stay programmes last approximately six months or more. These may be better suited to clients who are socially excluded, unemployed, in severe housing need, lacking in life skills, and prolific offenders. Supportive programmes provide accommodation, often following treatment in a rehabilitative programme, with specialist drug/alcohol and non-drug/alcohol related support. They are suitable for clients with low dependence on drugs and alcohol or who are now abstinent and have low care needs.

Services may utilise different 'philosophies', such as Faith Based, 12 Step or Therapeutic Community, which determine their approach. Some services may target specific groups and provide interventions and services appropriate to the needs of these groups, which may include drug-using pregnant women, drug and alcohol misusers with severe and enduring mental illness, and families and substance users in crisis. This chapter focuses on residential treatment programmes provided by Action on Addiction in England at Clouds House in Wiltshire and Hope House, London.

When established in 1983, Clouds House provided a programme based on the Hazelden, or Minnesota, treatment model. Clients were predominately alcoholics and there was a strong link to the 12 Step fellowship of Alcoholics Anonymous (AA). AA was formed in Ohio, USA in 1935, publishing its first basic textbook, 'Alcoholics Anonymous', in 1939. The AA 12 Step programme, which rather than simply aiming for abstinence from alcohol offers a way to recover from alcoholism, incorporates a spiritual approach which views alcoholism as an illness. Regular attendance at AA meetings and engagement with other AA members is the cornerstone of their approach. Membership in 2013 had grown to over 2 million (Alcoholics Anonymous, 2015).

The Clouds House programme began to include people addicted to drugs and this coincided with the emergence and growth of Narcotics Anonymous (NA) in the UK using an adaptation of the AA programme. Many of the counselling staff were themselves in recovery, and used their direct experience of addiction together with their membership of the fellowships as the basis of their approach. From diverse backgrounds, with some having formal counselling training and others coming from other fields such as education or the clergy, their role could be seen as more akin to 'professional AA sponsors' whose primary aim was to introduce clients to the first five steps of the 12 Step programme and prepare them for regular attendance at AA meetings.

Over the years there have been many changes in both the content of the programme and the way it is delivered, including the salience of 12 Step assignments, developments in the detoxification regimen, the management of mental health issues and greater use of complementary therapies such as acupuncture, reflexology, shiatsu massage, relaxation techniques and physical exercise. The psychosocial programme has incorporated interpersonal group therapy, cognitive behavioural therapy, motivational interviewing, cognitive analytic therapy, art psychotherapy, creative writing and a specialised supervision model for staff.

Two important developments in the work of the charity as a whole came directly from the experience of Clouds House. These were the recognition that in addition to their involvement in treatment, families of addicted people needed and deserved help in their own right, irrespective of whether the addicted person was seeking help. This led to the formation of Families Plus (now For Families) in 1989 whose activities are described elsewhere in this book. The other significant development was the recognition that there was a need for a specific training programme to ensure that counselling staff were able to deliver the programme effectively. This led to the establishment of a formal training programme in 1987 and the subsequent creation of the Centre for Addiction Treatment Studies, also described elsewhere in this book.

The need for a residential environment

For some people who have problems with alcohol or other drug use, receiving treatment in the community, close to their families and familiar surroundings, will provide an effective and realistic start to their recovery journey. Returning home from the treatment programme each evening can reinforce recovery in the context in which it will continue in the long term, and allow those around them to see (and adjust to) how their recovery is progressing. Action on Addiction has many years of experience delivering this model of treatment with much success.

For others, however, the familiar context of the community will contain environmental and relational triggers to addiction that may well, in the short term, be overwhelming, presenting a barrier to establishing and maintaining abstinence and recovery. For those in such a position, residential treatment offers a relatively short-term respite from the day to day pressures of living with addiction and provides a safe space in which to build a foundation for long-term recovery. The twenty-four hour nature of the experience, with others who are on a similar journey and where the focus on addressing addiction and building recovery is not lost or diluted, provides a containment that allows feelings and situations that would otherwise be too overwhelming to be tolerated, understood and managed.

It is not uncommon for people to question the validity of this approach. They may say that it does not teach people to deal with real life in the real world. That it provides a bubble that feels safe at the time but which at best may give a false sense of security or at worst result in people being ill-equipped to deal with the harsh realities of life when they leave treatment. It is important to recognise, however, that some people may be so entrenched in the day to day chaos of addiction, with few recovery resources available to them, that residential treatment provides the only realistic way to establish a recovery foothold. The idea that it is not real (because it is distanced from the pressures and threats of the environment in which addiction operates) is a misconception. The reality of residential treatment is that it gives temporary relief from the addictive environment: it offers the addicted person the opportunity to face up to and deal with the relational and behavioural problems that their addiction otherwise leads them to avoid.

To some extent this turns the idea of what is real on its head. The real world is internal as well as external and treatment can allow a person to make sense of the relationship between these often opposing aspects of their life in a different way, and intensify the recovery experience. The currency of the treatment environment is honesty and trust – two things that are usually absent in an addict's day to day functioning. It is belief-driven in the sense that it promotes the idea that optimism can replace hopelessness.

What people can recognise and change about themselves in the treatment environment will become directly transferable to their everyday life and relationships outside of treatment. The residential setting aims to allow people to learn how to do this in a manageable and sustainable way. It provides a safe place to eat, sleep and reflect on what needs to be done to find and sustain a healthier lifestyle in the company of like-minded people. The surroundings have a powerful effect on how people think and feel. A calm and quiet environment can ameliorate the anxiety which keeps them stuck. It is the short-term respite from the overwhelming situations that accompany addiction which will allow the addicted person to build the resources necessary to survive and thrive upon their return to the reality of the world outside. I have often heard clients talk about the importance of feeling cared for and how this, especially early on in treatment, can provide a sense of safety and containment that allows them to concentrate on what they are doing. Having someone to talk to at any time of the day or night, whether staff or peers, contributes to this feeling of being safe and contained.

Community culture and peer support

When people are thrown together in the face of adversity something powerful can happen that can awaken a shared sense of purpose based on the need to survive. Most people who come to residential treatment have tried, with varying degrees of success, to be free of their addiction, and many have come to the conclusion that they cannot do this alone. Thus, one of the important components of the treatment programme is to introduce clients to the concepts of self-help, mutual aid and peer support. As part of the treatment process clients will be introduced to 12 Step fellowships such as Narcotics Anonymous and Alcoholics Anonymous and other peer-support groups such as SMART Recovery, which offer a widely available and free long-term recovery resource.

In residential addiction treatment there is a focus on promoting a sense of community spirit and peer support that can become a springboard into long-term recovery. The mechanism of how this works is profound and involves people seeing beyond their differences and focusing on what they have in common. For those who are struggling to be free of addiction, the commonalities are not far below the surface: fear, anxiety, low self-esteem and hopelessness. The individual client in treatment will have the opportunity to recognise the personal obstacles to engaging with peer support and mutual aid groups and to modify their behaviour accordingly, allowing them to successfully engage with other recovering people. This is not just about plugging into a network of support and receiving help; it is also about discovering what they have to give of themselves to others. This process is enhanced by the fact that the treatment community is not static. Each week new clients arrive and existing clients complete treatment and move on. This is an important aspect of the model as it means that clients can move from the position of newcomer, being supported by more senior peers, to themselves becoming senior members of the community able to support and encourage those new to the programme. This can be the source of an increase in self-esteem which can strengthen the prospects of a sustained recovery.

An important ingredient of this kind of treatment is the mixed client group. At Action on Addiction, we provide treatment for men and women (the latter usually comprising around 40 per cent of the treatment population) aged from 18 upwards (82 is our eldest so far), from a wide range of ethnic, social, economic, educational and cultural backgrounds. There is something very powerful about this client mix, where the usual cultural and social boundaries lose their significance and the currency of treatment becomes a person's humanity rather than their status. It seems to allow social interactions that in everyday society would be unlikely but which can contribute significantly to personal growth and change. This is the engine that drives the treatment community. What can be recognised about a person's behaviour (by themselves and others) and subsequently illuminated and understood, can give that person the opportunity to experiment with different ways of relating to self and others and to change behaviours that limit their lives.

The Action on Addiction residential programmes are designed to combine the power and benefit of peer support and mutual aid with a structured psychosocial programme which directly addresses the client's addiction. In effect the programmes become a place for clients to learn how to benefit from, and contribute to, mutual aid: with the aim that it will enable them to use this knowledge and experience to maintain abstinent recovery beyond treatment in the long term. In order to achieve this we separate our treatment into first-stage and second-stage programmes.

First-stage treatment

The first aim is to establish abstinence and to build a solid and sustainable foundation for long-term recovery. The first responsibility is to stabilise health which for the majority will involve a process of withdrawal from the substances they are dependent upon. This process is managed by a medical team who are on-site twenty-four hours a day. Abstinence is necessary but not sufficient for recovery. It is not just about giving up drugs and alcohol but about adopting a new lifestyle that allows growth, health and peace of mind to flourish. Clients in first-stage are able to shift their view of the purpose of treatment from being about survival to living a healthier and more rewarding life.

People are thoroughly assessed prior to treatment and, depending on their individual circumstances and recovery resources, engage in a programme of four or six weeks. Most clients spend the first two weeks in the process of detoxification, and experience two to four weeks engagement in the therapeutic programme whilst drug-free. This is important as it allows them to gain a different perspective on their interactions with others and to modify the view they have of themselves: from addicted person to recovering person. This can have a significant effect in building two important resources for recovery: self-esteem and self-efficacy. We have recognised that the body heals quicker than the mind and that people are very vulnerable following detoxification. They are susceptible to thinking that, because they are drug-free, addiction has lost its power. This is a dangerous underestimation of psychological dependence, and it is crucially important to address this during detoxification.

The programme provides a structure, replacing what is often the chaotic and meaningless pursuit of addiction with a containing framework. The art of treatment lies in managing how tight or loose this framework needs to be at any given time. If too tight it stifles the clients' self-efficacy and breeds dependence on the staff. Too loose and addiction can get a foot in the door, treatment loses its meaning, with the danger of clients feeling aimless and demotivated. Both of these positions undermine the ethos of the recovery community and so the treatment team constantly strives to find the balance between these extremes. It requires a high level of communication between staff to keep in touch with what is going on. Through regular team meetings and group supervision sessions, information about the way the community is functioning can be exchanged and reflected upon. This allows the staff to manage the treatment environment with flexibility and sensitivity.

Recovery is a creative process and creative therapeutic activities play an important role in treatment. Helping clients to re-connect with their creativity is important because the process of building a new identity as a recovering person is central to recovery. Twice-weekly art therapy groups and creative writing sessions are designed to allow clients to approach self-exploration from different perspectives. The groups are structured to complement and reinforce the interpersonal aspects of the treatment programme by allowing reflection and active group discussion of the work created individually.

Second-stage treatment

For some people the process of building and consolidating recovery needs more time than first-stage treatment provides. The aim of second-stage is to continue strengthening both internal and external resources, with recognition that there may be issues which require further exploration and support. It is important that this programme enables the client to take more responsibility for managing their recovery and to engage with the world in a more proactive way. As the journey of recovery is one of moving from dependence, through inter-dependence to independence, the second-stage environment and programme loosens the boundaries of the treatment container, progressively shifting the balance from structured treatment activities towards self-determined and managed recovery. Thus, the structured treatment programme occupies the morning to early afternoon, with the clients being responsible for organising and managing their remaining time, including attendance at and affiliation to mutual aid activities. The time-frame for this process depends to a great extent on the individual's capacity and resources but in order to give the client a realistic chance of making these changes the treatment episode is usually between 12 and 24 weeks in duration.

Hope House

Established in 1988 as an eight-bedded unit in Maida Vale, London, Hope House is our second-stage treatment centre for women. In 2009 it moved to the suburb of Clapham, expanding capacity to 23 beds. The Hope House treatment programme is based on the same guiding principles, theoretical underpinnings and delivery structure as the Clouds House model. However, although there is much in common, there are some important differences in the client group, the therapeutic aims and length of treatment, which require specific approaches and delivery. The female-only (clients and staff) setting provides a safe and containing environment in which treatment and recovery can flourish.

We have recognised that many women's addiction problems are compounded by other factors such as unhealthy relationships (often with men), trauma, parenting issues and eating disorders. It has been our experience that in a mixed-gender first-stage treatment programme these issues are often brought to the fore, highlighting the need for a safe and contained environment in which women can continue their recovery. For many of the women it may be a long (or the first) time that they have been able to experience, understand and develop healthy relationships with other women as, for many, their often unhealthy relationships with men may have precluded this. The absence of men is significant as it allows the women to create a safe haven in which to address some of the issues which may have been hidden or avoided. Exploring these issues can feel very risky and the identification with each other's histories and experiences requires high levels of containment.

The Hope House second-stage treatment programme combines structured treatment for half of the day with the opportunity for clients to self-structure their remaining time. This will include regular attendance at the self-help fellowships. The programme duration is 12 weeks. As in first-stage treatment there is an ongoing process of assessment and adjustment of the treatment plan and as a result of this process some women remain in treatment for a further 12-week period.

The aim of the programme is twofold: to help clients deal with the important issues which, if left unaddressed, may make maintenance of long-term recovery difficult or impossible; and to provide a framework for their reintegration into wider society. This requires a measured approach that achieves a delicate balance between areas which can contain conflicting and difficult-to-manage feelings. For many who are parents this will include building, or rebuilding, relationships with their children. For those who are estranged from their children, the staff team will be able to assist with the process of managing the reality of the situation, often liaising with social services and the courts.

During weekdays lunch is provided by staff but the rest of the time the clients organise and prepare their own meals. This will be a particular challenge for clients who have a difficult relationship with food and eating. As a result there are regular 'food groups' where the clients can talk with and gain support from others with similar issues. As with Clouds House, we do not treat anorexia and the focus is on peer support, reflection and self-regulation rather than control.

Understanding addiction as a relationship

Those coming to residential treatment have to some extent begun to face up to the fact that their relationship with drugs and alcohol (or behaviours such as gambling or sexual acting out) can be highly destructive. Although it is clear that alcohol and drug misuse starts as a response to any number of situations and internal states, as it develops into addiction it takes on a self-perpetuating life of its own. The reality is that addiction becomes the primary relationship and making the choice to be abstinent involves a process of letting go, and experiencing concomitant grieving. This has serious implications for families and other significant persons who often feel that they have been relegated to second place on the list.

The boundaries of abstinence

The goal of treatment is the establishment and maintenance of abstinence from all mood-altering substances. This goal takes into account the vulnerability that dependent people have to cross-addiction or substitution, and addresses the potential for relapse. However, this raises questions about where the boundaries of abstinence are. Many of our clients smoke cigarettes and whilst we limit this activity to some extent in treatment by not allowing smoking in the building there remains the issue that many clients are addicted to nicotine and do not wish to give it up. Although most acknowledge the long-term negative health consequences, they see it as a problem that can be dealt with at some point in the future. At present we take a pragmatic approach to this, offering support with smoking cessation and encouraging clients to view smoking as part of their addiction.

This raises important questions for us as a treatment provider: by allowing clients to smoke in treatment, are we colluding with addiction? This is an area which needs to be addressed and resolved. Our clients are currently taking responsibility for deciding where their personal boundaries of addiction are with regard to nicotine. The role of treatment is to educate and illuminate the issues around the nature of their relationships with substances and behaviours in order for the client to make informed decisions about their behaviour. It goes beyond cigarettes and includes their relationship with food, exercise, relationships and sex.

Therefore the usefulness of understanding addiction as a particular kind of consuming relationship is that the recovering person can take responsibility for recognising when they are engaged in an addictive relationship, and choose to abstain from it. However, they cannot do this alone; addicts in isolation are susceptible to convincing themselves that what they are doing is not addiction. This is often called denial. The collective wisdom and experience of groups and communities of recovering people offers the addicted person a chance to escape from the trap of self-delusion. This requires that they trust others, and for many it is easier to trust someone who has been there and established recovery themselves.

Thinking about the family

Addiction does not exist in isolation: it always has a context and for most people that involves being part of a family. It does not make sense to address someone's addiction without paying attention to the context in which it operates. Addiction can have a profound impact, influencing behaviour and undermining relationships. The negative effects of addiction are felt across the family and it is our view that you do not have to be an addict to suffer from addiction. There is great benefit in including families in the treatment process, giving both the addict and their families the best prospect of creating and maintaining recovery. Our residential treatment programmes always keep this in mind and aim to include family members wherever possible.

The individual and the group

The individual needs of clients can be identified and addressed in a number of ways by the multidisciplinary team. Each client is allocated a 'focal counsellor' upon admission. This member of staff will be responsible for the individual case management of the client and will consult with members of the team and other professionals as required. The relevance of medical and psychiatric issues will be considered. The issues identified are prioritised, and those most relevant to the establishment of recovery are written into an individual plan. This plan sets achievable and measurable goals in each area, and suggests assignments to help the client move towards these goals. The assignments include individual study and reflective exercises, as well as group activities. In addition to case management the counsellor will help the client to understand the importance of interpersonal relationships, guiding them to effectively engage with the group and wider community. This is a crucially important aspect of the programme as it is helping the client to reformulate their issues and problems in an interpersonal context, reinforcing the idea that the community is the engine of recovery.

The main focus of the treatment community is group. This can range from formal group therapy sessions, to educational lectures and workshops, to socially focused activities such as country walks, singing and spending time together in the main lounge. Clients attend 90-minute group therapy sessions five times per week. The core model is Yalom's Interpersonal Group Therapy Model (Yalom, 1995). This reformulates the client's problem behaviours and symptoms as interpersonal problems, and then gets the group to work in the 'here and now' on the interpersonal process that may be occurring between the group members. The central idea is that people are not getting the satisfaction they would like from their relationships with others, and that problem behaviours (including inappropriate drug or alcohol use) are developed as a way of coping with this. Improving interpersonal functioning is thus a central and explicit task of our treatment, perhaps the most important one. It also serves as a kind of interpersonal relapse prevention training. Group therapy creates, for most clients, a feeling of bonding and belonging and is very highly valued by our completing clients.

Elements of the treatment programme

The programme is characterised by an integration of therapies that are usually seen as individual (such as the development of coping skills) with those that are clearly relational or social. There are seven major elements of our treatment programme.

The 12 Step approach

This conceptualises a person's inability to control or limit their drink or drug use as 'powerlessness'. The suggested response is to accept that abstinence is the only realistic approach, rather than trying to control consumption, and that this will allow the dependent person to be free from the struggle of addiction. In order to achieve and maintain abstinence the steps provide a framework for a new way of living and dealing with life's challenges. Central to this is the concept of 'higher power' which is left to individual members to define but is often seen to be God or the power of the group/fellowship. Although both Clouds House and Hope House introduce clients to the 12 Step approach and encourage active participation in the self-help fellowships, it is not necessary for clients to be convinced of their commitment to this upon admission. If someone is adamant that they are not interested in exploring 12 Step then we would recommend that they look elsewhere. However, if they are open-minded about exploring its benefits we will work with them on that basis.

Cognitive behavioural therapy

Functional analysis is used to identify why and in what circumstances a client uses alcohol or drugs, identifying high-risk relapse situations and determining what they need to do to either avoid or cope with whatever triggers use. Relapse prevention workshops enhance coping skills and increase self-efficacy and cognitive therapy is used for anxiety and anger management.

Interpersonal therapy

This aims to improve interpersonal relating and the self-to-self relationship. This is primarily achieved through interpersonal group therapy and the monitoring of individually identified problematic interpersonal and self-management procedures.

Health behaviours

This educational programme is designed to increase health behaviours, improve sleep pattern, teach relaxation skills and inform the client about the benefits of good diet and exercise. Also included is information about the management of and reduction of transmission risk for viral infections, particularly Hepatitis C and HIV. In addition there is an opportunity to experience a variety of complementary therapies.

Personal meaning

The exploration of personal meaning and purpose aims to reduce feelings of emptiness and boredom and increase hopefulness. It involves an exploration of beliefs and values and may or may not include a spiritual aspect, depending on the individual client's inclination.

Family

Family work offers the opportunity to help family members assess their relationship with the addicted person, how they have adapted to and coped with the problem, and what kind of adjustments might be desirable to facilitate better relationships in the future, to start the process of healing past hurts, and to anticipate possible setbacks. Family members also have an opportunity to learn about the treatment process.

Complex needs/dual diagnosis

Complex needs can include issues such as historical trauma/abuse, issues of loss and abandonment, patterns of forming unhealthy and destructive relationships with others, homelessness and self-harming behaviours. Dually diagnosed clients will have, in addition to substance dependence, a formal mental health diagnosis such as schizophrenia, anxiety disorder or personality disorder. For those clients who have complex needs in addition to their substance dependence, or are dually diagnosed, there is an individual programme of assessment where additional treatments or interventions are considered.

It is important to understand that all of these elements are at play at all times during treatment and that it is vital to view them in the context of the 24 hour a day experience of the treatment community. In this way the psychosocial programme can be understood as part of the wider experience of the clients sharing activities such as mealtimes, relaxation, walks in the countryside. The bedrooms at Clouds and Hope House are shared, providing the opportunity for mutual support, safety and companionship. For addicted people, who often have been isolated and lonely, this can prove (often after some apprehension) to be an important part of their treatment and recovery experience.

Assessing psychosocial issues

Although addiction is indiscriminate in who it chooses, not all addicts embark on their recovery journey from an equal position. A person's ability to recover can be influenced by the internal and external resources available to them. Having (or not having) a family, a secure place to live, a job, an education, social skills, money, will be significant to sustaining recovery. Action on Addiction uses the internationally recognised Assessment of Recovery Capital tool (ARC) to measure the quantity and quality of resources an individual has that can be used to facilitate and sustain long-term recovery. The results are depicted in the form of a bar-graph, which can be used as a visual aid at various stages in the recovery journey to enable clients to see where they currently are, the progress they have made and what they can continue to work on. Similarly, we also use the Action on Addiction 'Fit-to-12 Step' tool to evaluate how clients can make best use of the 12 Step support network. As well as being useful in assessment and recovery planning, it is also a meaningful way of evaluating the viability of recovery in the longer term.

De-selection from the programme

This can be one of the most difficult aspects of managing the treatment community. For the treatment team there is always a challenge in balancing the needs of the individual client with the safety and wellbeing of the treatment community as a whole. Because clients have made a huge personal commitment to abstinence when they enter treatment they are entitled to expect the treatment environment to be drug and alcohol free, safe from threats of violence, intimidation or discrimination.

It is sometimes only when a client has broken the boundaries which are designed to maintain this safety, such as by consuming drugs or alcohol whilst in treatment, that they understand how this is a personal obstacle to recovery. In such instances an individual may have gained valuable insight into their addiction from which they can learn, with the potential to move on in their recovery. However, breaking these boundaries is also deeply undermining of the ethos of safety and containment that is central to the treatment community. In these situations, despite the potential for individual growth, it is rare for the person who has transgressed to be able to remain in treatment. They will of course be encouraged and supported wherever possible to use what they have learned to continue their recovery. This will usually involve referral back to the referring agency or care-manager, referral to other services in their locale and attending self-help groups.

Conclusion

The UK national treatment system, which is designed to address the whole spectrum of substance misuse issues from problematic drug and alcohol use to severe dependence, is organised into treatment tiers. Residential treatment (Tier 4) is aimed at helping those who are dependent, often severely, on alcohol and/or drugs. The National Treatment Outcome Research Study (NTORS) (Gossop, Marsden & Stewart, 1998: 6) concluded that 'clients in the residential programmes were some of the most severely disturbed, and these clients made some of the greatest treatment gains'. A follow-up study found that although not all clients did well, 'the finding of reductions in problem behaviours together with the relative stability of outcomes between 1 year and 4–5 years is both interesting and important' (Gossop et al., 2003: 301).

In summary, residential treatment offers an intensity of experience that removes people from the networks which support addiction and encourages concentration on recovery. The alcohol and drug free environment and culture of recovery within a group setting is an antidote to isolation. It may also provide respite for others at home who are at risk. The containment of the managed environment and structured programme counters the characteristic chaos of addiction. The community of individuals working together towards shared goals fosters new healthier norms in interpersonal relationships. The message we give to clients is that long-term recovery requires a robust network of people who are supportive of recovery, combined with the practical application of recovery orientated behaviours. Just like addiction, recovery requires practice and repetition. As the National Treatment Agency (2012: 11) concluded, 'Residential rehabilitation is a vital and potent component of the drug and alcohol treatment system and should continue to be so . . . as one potential element of a successful recovery journey.'

References

Alcoholics Anonymous (2015) *AA Fact File. SMF-132*. Available at: http://www.aa.org/assets/en_US/pressmedia/m-24-aa-fact-file (accessed 14/04/2015).

Gossop M, Marsden J and Stewart D (1998) *NTORS at One Year. The National Treatment Outcome Research Study: Changes in Substance Use, Health and Criminal Behaviour One Year after Intake*. Department of Health. Available at: http://www.dh.gov.uk/prod_consum_dh/groups/dh_digitalassets/@dh/@en/documents/digitalasset/dh_4076746.pdf (accessed 14/04/2015).

Gossop M, Marsden J, Stewart D and Kidd T (2003) The National Treatment Outcome Research Study (NTORS): 4–5 year follow-up results. *Addiction* 98(3): 291–303.

National Treatment Agency (2012) *The Role of Residential Rehab in an Integrated Treatment System*. Public Health England. Available at: http://www.nta.nhs.uk/publications.aspx?category=Residential+services+-+inpatient+and+rehabilitation (accessed 14/04/2015).

Yalom ID (1995) *The Theory and Practice of Group Psychotherapy*. New York: Basic Books.

Part III

Action for families and young people

Chapter 5

Families

You don't have to be addicted to suffer from addiction

Nick Barton

The number of people living with or relating personally to people with addictions is difficult to quantify precisely but it is generally accepted that the numbers are very significant. Conservative estimates work on a ratio of four family members to each addicted person, which would mean in the UK alone there are somewhere between 5 and 12 million people in this situation (Velleman and Templeton, 2007). A significant sub-group within that figure are 1 million UK children living with parental drug misuse and 3.4 million children living with parental alcohol misuse (Manning et al., 2009). If scaled up internationally, and further widened to encompass families where a member is abusing substances but has yet to warrant a diagnosis of an addiction, the population to which we are referring is an extremely large one (the word 'multitude' springs to mind) and should be taken very seriously indeed.

It appears that despite some contextual differences, the experience and harmful impact of the substance misuse of a family member are remarkably similar all over the world (Orford et al., 2005). To quote these authors, '. . . living with a relative with a drinking or drug problem is a very particular experience . . . It is bad for the health of the family members and for the health of the family as a whole' (Orford et al., 2005: 117).

This chapter will look at the origins and evolution of the work of the UK charity Action on Addiction with families affected by addiction, explaining in the process the thinking behind the variety of specific interventions that the charity has developed and the overall approach it takes to families in the context of responding to addiction. It will also discuss how the theoretical basis of practice, and the knowledge, understanding and skills of the workforce needed to change accordingly. It will close by making an argument that it would be in society's interest for the addiction field as a whole to think beyond the individual, and to make a bold and positive investment in a much more family-centred response to the needs of people affected by addiction.

In 1986, gathered in a somewhat faded retreat centre in Warminster, England, were sixteen adults who identified themselves as family members; in other words, people who were at that time, or had been previously, in a personal relationship with someone suffering from an addiction. The addicted person in their lives did not have to be in recovery, in treatment or even be help-seeking at the time. The people who gathered in Warminster were from various parts of the UK as well as abroad, and did not know each other. There was nervous anticipation. They had arrived to take part in what was and is still known as the Family Programme.

In welcoming our guests to the first gathering we, the facilitators, said we suspected that some might have come to learn how to fix the addicted person in their life or at least to understand why they were as they were. There was some eager nodding as if a curative formula was about to be revealed. 'We are afraid', we carried on, 'we are not going to do that . . . because we can't.' Heads went down. 'What we are going to do', we continued nonetheless in positive tone, 'is ask you a simple question, and that is: How are *you*?' We very deliberately placed emphasis on the 'you'. There was a brief pause before several people broke down in tears.

While we had foreseen the probability of a moment for reflection, we had not expected our question to demolish some clearly fragile defences. But our simple solicitation had gone to the heart of the reason we had invited these people to our new programme: that they had lost touch with their own needs. So focused had they become on the one with the addiction that they no longer paused to consider their own welfare. There was, in their minds, no time for that. Everything had come to depend on change occurring in the one they loved. But away from the object of their obsession, an unexpected empathy for their wellbeing, even from strangers, was too much to deflect, so raw were they.

This was a very important moment in the life of the charity and the development of its challenge to addiction. It signalled a clear acknowledgement that the people it had been established to serve included not only anyone with the obvious manifestations of addiction but also those relating personally to them, including spouses, partners, parents, grandparents, offspring, siblings, friends and even colleagues at work. It also recognised the necessity of responding to families and their non-addicted members in their own right, rather than as had previously been the case, solely in relation to the person with the addiction, the 'identified patient'. The latter arrangement had generally been the order of the day across the addiction field, including within our own services, where families were commonly considered peripheral to the main concern, which was seen as being the treatment of the addicted person. Unrecognised at the time was the fact that this exclusive approach directly paralleled the fixation of the families themselves. The underlying belief or assumption was: focus on getting the addicted person successfully treated and all will be well. This approach was, like addiction itself, counterproductive, and much of the professional world was in effect colluding with the dynamics of addiction while firmly believing it was doing the very opposite.

The brief residential programme for family members

The Family Programme is a five-day (midday Monday to midday Friday) structured residential experience devised by some of us working at the residential treatment centre Clouds House which was run by the then charity, the Life-Anew Trust. This later became Clouds, which in turn was subsumed into the new Action on Addiction by a merger in 2007 with two other charities. The Family Programme mixes interpersonal group therapy and workshops that address typical issues such as how addiction affects families, family roles, managing stress, understanding powerful emotions, healthy coping, self-care and self-esteem.

However, many years priors to this, taking inspiration from the mutual aid fellowships of Alcoholics Anonymous and Narcotics Anonymous, some family members had formed their own mutual aid groups, calling them respectively Al-Anon (alcohol, formed in 1951) and Families Anonymous (drugs, formed in 1971). The basis of mutual aid consists of help and support reciprocally exchanged between people in similar situations. This group model formed the foundation of professionally delivered abstinence-based rehabilitative treatment programmes in the UK, and is often referred to as the Minnesota Model as a reflection of its geographical origins. It was therefore no great leap that mutual aid should be placed at the core of the brief residential programme for family members. People more or less in the same situation identify with each other and, with professional assistance in a safe setting, come to a greater understanding of how addiction has consumed them too, a process that helps them to find ways to reclaim their lives. Taking time out and away from the focus of their obsession, which is the addicted person, allows them to reconnect with their own needs. It is in a real sense partly a process of withdrawal. Like any withdrawal process it is not without discomfort. Coming to terms with powerlessness over the other person after having put so much time and energy into the struggle to get them to change is a difficult adjustment to make. But as with the person who lets go of their drug, new possibilities open up. The world expands rather than, as it does with obsession, and as it does with addiction, inexorably contracting.

At Clouds House, the charity's residential treatment centre in Wiltshire, England, the families of clients had previously been viewed solely as a source of information, or perhaps, evidence. More crudely it might be said they were invited to 'dish the dirt' on the addicted person in treatment in order to break that person's presumed denial as to the nature and extent of their addiction problem. The family was sent forms to fill in that became, in effect, the charge sheet of the family's experience of living with addiction and its unpleasant consequences. While family visiting days did include an invitation to a discussion of the principles and benefits of Al-Anon and Families Anonymous, the two mutual aid fellowships for families, the systemic approach that was to develop later was some way off.

The assumption underpinning any involvement of families was that the addicted person adversely affected the other members of the family unilaterally. It was a one way street. This was an understandable viewpoint given the visible and tangible impact of a family member's addiction, but it subtly fostered the very censorious and moralistic view that the philosophy of the treatment programme hoped to avoid. If the reverse relational influence, family on addict, was ever considered it was generally with the idea that families could encourage their overtly addicted family members into treatment and support them to stay there, as well as provide some sort of unpaid aftercare. While that may often be the case and there is evidence to support its value, the idea that members of families or the family system as whole might have been co-opted to play a dynamic part in initiating or sustaining addiction was rarely, if ever, given serious consideration. Any suggestion to family members that they might not only be affected by, but also might affect the other person, was usually met with vigorously defensive rebuttal. They tended to react as if they were being blamed for the addiction. 'It's not my fault. I'm not the one with the problem, it's him/her.' It is not hard to see why they would take this position. In a curious way, this is the flip side to the blame that addicted people sometimes aim at their families in order to avoid responsibility for their own behaviour. If we have learnt nothing else we can at least see that blame, in whichever direction it is aimed, is an unhelpful distraction that delays meaningful engagement with a process that can help everyone.

Helping distressed family members understand that their tendency to focus exclusively on the addicted person and their progress or otherwise towards recovery may not be helpful either to them or their addicted loved one remains a particular challenge. No matter how kindly you ask 'How are you?' it is clear many family members would much rather continue to focus on the other person. That is seen as where the problem lies and where the solution is to be found. But again it mirrors to some extent the difficulty the addicted person has in letting go of the relationship to their substance or behaviour.

It became increasingly clear to the team at Clouds House that families had an essential part to play in treatment, and eventually specialist family counsellors were recruited to serve as integral members of the multidisciplinary treatment team. While providing much needed dedicated support to families, this also served to ensure that the family perspective and context was held in the collective therapeutic mind of the team and taken fully into account in treatment planning and delivery. This was not about attaching an interesting side line to the approach current at the time but a different way of thinking that was continuing to emerge and drive practice. It was also no longer acceptable to leave family members to stew in their distress or communicate with them solely in relation to the addicted person but to think about them as members of a system as well as to provide for them in their own right. Thinking systemically became central. It was no longer acceptable within the charity's addiction services to think of helping someone without reference to the context of their lives as a whole or their most important relationships, which were such an affecting part of that context. It is the 'affect' part of the word affecting that is so important here. The excitation and mediation of emotion plays the pivotal role in addiction and there are few things more capable of stirring emotions than family relationships.

It was not until later that families were identified as critical elements in the concept of 'recovery capital', the personal and social resources that an addicted person has at his or her disposal to aid the process of recovery (Granfield and Cloud, 2001). The lack of family support constitutes a considerable deficit where such resources are concerned. Nevertheless, it took persistence to ensure that the approach of the core treatment programme which addressed the needs of individuals, albeit in the context of a programme based on mutual aid, included the involvement of families. Naturally there was resistance. Addictions counsellors often find it hard to see beyond the individual client in whose interests they work and whose care they are asked to manage. This may well be because clients are assigned to their care as individuals and that individual is the one they actually see and engage with most of the time. It may also be because of the anxiety arising out of dealing with more than one person, especially for counsellors untrained in this particular dimension and, more obscurely, because it risks putting them in touch with issues arising in their own families of origin.

Once again there is a parallel. The counsellor may unwittingly come to mimic the exclusivity of the family member's concern. They can find themselves reacting to their client's behaviour in treatment just as a member of the family would. They may become anxiously controlling, judgemental, even punitive or dismissive. Or, they may become overly cosseting and protective. They may inadvertently 'enable' the addiction, as it has often been termed. It is essential that counsellors receive regular clinical supervision to help them maintain an appropriate perspective on their relationship with clients. Unconsciously, clients frequently invite those helping them to adopt roles that replicate historic relationships. These invitations have to be recognised for what they are, as well as understood as sources of vital information and insight.

The new approach was given encouragement by the findings of an independent evaluation of the outcomes of Clouds House. A 30-month follow-up study undertaken by psychologist Alex Georgakis (1995) indicated that those who involved their families tended to do better than those who did not. While caveats must inevitably be expressed because some people would have had families with whom they could engage, and others were in no position to involve their families in the first place, and it was better that some did not, the principle holds up. Not long afterwards the brief residential programme for family members was also submitted to independent evaluation (Georgakis and Shepherd, 1997). That study arrived at two findings of particular note. The first was that those attending the residential programme for family members experienced a range of mental (anxiety, depression, low self-esteem) and physical (aches and pains, tension, weariness, susceptibility to infection) symptoms of distress that were measurable by standardised tests and which were shown by these tests to be of a surprising degree of severity. Secondly, despite the significant impairment to health, a relatively brief intervention could bring significant relief to these symptoms and this relief appeared to last for at least a year rather than fading on return to home life as might have been expected.

In 1998 the decision was taken to invest in a visible commitment to working with families affected by addiction by establishing a specialist division within the then charity of Clouds. Rather than members of the residential treatment team continuing to undertake programmes on behalf of families, a separate entity was created with its own team, resources, and strategic plans to serve its own constituency of beneficiaries. It was given the name Families Plus to signal two things: that we were positive about addressing the needs of families within the framework of an addiction charity, and that our intention was to encompass all those personally affected by another person's addiction. Six years after the merger in 2007 of three charities that resulted in the current Action on Addiction, Families Plus was superseded by Action on Addiction: For Families. By this time the charity's response to the needs of families affected by addiction had matured and diversified.

The workforce

It is all very well to recognise that families affected by addiction need specialist help and support but it is quite another to provide anything meaningful by way of response to the need. Because the field had largely relegated families to the periphery, if not simply discounted or perhaps never even considered the value of including them in the treatment plans of their addicted loved ones, expertise was in very short supply. A workforce with the capability essential to providing an effective specialist service for families did not exist. Something had to be done to address this deficiency both where Clouds' immediate plans were concerned but also at a strategic level nationally.

Over the ten years that Clouds was gradually fashioning a dedicated and direct response to families, there was a comparatively well-developed field of generic family therapy in the UK with leaders such as the Institute of Marital Studies at the Tavistock Centre or the Institute of Family Therapy but the knowledge and skills had not yet come to encompass addiction and its effect on families. At about the same time others in the academic world (particularly such luminaries as Professors Richard Velleman (University of Bath) and Jim Orford (University of Birmingham) were urging the field to recognise the effect of addiction on families. Adfam, a charity founded by a parent of a heroin addict, was established in 1984. Professor Griffith Edwards, of worldwide renown and co-founder of the National Addiction Centre, was speaking cogently of the need to take a family inclusive approach to addiction. As is so often the case, a number of players were being carried in the same direction by the current of an underlying imperative, though not necessarily in co-ordinated fashion or at the same speed.

In the development of our own expertise combining knowledge and skills of family therapy and addiction treatment, an important step was for selected personnel to acquire the know-how our workforce did not possess. The charity Clouds had seen the need for addictions counsellors to be trained to a much higher standard than ever before and in the late 1980s it embarked on a project to that resulted in the foundation of the Centre for Addiction Treatment Studies (CATS). The charity became a franchised partner of the University of Bath, designing and teaching a Foundation and an Honours degree in Addictions Counselling. Where working with families was concerned, professional education was directed at three different constituencies:

1 people in the addiction field wishing to work with families in a specialist way
2 people seeking to become rounded addictions counsellors/practitioners/therapists, and
3 members of the workforce of universal services who, in the course of their work, inevitably come into contact with families affected by addiction.

The degree courses taught by the Centre (or CATS as it is generally known) include a module on Working with Families Affected by Substance Misuse. This means that graduate counsellors who spread out across the addiction field to work in a variety of settings bring a much more rounded and integrated view to their therapeutic endeavours. They in turn may help to influence for the better thinking and practice within their current and subsequent places of work.

Systems theory

Key to the training of people to work effectively with families affected by addiction, as it is in any serious attempt at family-related work, is the need to understand systems theory. The essence of systems theory as developed by Dr Murray Bowen in the US and others (www.thebowencenter.org) is that the individual parts of any socially constructed group affect the whole, and vice versa; that the interrelationships between family members and between individuals and others affect family and individual functioning for good or ill. Throw in a powerful dynamic like addiction and the system rearranges itself to accommodate the demands of this force. Addiction is powerful, self-protecting, and will co-opt allies to maintain itself. This may result in family members assuming new roles or variations of old ones in an unwitting collusion with addiction. New unhealthy norms which go largely unrecognised are created; and so addiction prospers.

Clinical supervision

Clinical supervision has long been understood to be an essential adjunct to effective and ethical psychotherapy practice as well as in psychosocial addiction treatment programmes serving individual adults. It did not take long to appreciate that it was equally relevant to working with families affected by addiction. In fact, the range of scenarios played out in family relationships and the powerfully affecting dynamics, suggested it might have an even more important role to play. The potential for practitioners working without recourse to an independent reflective supervisor to be tripped up by their personal blind spots, and thus to adopt counterproductive roles and reactions, is clear. It is especially important when safeguarding issues are in play.

Carer support groups

Not everyone can or wants to participate in a residential experience and so we decided that a model of support was needed that was more easily accessible in local communities for family members. With the help of funding from the UK Home Office's Recovered Assets Fund we devised a low-threshold, professionally facilitated support group which we called the Carer Support Group. The name was chosen in recognition that family members of people with an addiction were in a similar situation to families coping with disabilities or other life-threatening illnesses. The basis of the intervention is a two-hour weekly workshop dealing with issues arising in the lives of participants and promoting a practical approach to self-care. Topics include: dealing with shame and guilt, letting go, setting boundaries and family roles. The groups are encouraged to develop a mutually supportive safe environment in which trust and openness may flourish.

Counselling for individuals and couples

From the earliest forays into work with families, we have offered both individual and couples counselling. Sometimes these are provided on a standalone basis or as support to complement other programmes. Behavioural couples therapy is an addiction-related intervention underpinned by evidence (O'Farrell and Fals-Stewart, 2000).

M-PACT

In 2003, the UK government's Advisory Council on the Misuse of Drugs published its *Hidden Harm* report that drew attention to the plight of children living with addicted parents and other adults, and to the potential impact on their future well-being, including the risk of developing substance misuse problems. The phrase Hidden Harm has entered the vernacular as the catch-all term for the effects of parental substance misuse. The harm is hidden because of the stigma that attaches to addiction, the shame this engenders and the chronic fear within families of intervention by statutory agencies. *Hidden Harm* highlighted both the actual risks of harm and its potential long-lasting impact. The report, and its follow-up publication (Advisory Council on the Misuse of Drugs, 2007), made no fewer than 48 separate recommendations.

In the meantime, the team at Families Plus had been approached by two clients who were themselves parents and who challenged the fact that the service did not in any way directly provide for children. With this challenge and given the inescapable conclusions of the *Hidden Harm* report, the Families Plus team decided to take action. At the same time, we realised the need to collect data on the number of dependent children that were in the care of the individual adults we were treating. This is still not universal practice but, in our view, if children are to be properly protected, it should be.

The first thing was to select a manageable number of the most strategically important of *Hidden Harm*'s multiple recommendations and we settled (with some paraphrasing) on the following:

1 Devise an intervention to respond to the needs of the children
2 Make it as widely available and accessible as possible
3 Develop a workforce capable of delivering such a programme.

The team then held several focus groups with parents, and their children where possible, to explore what they thought would help. Background research was undertaken to see whether an intervention already existed and this uncovered the Strengthening Families Program (SFP) (Kumpfer, Molgaard and Spoth, 1996). This programme has an uncomplicated structure, focuses on strengths rather than deficiencies, was well supported by evidence, and had been selected by the US National Institute of Drug Abuse as one of three programmes for replication. The SFP model was being adapted for the UK by Dr Debby Allen at Oxford Brookes University but not specifically for use with families affected by parental addiction. We therefore undertook to make this adaptation and, after a great deal of careful work on constructing a manual, piloted the first Moving Parents and Children Together (M-PACT) programme and commissioned a formal evaluation (see chapter by Lorna Templeton in the present volume).

As with the treatment of individuals, the M-PACT programme is designed with a strong element of mutual aid included, as it brings different families together to work collectively at the same time on the issue they have in common. The M-PACT programme responds both to the needs of the individuals (adults and children) within the family and to the family as a whole. It has restorative as well as preventative potential. An addicted adult may come to recognise the need for treatment; a non-addicted adult may develop better self-care and more confident parenting; while a child may feel that, having had their reality recognised at last, they can reap a variety of benefits, including re-orienting themselves to priorities more appropriate to their stage in life. The family may loosen the insidious organising grip of addiction, improve interpersonal relationships and re-set its culture to embrace healthier norms.

The families who take part in M-PACT illustrate how addiction takes hold of a family to the point where it becomes the organising dynamic, determining many aspects of family culture and function. The systemic view held by M-PACT practitioners provides protection against the trap of blame, and allows the family to focus on releasing addiction's hold over their lives, both individually and as a unit. To understand that hold it is necessary to understand addiction itself. We think that is best done by its characterisation as an all-consuming relationship with a substance or behaviour. Self-perpetuation is in the very nature of addiction. This is achieved partly by the self-delusion that what is happening is not, and that what is getting worse is not really a problem at all. This delusion often intensifies as the problem worsens. The greatest encouragement to this harmful process is secrecy and the tacit acceptance that the family should not 'go there'. Honest communication goes underground as it becomes increasingly difficult to face up to it, and so distortion of roles and relationships takes over as a way of coping with the situation. Fear (mostly of loss of one kind or another) dominates but is expressed only in acting out, inverted emotions or symptoms. Anger festers and frequently erupts.

Shame stalks the home. It is a mighty uncomfortable place to be, especially for the children who in the case of parental addiction often participate in a reversal of roles that sees them become their parents' carers.

National policy

There are very good reasons, including economic ones, for much greater consideration at a policy level of families affected by addiction. This is not based solely on charitable empathy for suffering people. Such an approach will not only benefit families and their individual members but greatly enhance the effectiveness of the treatment system and thereby the prospects for wellbeing of the local community as a whole. Therefore there are significant health economic benefits to be had. It is clear that the mental and physical health of people relating closely to someone with an addiction are adversely affected to a significant degree. The ways they deal with their symptomatic distress often makes matters worse or at least adds to the burden on resources. If we multiply those symptoms which cut across both physical and mental health by the numbers of people (millions) who experience them, and then add in the cost of the resources being drawn on both formally and informally to ameliorate their distress, sometimes quite counterproductively, we should see that we are looking at a major public health issue, the equivalent of an epidemic. This would of course be daunting were it not for the fact that relatively brief interventions can alleviate those symptoms and set a family on course for a much healthier life, sustainable over the long term. What is more, it is likely that supporting family members in this way may also have a consequential benefit to the addicted person. Their recovery capital is greatly enhanced.

While there has been progress in bringing the involvement of families to the fore in the arenas of both policy and practice, and the UK National Drug Strategy of 2010 (HM Government, 2010) was encouraging in this regard, the perspective set out above suggests we need to go much further. Interventions that encompass the family need to be routinely included in the specifications issued by commissioners when inviting treatment providers to tender for service contracts. It is of course a difficult proposition because the mind-set that makes the addicted person the centre of therapeutic attention and therefore the focus for investment is profoundly entrenched. But at a time when economic constraints count for so much, we are obliged to look for imaginative responses that increase the possible returns on public or charitable funds expended. We have no doubt that with well-informed investment in family-focused interventions in the addiction field the public health gain will be significant. We have to change the attitude from seeing it as nice-to-have to recognition that it is essential. It is time for everyone involved at every level to think beyond the individual, from the outset.

Case study

The case study below illustrates the powerfully destructive hold addiction can have on a family, including the many facets of 'collateral damage'. It also more hopefully underlines the value of a response that encompasses the whole family and one that includes help for individual members as well as the unit as a whole.

Family profile

Mother: Alcohol misuser; Father: Non-user; Sons: Kevin aged 21, Mal aged 19; Daughter: Tracy aged 14. The mother had been drinking alcoholically for over 10 years. When intoxicated she became verbally abusive to her family and had been arrested several times for drunk and disorderly behaviour and indecent exposure whilst under the influence. She had attempted suicide several times. All three young people spoke about being unable to remember a time when their mother did not drink. They all agreed that the only time when things were OK at home was when their mother was out or asleep. The father worked long hours. Kevin spent most of his time away from home preferring to stay at his girlfriend's flat. Mal had put university on hold because he felt he could not leave his sister in the house without his protection. He had several police cautions for antisocial behaviour. The mother's previous engagements with local Drug and Alcohol Services had not resulted in any significant changes for her or the family.

Things came to a head after a particularly disturbing incident when the mother smashed up the house after drinking several bottles of wine. She broke furniture and electrical equipment and proceeded to violently threaten Tracy, swearing at her and spitting directly into her face. Tracy became frightened and in desperation called the police. Children's Services became involved with the family and as a direct consequence a child protection plan was implemented. Tracy was diagnosed with depression due to living with her mother's alcohol misuse and was prescribed antidepressants by a doctor. She had been regularly self-harming, cutting her arms and legs as a way to cope. On one occasion she attempted to take her own life by overdosing on over-the-counter medication. Her school attendance was poor, her grades were going down and it was observed that she was struggling in her peer group.

Tracy and her mother were referred to the Moving Parents and Children Together Programme (M-PACT) by social care. The father was unable to attend due to work commitments. An assessment took place in the family home and it was noted how all of the doors downstairs had holes in them where they had been punched and kicked. The mother presented as being paranoid one minute and very angry the next. At one point she fell to her knees and begged for help. The atmosphere in the house was described as being toxic. Tracy felt she was to blame for her mother's drinking. She felt unloved and very alone. None of her friends visited her at home because of the changeable behaviour of her mum.

Mother and daughter were offered a place on the M-PACT programme. Before the start the mother cut her wrist with a shard of glass and smashed up the house once again. During the M-PACT programme Tracy was able to verbalise what it was like living with addiction. Surprisingly quickly her mother came to realise just how much she had affected her children. Listening to the effects of her substance misuse on others provided the mother with a degree of insight such that she began to talk of wanting recovery. It was noticed that both of their levels of confidence and courage developed throughout the programme. The mother's case for referral to residential rehabilitation was supported and she entered a facility. Despite a history of long-term alcohol abuse this was the first time she had gone into treatment. While the mother was away, the father completed a five-day residential programme for relatives and friends affected by someone else's addiction. The programme offered information about addiction and its effects on others, guidance on related subjects such as stress and self-care as well as group therapy where opportunities were available to explore personal issues and receive help and support.

After a six-week stay the mother left residential treatment and continued to gain support from attending local aftercare services and AA meetings. The father became a regular member of a weekly carer support group for people affected by another's substance misuse. Together mother, father and daughter attended facilitated family meetings where they were encouraged to communicate honestly in age appropriate ways and to listen to one another's opinions and needs. Mother and father engaged in couples counselling and personal therapy. They decided to separate but did so on good terms. Their relationship moved to a warm friendship whereby all of the family were able to spend time together. Social Care closed the case as child protection was no longer appropriate. Tracy stopped self-harming and was taken off antidepressants. She has now left school after obtaining good academic grades and is in her second year at Art College. Her mother returned to full time work. She did have one relapse but was able to learn from this incident and has remained abstinent since. Mal had several personal therapy sessions for his experiences and is now in the process of joining the RAF. Kevin spends a lot more time at the family home with his girlfriend. All relationships within the family have improved considerably.

References

Advisory Council on the Misuse of Drugs (2003) *Hidden Harm: Responding to the Needs of Children of Problem Drug Users*. London: The Stationery Office.

Advisory Council on the Misuse of Drugs (2007) *Hidden Harm Three Years On: Realities, Challenges and Opportunities*. London: The Stationery Office.

Georgakis A (1995) *Clouds House: An Evaluation of a Residential Alcohol and Drug Dependency Treatment Centre*. Unpublished report available from: Nick.Barton@actiononaddiction.org.uk.

Georgakis A and Shepherd S (1997) *Clouds Family Programme: An Interim Evaluation*. Unpublished report available from: Nick.Barton@actiononaddiction.org.uk.

Granfield R and Cloud W (2001) Social context and 'natural recovery': the role of social capital in the resolution of drug associated problems. *Substance Use and Misuse* 36(11): 1543–1570.

HM Government (2010) *Drug Strategy 2010 Reducing Demand, Restricting Supply, Building Recovery: Supporting People to Live a Drug Free Life*. Available at: https://www.gov.uk/government/publications/drug-strategy-2010--2 (accessed 08/04/2015).

Kumpfer KL, Molgaard V and Spoth R (1996) The strengthening families program for the prevention of delinquency and drug use. In: Peters RDeV and McMahon RJ (eds.) *Preventing Childhood Disorders, Substance Abuse, and Delinquency*. Banff International Behavioral Science series. Thousand Oaks, CA: Sage Publications, 241–267.

Manning V, Best DW, Faulkner N and Titherington E (2009) New estimates of the number of children living with substance misusing parents: results from UK National Household Surveys. *BMC Public Health* 9: 377.

O'Farrell TJ and Fals-Stewart W (2000) Behavioural couples therapy for alcoholism and drug abuse. *Journal of Substance Abuse Treatment* 18(1): 51–54.

Orford J, Natera G, Copello A, Atkinson C, Tiburcio M, Velleman R, Crundall I, Mora J, Templeton L and Walley G (2005) *Coping with Alcohol and Drug Problems: The Experiences of Family Members in Three Contrasting Cultures*. Hove: Routledge.

Velleman R and Templeton L (2007) Understanding and modifying the impact of parents' substance misuse on children. *Advances in Psychiatric Treatment* 13: 79–89.

Chapter 6

M-PACT

Supporting families affected by parental substance misuse

Lorna Templeton

The M-PACT (Moving Parents and Children Together) programme is a structured whole family intervention which aims to guide families through the dual processes of understanding how addiction has negatively affected them and their family, and finding a way to make positive changes as individuals and families to overcome those negative effects. M-PACT was introduced in England in 2006 and, as it comes to its tenth anniversary, approaching 400 families have engaged with the programme. This chapter will cover the research, practice and policy context in which M-PACT was introduced, and in which it has since developed. An overview of the M-PACT programme, and the model which underpins it, will follow. This will include a profile of families attending and completing the programme, and findings from research indicating how M-PACT helps children, parents and families. Finally, the future and sustainability of M-PACT will be discussed, within the continually changing national and local context in which it operates.

Understanding the rationale for M-PACT

The M-PACT programme was developed in response to the report *Hidden Harm* (Advisory Council on the Misuse of Drugs, 2003), a seminal publication which brought the plight of the children of parental substance users to the fore, coupled with a plea from families asking the UK charity Action on Addiction to do more for children (Altobelli and Payne, 2014; Barton and Gulliver, 2009). In particular, the aim of M-PACT focused on three of *Hidden Harm's* 48 recommendations:

1 To develop dedicated services to respond to the specific needs of children;
2 To make these services widely available and accessible; and
3 To have a specially trained workforce delivering such services.

Since its inception M-PACT has operated in a context which has continued to stress both the size of the problem and how parental substance misuse can affect children in both the short and the long term. Estimates of prevalence highlight a problem far greater than the figures indicated in the *Hidden Harm* report, which focused on the children of drug misusers and did not closely consider the much more sizeable population of children of alcohol misusers. The headline figures from Manning et al. (2009), one of the most comprehensive studies (indeed, one of the few studies) since *Hidden Harm* in 2003 about the size of the problem, showed an estimate of nearly 3.5 million children under 16 years of age living with one or more parent with an alcohol problem, ranging from binge-drinking to dependent use. A further 335,000 were estimated to be living with a parent with a drug problem, a figure which increases to approximately one million children where a parent has used illegal drugs in the previous year (Manning et al., 2009). Furthermore, parental substance misuse is one of the most common issues on social worker caseloads, and a factor which is associated with poorer welfare outcomes , increased rates of re-referrals, and serious case reviews (Brandon, Bailey and Belderson, 2010; Cleaver et al., 2007; Forrester and Harwin, 2011). However, it should be noted that M-PACT aims to reach any family which is affected by addiction, not just those at the severe end of the spectrum where child and family services are involved.

A considerable library of evidence is now available which documents how all domains of a child's life, their development and environment, can be negatively affected by parental substance misuse (Adamson and Templeton, 2012; Cleaver, Unell and Aldgate, 2011; Houmoller et al., 2011). A critical element of this is how parenting, family life and family relationships can be adversely affected and dominated by substance misuse and its effects, circumstances which are often exacerbated by the presence of other commonly co-existing family and social difficulties, particularly mental health problems and domestic abuse (Brandon, Bailey and Belderson, 2010; Cleaver et al., 2007; Kroll and Taylor, 2003). An important finding from a study with 164 adult children of problem drinkers was that, when reflecting on their childhood experiences, many identified the disruption and disharmony (including high levels of violence) that the drinking had on family life as more impactful than the drinking itself (Velleman and Orford, 1999). Substance misusing parents can cause harm to their children in a variety of ways. Holmila, Itapuisto and Ilva (2011) point out that while there are some intended harmful acts such as violence or sadism, the majority of the harm derives from the unintended consequences of substance misuse. These consequences include poverty, reduced social status, and a general lack of care, support and attention. These harms can have a far-reaching impact on children's present and future lives.

Thus, it can be seen that children face considerable challenges and risks through living with parental substance misuse, with poor outcomes more likely where there are cumulative stressors alongside the alcohol and/or other drug use, and where the impact on family life and relationships is greater. However, it has also been recognised that children often respond to their circumstances with 'active agency', which they draw upon to take control by the coping strategies they adopt, the support they seek, and what they choose to share about their circumstances with others (Backett-Milburn et al., 2008; Hill, 2015; Holmila, Itapuisto and Ilva, 2011; Houmoller et al., 2011). Attempting to have some degree of control over their circumstances is just one of many protective factors which, if present, can build resilience in children who are exposed to parental substance misuse. It is now widely recognised that there are a number of processes, operating at individual, familial and environmental levels, which can reduce or prevent the impact of a risk factor by the way 'protective factors modify or transform responses to adverse events so that families avoid negative outcomes' (Benzies and Mychasiuk, 2009: 104). The presence of such protective factors can help to build resilience in children and families, with resilience defined as the ability to 'respond positively to an adverse event and emerge strengthened, more resourceful and more confident' (Benzies and Mychasiuk, 2009: 104).

However, resilience is more complex than this in a number of ways. It is a process rather than a static trait or outcome, and the combination of both protective and risk factors or processes will be different for every individual or family. Furthermore, protective factors can change over time, and some may be helpful in the short term but less so in the long term, in response to different circumstances. Confusingly, the presence of a protective factor, such as a child doing well at school, may in fact mask the problems they are experiencing, including other risk factors to which they may be exposed.

This all means that, as it becomes more common for services and interventions to balance risk reduction and safeguarding with building resilience, it is essential that practitioners have an adequate understanding of protective factors, resilience and their inherent complexities (Adamson and Templeton, 2012; Benzies and Mychasiuk, 2009; Velleman and Templeton, 2007). For example, a study in Scotland with 38 young people (aged 15–27 years) with at least one parent with an alcohol or drug problem highlighted that identified coping strategies and support were '*often fragile and conditional*' (Bancroft et al., 2004: ix), could be '*a double-edged sword*' (Backett-Milburn et al., 2008: 477); and furthermore that, '. . . *the protective factors classically thought to promote resilience were seldom in place for these children unconditionally and without associated costs*' (Backett-Milburn et al., 2008: 476) (emphasis added).

However, protective factors located within the family, particularly in terms of parenting and parent–child relationships, seem to be central to building resilience in children affected by parental substance misuse. The early years and key stages of a child's development appear to be critical times at which children can be at increased risk of poor outcomes and when a protective factor or process can be most influential (Velleman and Templeton, 2007). A review of randomised controlled trials of interventions for parents and/or children where there was parental substance abuse, although including only four studies, cautiously reported that focusing on parenting and family functioning appears to contribute to improved outcomes for children (Calhoun et al., 2015).

Research has also identified other factors which seem to be important. For example, a US study (Moe, Johnson and Wade, 2007) carried out qualitative interviews with 149 children aged 7 to 13 years who had a substance-misusing parent, and three themes emerged from children's comments about what is important with regards to resilience. First, in terms of substance misuse behaviour, children talked about the need for their parents and themselves to be free of substance misuse. Second, children held clear perceptions about the substance misuse behaviour, including not feeling guilty about their parent's drug/alcohol misuse, the important role of treatment and recovery, and parents as role-models (both negative and positive). Finally, children talked about internal resources, centred on their ability to express their feelings, knowing the truth about their parent's addiction and recognising the different choices, attitudes and activities which can encourage a sense of resilience. Based on these findings, the authors identified three ways in which practitioners can help support children to develop their own characteristics of resilience; namely, providing children with a venue in which to express their feelings, educating them about substance misuse, and showing them that there are other ways to live (Moe, Johnson and Wade, 2007).

In summary, it seems that attempts to help children and families affected by parental substance misuse should, first, target the ways in which families, and the relationships and individuals within them, are affected; second, offer help within a family context rather than with children in a vacuum; and, third, balance attention to issues of risk and safeguarding with efforts to manipulate protective factors and processes in order to build resilience. However, despite a significant growth in services and interventions for children and families over the last ten plus years, there is still a lack of firm estimates for how many children and families are affected by parental substance misuse, a postcode lottery of service availability, a dearth of evidence for what works best, a lack of clear understanding of how to build resilience and sustain positive change in the long term, and the need to best understand how to commission and deliver services (Adamson and Templeton, 2012; Clay and Corlyon, 2010; Manning, Clifton and McDonald, 2014). Nevertheless, the M-PACT UK rollout is making an important contribution towards filling these gaps.

The M-PACT programme

M-PACT is influenced by the Strengthening Families Program, a preventative and skills-based programme for vulnerable families, originally introduced in the USA but now successfully translated to the UK. M-PACT is a therapeutic whole family programme, which aims to support children within a holistic family context and to give them a safe voice. The 'M' of M-PACT stands for 'moving' and this comprises two elements: 'parents and children coming together after the fragmentation caused by addiction, and then moving forward as individuals and as a family' (Barton and Gulliver, 2009: 12). More specifically the aims of M-PACT are to reduce patterns of harmful behaviour associated with the parental substance misuse; reduce conflict by improving communication and family relationships; increase knowledge and awareness around addiction and how it affects everyone within the family; and identify individual and family strengths on which positive change can be based. Furthermore, M-PACT believes in working with whole family units to bring about change; targeting individual and family strengths to build resilience; and mutual aid through bringing together a number of families who are struggling with parental addiction.

Each M-PACT programme brings up to a maximum of eight families together for eight weekly meetings. A 'family' is broadly defined but typically includes at least one child of eligible age (8–17 years) with one or more adults, most commonly the parent with the identified alcohol or drug problem (who does not necessarily have to be abstinent but who must be engaged in treatment or stable on medication, and cannot attend programme sessions if intoxicated) but sometimes other non-using adults (with or without the attendance of the using parent). Each family completes a comprehensive assessment prior to being offered a place on a programme. The eight programme sessions run weekly for two and a half hours, with opportunities for follow-up through both an individual review with each family shortly after the final session, and a reunion roughly three months later which brings the families together again for the final time. Each of the M-PACT sessions focuses on a different core topic, with time at each session for children and adults to work separately as well as time when all participants work together in a group. There are seven core topics: introductions; two sessions on making sense of addiction; my family and communicating with those you care about; feelings and beliefs about yourself; individual and family first aid kits and toolboxes; endings. In addition, there are creative and social aspects which run throughout the programme. Attendance can be supported by a crèche for younger children and help with transport to and from the programme venue.

Four facilitators deliver each programme, sometimes supported by additional staff or volunteers. To guide M-PACT practice and ensure fidelity to its model there is a comprehensive practitioner manual, supported by intensive training (which is accredited by the University of Bath) and clinical supervision. Organisations or local collaborations wishing to deliver M-PACT must do so under licensed agreement (requirements cover staff training, delivery of one or more programmes within a defined time period, and the collection and submission of data on the work done).

Engagement with M-PACT

The first programme was run in 2006, and by the end of May 2015 there were 31 licensed M-PACT sites. The majority of these sites are in a range of community settings across England (there is one site in Wales and one in the Channel Islands), but there are also a small number of prisons where M-PACT is available. A partnership with Place2Be has seen the introduction of M-PACT at schools in four sites across England, while another collaboration, with the Amy Winehouse Foundation, is supporting the delivery of M-PACT across London.

Based on end of programme reports submitted by licence holders, by the end of May 2015 a total of 342 practitioners (from a wide range of disciplines) have been trained and have successfully delivered 98 programmes. A total of 368 families, involving 566 children and 502 adults (most commonly the parent with the drug or alcohol problem), have engaged with M-PACT. The national retention rate is high; in 84 per cent of families who start a programme, one or more individuals within that family completed Session 8.

All M-PACT programmes are required to collect basic data on each person who engages with M-PACT and on the sessions that they attend. From data available on 477 participants (who attended programmes at 21 licensed sites) it can be seen that:

- Participants come from 175 families and include 252 children, 134 adult users and 63 other non-using adults (usually a parent). Family size ranges between one and six individuals, but in just over three-quarters of families there were either two or three participants who engaged with M-PACT.
- Gender – more than half of children, nearly two-thirds of adult substance users, and approximately three-quarters of adult non substance-users are female.
- Age – the mean age of children is 12 years (range 8–19 years), the mean age of adult users is 38 years (range 24–54 years), and the mean age of adult non-users is 41 years (range 24–68 years).
- Ethnic status – the majority of all participants are White British.
- Substances used – problems with alcohol or illegal drugs (predominantly heroin and the opiates) are most common, although for a significant proportion of families the problems involved combinations of alcohol, illegal drugs and prescribed medication.
- Referral source – referrals to community programmes are most likely to come from statutory (adult or child) services or to be self-referrals. Referrals to prison programmes tend to come from within the prison, while the majority of referrals to the Place2Be programmes come from within the school setting.

How M-PACT benefits participants

Evaluation has been a core element of the programme since the first pilot in 2006. There is a solid qualitative evidence base for how M-PACT benefits children, adults and families. Drawing on interviews from 73 participants who completed 13 programmes, Templeton (2014) identified four themes to capture these benefits. These themes are supported by data from evaluation of the first programmes delivered in a prison setting, and also by emerging findings from the delivery of M-PACT through the school setting. The themes are: shared experiences; understanding addiction; communication; and healthier, safer, more cohesive families.

Shared experiences

Participants find it beneficial to meet, talk to and listen to others with similar experiences. This helps them to realise that parental substance misuse is a very common problem which affects a great number of families, thereby normalising their experiences while also offering peer support.

> We were all in it together so we all supported each other. (adult, community)
>
> It felt like it weren't just me who was living in a bad situation and wishing that my family could change. (child, community)
>
> It was good to tell someone about my feelings because I never get to tell anyone about my feelings. (child, community)

Understanding addiction

This involves a reciprocal process whereby parents accept greater responsibility for their problems, and children realise that the problems are not their fault and they are not to blame.

> M-PACT has made me realise what I was doing to these children. (mother, Place2Be)
>
> Every now and then I reflect on it and think that's why that's happening . . . and now I know why. (child, community)
>
> It highlighted my shortcomings. I was not playing the role I should have been playing as a father. (parent, community)
>
> I can't really change my parent, I have to learn to live with that . . . . getting on with my life and not letting problems affect me. (child, community)

Communication

There are a number of ways in which M-PACT supports improvements in communication about addiction and general communication within families. This includes changing communication styles, talking openly and appropriately about addiction, listening to children, and a reduction in arguments and conflict.

> Before we went to M-PACT, we never used to talk, we used to always shout at each other . . . but now we're getting on. (children, Place2Be)
>
> It's changed our relationship towards my family . . . . they've got a better relationship and they talk softly. (child of prisoner)
>
> [I've learned] to be calm, to actually listen properly to what they were saying not just the bits and pieces I wanted to hear. I think it's really helped me. (adult, community)
>
> Forcing the family to think about issues that we didn't talk about at home. (adult, community)
>
> We all get along, like before we all used to scream at each other and now we can talk to each other properly. (mother, Place2Be)

Healthier, safer, more united families

Families are more cohesive and have stronger relationships, and individuals and families can keep themselves safe.

> We felt like our family had drifted apart and we weren't a family any more but now we are, I realise, a special little family. (female partner of prisoner)
>
> I know how to keep myself safe and what to do to keep myself happy. (child, community)
>
> You won't fight for yourself but you'll fight for your children, I just want them to feel safe with me and not think what's mummy going to do now, I want them to feel safe and secure, and therefore happy. (adult, community)
>
> I know my brother and mum a bit more better than I used to, it brought us closer together . . . . normally I'm out playing with my mates, and [my brother] out with his mates, and mum in her room. Now . . . we all sit downstairs, watch TV, eat dinner together, which we never used to do before. (child, community)

There is also evidence that M-PACT can contribute to a range of other outcomes, including parents engaging in drug or alcohol treatment; children who are more confident, less angry and distressed, and who do better at school; and having a child protection plan removed.

> I think it helped because I ain't getting bullied no more . . . . I used to hate going to school . . . cos people used to call me names and that, but no-one does that no more. (child, community)
>
> If I didn't do that course I don't honestly know if I would have stayed clean, but to be put in that position, and given another chance with social services . . . .It was a fantastic programme, I can't fault it. (parent, Place2Be)
>
> I think this sentence has done more for me than any other sentence . . . . M-PACT has been a major part [of that], it's turned my thinking around . . . . I'm [in my 40s] and nothing has ever made me change my way of thinking. (male prisoner)
>
> It really helps you to build your confidence. First when I went there I was really shy even though I didn't know anything. The second week I was still really shy but when we were ending I was really confident. I felt like, in English, I can actually read out loud. (girl, Place2Be)

Finally, given the entrenched nature of the problems of many of the families who engage with M-PACT, it is inevitable that a brief programme will not be all that some families require, but it is also important that the intervention is time-limited so families do not become overly dependent on such support (Roberts, 2015). Therefore, an important feature of M-PACT is the post-programme review with each family which can help identify, signpost and refer individuals and families to other local services as required. Indeed, this need for further support is a key driver behind the collaboration with Place2Be, where children can also receive support from a school-based service before, during or after (or combinations thereof) an M-PACT programme.

An economic assessment, using a social return on investment (SROI) methodology applied to five M-PACT sites, reported that (depending on the level of caution applied to the figures included in the model, and on the proxy measures included) for every £1 spent, an M-PACT programme can save between £2.76 and £6.53 in the first year after engagement of a family (Interface Enterprises, 2013).

Learning and looking ahead

M-PACT embodies in a number of ways an integrated approach to supporting families affected by substance misuse. It brings together using and non-using adults with children, it brings together a number of families for each programme, and it considers both risk and resilience in the support which is offered. At a delivery level, most M-PACT teams are themselves multi-disciplinary and from a range of universal, health, social care and criminal justice settings. M-PACT is also at the heart of the holistic and recovery framework which drives the work of the UK charity Action on Addiction, and it is integrated with a number of its services.

Alongside this there are encouraging findings that, certainly in the short term, M-PACT can effect real change for individuals and families, that the programme itself brings economic value, and has demonstrated its potential in community, prison and universal settings. The ways in which M-PACT helps children, adults and families align with the aims of the programme. Moreover, it seems as if the programme can target some of the key individual and familial protective factors which are believed to create resilience in this population (Moe, Johnson and Wade, 2007; Velleman and Templeton, 2007). These findings also mirror those from the evaluations of other UK services and interventions (Adamson and Templeton, 2012; Cass and Fernandes, 2014; Clay and Corlyon, 2010), as well as general findings from other family group programmes which have highlighted that success can be a result of positive therapeutic factors such as group cohesion, observational experiences (such as being with others with similar experiences) and confidence in the therapists (Lemmens et al., 2009).

However, there is a need for further research (such as quasi experimental or randomised controlled trials) to more accurately assess whether the benefits of M-PACT can be attributed to the programme itself or to other factors; to understand what is effective in building resilience; and to investigate how positive change can be maintained in the longer term (Adamson and Templeton, 2012; Calhoun et al., 2015). In a practice and policy climate which is highly outcome-focused, the challenges of measuring longer-term change associated with family interventions have been highlighted (Tunstill and Blewett, 2015). This means that the measurement of what have been called 'interim outcomes' (or what Tunstill and Blewett call 'steps along the way') takes on greater significance, particularly when the complexities of many of the families who engage with M-PACT mean that outcomes cannot be straightforwardly measured. Moreover, while significant positive change in all areas is unlikely in the short term, a consideration of interim outcomes is helpful because '[it] is not to say that the small but important improvements taking place in the family are not crucial to the entire journey being made by the child and her/his family' (Tunstill and Blewett, 2015: 240). Furthermore, there is a need to develop services which offer early intervention with families, rather than the current pressure to intervene predominantly with families who are known to children and families statutory services (Adamson and Templeton, 2012; Manning, Clifton and McDonald, 2014).

M-PACT has achieved much in its first ten years and is continuing to develop in response to the need and the different settings in which it is being introduced. While it was, and still is, a clear response to *Hidden Harm*, the need for a service like M-PACT is as great, if not greater, then when it was conceived in 2006. Hence, M-PACT remains a unique and innovative response to a highly common problem, yet one where it is possible to effect positive change for children and their families. As M-PACT evolves it will hopefully continue to make a valuable and essential contribution to practice, policy and research in this area, including extending the diversity of families who engage with the programme (for example, to include younger children and those from a range of black and minority ethnic groups), and working to sustain positive change in the long term.

References

Adamson J and Templeton L (2012) *Silent Voices: Supporting Children and Young People Affected by Parental Alcohol Misuse*. London: Report to the Office of the Children's Commissioner in England.

Advisory Council on the Misuse of Drugs (2003) *Hidden Harm: Responding to the Needs of Children of Problem Drug Users*. London: Advisory Council on the Misuse of Drugs.

Altobelli C and Payne C (2014) Noticing the Hidden Harm. *BACP Children and Young People* March: 4–8.

Backett-Milburn K, Wilson S, Bancroft A and Cunningham-Burley S (2008) Challenging childhoods: young people's accounts of 'getting by' in families with substance use problems. *Childhood* 15(4): 461–479.

Bancroft A, Wilson S, Cunningham-Burley S, Backett-Milburn K and Masters H (2004) *Parental Drug and Alcohol Misuse: Resilience and Transition Among Young People*. York: Joseph Rowntree Foundation.

Barton N and Gulliver E (2009) Moving together. *Drink and Drug News* 12 September: 12–13.

Benzies K and Mychasiuk R (2009) Fostering family resiliency: a review of the key protective factors. *Child and Family Social Work* 14(1): 103–114.

Brandon M, Bailey S and Belderson P (2010) *Building on the Learning from Serious Case Reviews: A Two-Year Analysis of Child Protection Database Notifications 2007–2009: Research Brief*. London: Department for Education.

Calhoun S, Conner E, Miller M and Messina N (2015) Improving the outcomes of children affected by parental substance abuse: a review of randomised controlled trials. *Substance Abuse and Rehabilitation* 6: 15–24.

Cass R and Fernandes P (2014) *Evaluation of FED UP: Interim Report*. London: NSPCC.

Clay D and Corlyon J (2010) A review of services for children and young people with drug-misusing carers. In: MacGregor S (ed.) *Responding to Drug Misuse: Research and Policy Priorities in Health and Social Care*. Hove: Routledge, 179–189.

Cleaver H, Nicholson D, Tarr S and Cleaver D (2007) *Child Protection, Domestic Violence and Parental Substance Misuse: Family Experiences and Effective Practice*. London: Jessica Kingsley.

Cleaver H, Unell I and Aldgate J (2011) *Children's Needs – Parenting Capacity. Child abuse: Parental Mental Illness, Learning Disability, Substance Misuse, and Domestic Violence* 2nd edn. London: The Stationery Office.

Forrester D and Harwin J (2011) *Parents Who Misuse Drugs and Alcohol: Effective Interventions in Social Work and Child Protection*. Chichester: John Wiley and Sons.

Hill L (2015) 'Don't make us talk!' Listening to and learning from children and young people living with parental alcohol problems. *Children and Society* 29(5): 344–354.

Holmila M, Itapuisto M and Ilva M (2011) Invisible victims or competent agents: opinions and ways of coping among children aged 12–18 years old with problem drinking parents. *Drugs: Education, Prevention and Policy* 18(3): 179–186.

Houmoller K, Bernays S, Wilson S and Rhodes T (2011) *Juggling Harm: Coping with Parental Substance Misuse*. London: London School of Hygiene and Tropical Medicine.

Interface Enterprises (2013) *SROI Analysis: A Social Return on Investment Analysis of the M-PACT (Moving Parents and Children Together) Programme*. East Knoyle, Wiltshire: Action on Addiction.

Kroll B and Taylor A (2003) *Parental Substance Use and Child Welfare*. London: Jessica Kingsley.

Lemmens G, Eisler I, Dierick P, Lietaer G and Demyttenaere K (2009) Therapeutic factors in a systemic multi-family group treatment for major depression: patients' and partners' perspectives. *Journal of Family Therapy* 31: 250–269.

Manning J, Clifton J and McDonald C (2014) *'I think you need someone to show you what help there is': Parental Alcohol Misuse: Uncovering and Responding to Children's Needs at a Local Level*. London: Office of the Children's Commissioner.

Manning V, Best D, Faulkner N and Titherington E (2009) New estimates of the number of children living with substance misusing parents: results from UK national household surveys. *BMC Public Health* 9: 377.

Moe J, Johnson J and Wade W (2007) Resilience in children of substance users: in their own words. *Substance Use and Misuse* 42(2–3): 381–398.

Roberts L (2015) Time to change? Exploring the impact of time-limited service provision in a family support service. *Child and Family Social Work* DOI:10.1111/cfs.12229.

Templeton L (2014) Supporting families living with parental substance misuse: the M-PACT (Moving Parents and Children Together) programme. *Child and Family Social Work* 19(1): 76–88.

Tunstill J and Blewett J (2015) Mapping the journey: outcome-focused practice and the role of interim outcomes in family support services. *Child and Family Social Work* 20(2): 234–243.

Velleman R and Orford J (1999) *Risk and Resilience: Adults Who Were the Children of Problem Drinkers*. Amsterdam: Harwood Academic.

Velleman R and Templeton L (2007) Understanding and modifying the impact of parents' substance misuse on children. *Advances in Psychiatric Treatment* 13(2): 79–89.

Chapter 7

Young people and substance misuse

The power of personality

Maeve O'Leary-Barrett and Patricia J Conrod

Introduction

Alcohol and drug misuse prevention programs are typically delivered within community, family, or school settings. Increasingly, schools are being highlighted as the most promising setting for the implementation of alcohol and drug prevention programs, and a recent review of evidence-based prevention programs suggests that the effects of school-based prevention approaches are more favorable than those resulting from community-based, family-based, and multifaceted programs (Emmers, Bekkering, & Hannes, 2015). Most school-based alcohol and drug use prevention programs are universal approaches, with the same intervention applied across the whole of the selected population, and are based on the social influence model. Programs aim to teach youth about the harms of substance misuse, to increase generic coping skills and to promote balanced attitudes about normative substance use behavior in adolescence, as youth are shown to overestimate alcohol use among their peers, which in turn influences individuals' own substance use (Lynch et al., 2015), although there are some conflicting views (Pape, 2012). However, a number of systematic reviews have concluded that the evidence in favor of universal school-based programs is limited (Foxcroft and Tsertsvadze, 2011; Faggiano et al., 2014). Some programs even show iatrogenic effects (Werch & Owen, 2002). One example is the Take Charge of Your Life program, which was associated with increased alcohol and cigarette use over five years among youth who had reported not using these substances at baseline relative to a no-treatment control group (Sloboda et al., 2009). Certain programs have been identified as being effective in reducing the incidence of drunkenness and binge drinking, for example Life Skills Training, the Unplugged program, Good Behaviour Game (Foxcroft & Tsertsvadze, 2012). However, these programs are relatively time- and resource-intensive, requiring a minimum of 12 one-hour sessions, and have only mild effects on alcohol and drug use outcomes. Several other evidence-based programs have also proven difficult to implement in school settings due to time and resource constraints (Faggiano et al., 2008; Stephens et al., 2009).

Recognizing these limitations, there is increasing interest in the use of brief alcohol interventions (BAIs) to target alcohol use in adolescents, as these have the benefit of being less costly and more feasible to implement in real-life settings. A recent systematic review of 185 studies indicated that BAIs have modest efficacy in reducing alcohol consumption and alcohol-related problems in adolescent and college age samples (Hennessy & Tanner-Smith, 2015; Tanner-Smith & Lipsey, 2015). Indeed, research has demonstrated that brief interventions are generally as effective as those with longer durations (Gottfredson & Wilson, 2003). Although initial research has demonstrated intervention effects of BAIs up to one year post-intervention, few studies to date have examined BAI efficacy for longer than one year post-intervention with adolescents, and studies with college age samples showed that effect sizes were non-significant by two years (Tanner-Smith & Lipsey, 2015).

Brief intervention approaches most commonly use cognitive behavioral or skills training and motivational interviewing approaches, and a recent meta-analysis suggests that interactive forms of program delivery are associated with heightened efficacy, as opposed to programs that focus on psycho-education only (Hennessy & Tanner-Smith, 2015). This finding is supported by an earlier review of effective school-based programs (Gottfredson & Wilson, 2003). Certain motivational interviewing exercises, such as decisional balancing and goal setting, are associated with larger effect sizes in brief interventions for adolescents (Tanner-Smith & Lipsey, 2015). The importance of using skilled group leaders who are well trained, supervised, and implement programs with fidelity has been highlighted by several studies (e.g. Sloboda et al., 2009). Serious consideration needs to be given to the potential adverse effects of grouping high-risk youth in interventions aimed at reducing deviant behavior, due to the negative influence that high-risk peers can have on one another, resulting in exacerbation of problem behaviors. It is suggested that the effects of such "deviancy training" may be reduced in the presence of a skilled group leader (Dishion & Dodge, 2005).

Selective approaches

Whilst experimentation with alcohol and drugs is a relatively normative behavior during adolescence, only a subset of substance users will progress to more problematic use. It is therefore of particular importance to identify and target those individuals who have a heightened risk of developing problematic misuse. Selective approaches to prevention differ from the universal programs in that they target known risk factors for addiction. Though less frequently implemented than universal programs, selective prevention approaches are associated with stronger intervention effects (Gottfredson & Wilson, 2003; Foxcroft & Tsertsvadze, 2011), and have the potential to have a large public health impact (Willenbring, 2013). Theoretically, targeting interventions to particular risk profiles facilitates change in a positive direction as interventions focus on etiological processes underlying problematic behaviors, thus addressing the root cause of the issue.

Longitudinal research has highlighted the importance of numerous risk factors on the development of early-onset substance misuse and addiction (Grant, Stinson, & Harford, 2001). Namely, the impact of family history, externalizing disorders, internalizing disorders, childhood adversity and trauma, high school drop-out, and personality factors is well established. Moreover, studies suggest that risk factors for addiction tend to cluster together (e.g. Krueger et al., 2002). It is increasingly suggested that personality factors may partially account for the relationship between other risk factors and addiction (e.g. Krueger, McGue, & Iacono, 2001). Indeed, some studies suggest that personality factors may mediate the relationship between genetic factors and substance misuse (e.g. Laucht et al., 2007).

Targeting personality risk factors for addiction offers a promising intervention approach in that personality traits are differentially associated with motives for substance use (Comeau, Stewart, & Loba, 2001), drugs of choice (Le Bon et al., 2004), patterns of coping (Connor-Smith & Flachsbart, 2007), and sensitivity to the effects of drugs (Conrod, Pihl, & Vassileva, 1998; Leyton et al., 2002). Personality-targeted interventions can thus address the vulnerability factors and specific motivations for misuse associated with a particular personality profile, enhancing the individual relevance and impact of an intervention.

Preventure: a personality-targeted approach

Four personality traits, namely hopelessness, anxiety-sensitivity, impulsivity, and sensation seeking have been associated with early-onset risk factors for addiction in youth. Each personality profile is associated with distinct motivational pathways to substance use, as well as risk factors for specific mental disorders (Castellanos-Ryan & Conrod, 2012). High-risk young people can be identified by using scores on a brief personality questionnaire, the Substance Use Risk Profile Scale (SURPS). The SURPS has been shown to have good sensitivity (72–91%) and specificity in predicting those who will develop substance use or mental health problems over an 18-month period in adolescence (Castellanos-Ryan et al., 2013). The four personality profiles of hopelessness, anxiety-sensitivity, impulsivity and sensation seeking are targeted in the Preventure (Personality Risk Education) program, a school-based, selective intervention for early-onset alcohol and illicit drug use. A central tenet of this personality-targeted approach is that youth are taught about their personality profiles in personality-matched groups, and interventions focus on personality-specific motivation for substance use, and other personality-specific problems (e.g. internalizing or externalizing symptoms). This contrasts with universal approaches, where youth are provided with general risk information about substance misuse, irrespective of their individual characteristics. Personality-matching is a key feature of the Preventure intervention design and has been shown to be crucial to intervention efficacy, as groups where personalities are not matched are no more effective than motivational control groups in affecting substance use (Conrod et al., 2000a).

With regards to the personality profiles in question, hopelessness is associated with the use of substances to dampen feelings of sadness or worthlessness, and is a risk factor for depressive disorders (Woicik et al., 2009; Krank et al., 2011). Fourteen-year olds with high levels of hopelessness have a three times greater odds of developing severe depressive symptoms over 18-months than youth without this high-risk profile (Castellanos-Ryan et al., 2013). Anxiety-sensitivity is a risk factor for addiction through the use of substances to dampen fears of the physical sensations of anxiety, and predicts a heightened risk of panic and anxiety disorders (Stewart & Kushner, 2001). Fourteen-year olds with high levels of anxiety-sensitivity have a 3.5 times greater odds of developing severe emotional problems over 18-months than youth without this high-risk profile (Castellanos-Ryan et al., 2013). Whilst anxiety-sensitivity appears to protect against substance use during adolescence, possibly due to avoidance of social situations that involve alcohol, or anxiety regarding the impact of alcohol use, this trait emerges as a risk factor for addiction in adulthood (Conrod et al., 2000a). Anxiety-sensitivity also predicts internalizing problems, which in themselves are risk factors for the development of problematic substance use (Hussong et al., 2011). With regards to the externalizing traits measured by the SURPS, impulsivity is associated with disinhibition over a range of behaviors, including conduct disorders, antisocial tendencies, attention-deficit/hyperactivity disorder, problem drinking and polysubstance use (Castellanos-Ryan & Conrod, 2012). Of the 14-year-olds identified as high-risk by the impulsivity scale 70–80% developed conduct or drug use problems within the next 18 months (Castellanos-Ryan et al., 2013). Impulsivity is a risk factor for early-onset alcohol use through multiple, as opposed to specific, drinking motives (Mackinnon et al., 2014). Lastly, sensation seeking is associated with risk-taking behaviors, including heavy alcohol use (Castellanos-Ryan & Conrod, 2012), but not with other forms of non-addictive psychopathology (Conrod et al., 2000b). Individuals with high levels of sensation seeking are shown to be sensitive to the rewarding properties of alcohol and to engage in binge drinking in order to maximize their enjoyment of alcohol (Woicik et al., 2009). Sensation seeking is associated with alcohol use for enhancement motives, to increase positive affect when fatigued, bored, or under-stimulated, or to increase enjoyment in social situations.

Preventure interventions in practice

The Preventure personality-targeted intervention program is based on the cognitive behavioral therapy (CBT) model, an approach which has been found to be effective in addressing substance use problems in adolescents. Interventions include psycho-educational material, and are delivered according to the "spirit" or essence of the motivational interviewing approach. A novel component to this intervention program is that all materials are targeted to each individual personality profile, making interventions personally relevant for each participant. The interventions are delivered over two 90-minute group sessions by a trained facilitator and co-facilitator, with an average of six personality-matched adolescents per group. The interventions are delivered following a manual, and include real life scenarios shared by young people in specifically organized focus groups. Particular attention is paid to ensuring that manuals are culturally appropriate, and materials have been specifically developed for youth in the United Kingdom, Canada, Australia, the Netherlands, and the Czech Republic. Throughout the group intervention, cognitive behavioral and motivational principles are presented and explored using examples of real life scenarios, as well as participants' personal experiences.

In the first session, participants are guided in a goal-setting exercise designed to enhance motivation to change behavior. Psycho-educational strategies are used to teach participants about the target personality variable and associated problematic coping behaviors (e.g. risk taking in youth with high levels of sensation seeking). Substance misuse is referred to as a problematic coping behavior across all personality profiles, and the groups discuss personality-specific motives for use (e.g. to cope with feelings of sadness in the hopelessness-prone group). Other non-substance-related personality-specific maladaptive coping behaviors are also presented, and a decisional balancing exercise is conducted in order to explore the short- and long-term consequences of a particular maladaptive coping strategy. Participants subsequently generate an alternative, more adaptive coping strategy, which they explore using a second decisional balancing exercise. The CBT model is then presented, and participants are guided through breaking down personal experiences according to the physical, cognitive and behavioral components of an emotional response. All exercises discuss thoughts, emotions, and behaviors in a personality-specific way, e.g. identifying situational triggers and cognitive distortions related to impulsivity.

In the second session, participants are encouraged to identify and challenge personality-specific cognitive distortions (e.g. negative, global, self-referent thinking for hopelessness-prone youth) that can lead to problematic behaviors. Participants are then assisted in completing a cognitive restructuring exercise using a personal example, which is associated with an alternative behavior that is in line with valued life goals.

The Preventure evidence base

The Preventure program has been evaluated in four separate randomized clinical trials in high schools in the United Kingdom (Conrod, Castellanos, & Mackie, 2008; Conrod et al., 2013); Canada (Conrod et al., 2006); and the Netherlands (Lammers et al., 2015). This brief program has resulted in delays and reductions in rates and growth of alcohol consumption, binge drinking, and severity of alcohol-related problems in selected high-risk youth up to a two-year period when delivered by trained psychologists (Conrod, Castellanos-Ryan, & Mackie, 2011; Lammers et al., 2015). Effect sizes for intervention effects on alcohol use are striking, as evaluated by numbers needed to treat (NNTs), which represent the number of participants who need to take part in the intervention in order to prevent one bad outcome, in this case binge drinking. NNTs at six months post-intervention were between four and six for alcohol users at baseline across three trials (Conrod et al., 2006; Conrod, Castellanos, & Mackie, 2008;

O'Leary-Barrett et al., 2010), and as low as two for sensation seeking youth who had consumed alcohol prior to the intervention, a particularly high risk group (Conrod, Castellanos, & Mackie, 2008). In addition, the Preventure interventions have resulted in reduced drug use rates and frequency, with high-risk youth who received interventions reporting a 30% reduced odds of taking up marijuana use, 80% reduced odds of taking up cocaine, and 50% reduced odds of taking up other drugs over a two-year period relative to their control counterparts (Conrod, Castellanos-Ryan, & Strang, 2010). The intervention was also associated with personality-specific effects on mental health symptoms and reckless behaviors over six months e.g. reduced depressive symptoms in hopelessness-prone youth, reduced panic attacks, and school avoidance in youth with high levels of anxiety-sensitivity, and reduced shoplifting in youth with high levels of impulsivity (Castellanos & Conrod, 2006). In recognition of these robust intervention effects, Preventure has been identified as a promising approach in a review of prevention programs for substance abuse and dependence in adolescents with comorbid disorders (Salvo et al., 2012).

In an effort to move towards a sustainable model of program implementation, a randomized controlled trial known as Adventure investigated the efficacy of the Preventure intervention model when delivered by school-based professionals, such as school counsellors, teachers, and special educational staff, who were trained and supervised by the research team (O'Leary-Barrett et al., 2010). This was considered an important step in addressing the implementation barriers faced by many evidence-based intervention programs, which are not sustainable in real-world settings without ongoing input from an external agency, a research team for example. In the Adventure trial, educational professionals attended a three-day training workshop, followed by a minimum of four hours' supervision in running through a full, two-session intervention with the trial therapist. Intervention facilitators included school counsellors, teachers, student support, and special educational needs staff.

The first day of the training workshop presented the rationale and evidence base for the personality-targeted approach, as well as an overview of the psycho-educational, cognitive behavioral and motivational components of the interventions. The second day focused on basic counselling skills (e.g. empathy, reflective listening) and general cognitive behavioral and motivational interviewing principles, using both didactic presentations and role play exercises. The third day reviewed the specific cognitive behavioral and motivational skills necessary for delivery of the Preventure interventions, and trainees were guided in carrying out the core components of the manual using role play exercises. Subsequent to completing the training workshop, trainees ran supervised interventions with groups of students in a different grade, who were not involved in the formal trial. A checklist was devised by the research team to measure whether facilitators demonstrated sufficient mastery of cognitive behavioral, motivational, and general counselling skills. Thirty-one trainees (84%) successfully completed the training and supervision and qualified as facilitators of the intervention. Trainees' adherence to the treatment protocol and intervention quality was monitored during the formal trial, both by trained members of the research team and an independent evaluator, using a scale designed specifically by the principal investigator (Patricia Conrod) and the trial therapist, as well as the Cognitive Therapy Scale (Young & Beck, 1980). The majority of facilitators were rated as having adequate counselling skills and treatment fidelity. Scores suggest the intervention facilitators achieved many of the goals of a cognitive behavioral therapy intervention in practice but did not perform at a therapeutic level equivalent to a trained clinical psychologist. Further details regarding the quality and fidelity of intervention delivery can be found in O'Leary-Barrett et al. (2010).

Evaluation of the Adventure trial results indicated that intervention effects over two years reported in previous trials were replicated, with high-risk youth reporting reduced rates and growth in alcohol consumption, binge drinking and alcohol-related problems (Conrod et al., 2013), and reductions in onset of cannabis use in youth most prone to early drug use, namely those with high levels of sensation seeking (Mahu et al., 2015). The interventions were also associated with significant reductions in internalizing and externalizing symptoms in high-risk youth over two years, as well as reductions in severe depressive and conduct problem symptoms (O'Leary-Barrett et al., 2013). In addition, some herd effects of the intervention on low-risk youth (who did not participate in the interventions) were observed, suggesting that the benefits of the targeted intervention may be transferred to the wider school population. Specifically, low-risk youth in intervention schools (where their high-risk peers participated in interventions) reported significantly reduced rates of alcohol consumption and binge drinking over two years, and a reduced growth in binge drinking relative to low-risk youth in control schools (Conrod et al., 2013). Whilst there is some variability in effect sizes across Preventure trials that may be attributable to sample characteristics (e.g. whether or not youth have initiated alcohol consumption prior to participating in the intervention), or the levels of training of intervention facilitators (Lammers et al., 2015), comparisons of the efficacy of personality-targeted interventions across studies nevertheless revealed similar effect sizes when delivered by trained psychologists and school-based staff (O'Leary-Barrett et al., 2010).

Mechanisms of action

In addition to the growing evidence base surrounding the Preventure program, current studies in our laboratory are focusing on understanding the mechanisms underlying this intervention program, in order to validate the theoretical model being used and to further enhance treatment effects. The study of intervention mechanisms is considered a necessary complement to efficacy research, and contributes significantly to improving clinical practice (Kazdin & Nock, 2003). Treatment processes are currently understudied, particularly within youth treatment studies and group interventions, and a recent review of the state of psychotherapy research called for randomized controlled trials to investigate both the efficacy and the mechanisms of interventions (Stiles, Hill, & Elliott 2014).

Preventure can be differentiated from many other prevention approaches in that it targets personality risk factors for both substance misuse and associated internalizing, and externalizing symptoms, and has demonstrated reductions in both substance misuse and mental health symptoms over a two-year period (Conrod, Castellanos-Ryan, & Strang, 2010; Conrod, Castellanos-Ryan, & Mackie, 2011; Conrod et al., 2013; O'Leary-Barrett et al., 2013). It was thus of interest to examine whether there is a causal relationship between changes in alcohol use and psychological well-being. A recent study has demonstrated that two-year intervention effects on binge drinking and alcohol-related problems are partially mediated by early changes in drinking behaviors in the six months post-intervention (O'Leary-Barrett et al., under revision). In addition, global improvements in mood in the six months post-intervention partially mediate two-year intervention effects on both internalizing and externalizing symptoms. These results emphasize the clinical significance of targeting early-onset drinking behaviors, which can then account for longer-term intervention effects on substance misuse. This is also supported by long-term investigations of family-focused universal prevention programs (Spoth et al., 2009; Spoth et al., 2014). The results also suggest that intervention effects on alcohol consumption and mental health symptoms may occur through both common and specific processes, likely reflecting a combination of mental health and early-onset drinking on adolescent mental health trajectories. We are currently investigating the more proximal processes through which this program has its effects, in an effort to identify the core, active therapeutic ingredients.

Future work

Future studies will expand on the existing efficacy data, and investigate whether the beneficial effects of the personality-targeted approach extend to the prevention of clinically significant addiction outcomes over a five-year period in adolescence. The Co-Venture project is an ongoing cluster randomized controlled trial that is evaluating the long-term efficacy of Preventure interventions in 31 high schools in Montreal, Canada. This clinical trial uses developmentally sensitive neuropsychological measures to examine whether preventing early-onset substance use produces benefits on intermediate neuropsychological outcomes, and employs a unique opportunity to investigate the possible causal associations between cognitive functioning and early-onset substance use. A second line of research, the CAP study with Australian adolescents, is examining whether intervention efficacy can be enhanced by combining the personality-targeted approach with an effective universal internet-based program (Newton et al., 2012). Finally, feasibility of a Czech adaptation of the Preventure programme is also reported in the literature (Maierová et al., 2015).

Conclusions

The Preventure program represents an extremely promising approach to youth alcohol and drug misuse prevention. This brief, targeted approach can be distinguished from traditional universal prevention programs in that it was designed on the basis of on etiological research that characterizes the personality and motivational profiles of individuals at heightened risk for early-onset and problematic substance misuse. Interventions are thus tailored to individuals' personality-specific risk factors for substance misuse, as well as associated mental health symptoms. To date, program efficacy has been evaluated in four randomized controlled trials, which have revealed reductions in alcohol and drug misuse, as well as in depressive, anxiety and conduct problem symptoms over a two-year period. Intervention effects were also replicated when delivered by trained school-based professionals, suggesting that this program has potential to be implemented within real-world settings. Preliminary process research suggests that the tailored nature of the interventions is key in contributing to its striking evidence base.

References

Castellanos N & Conrod PJ (2006) Brief interventions targeting personality risk factors for adolescent substance misuse reduce depression, panic and risk-taking behaviours. *Journal of Mental Health* 15(6): 645–658.

Castellanos-Ryan N & Conrod PJ (2012) Personality and substance misuse: evidence for a four factor model of vulnerability. In: Verster J, Brady K, Galanter M, & Conrod PJ (eds) *Drug Abuse and Addiction in Medical Illness*. Humana/Spring Press, 47–62.

Castellanos-Ryan N, O'Leary-Barrett M, Sully L, & Conrod, PJ (2013) Sensitivity and specificity of a brief personality screening instrument in predicting future substance use, emotional, and behavioral problems: 18-month predictive validity of the substance use risk profile scale. *Alcohol: Clinical and Experimental Research* 37(S1): E281–290.

Comeau N, Stewart SH, & Loba P (2001) The relations of trait anxiety, anxiety-sensitivity, and sensation seeking to adolescents' motivations for alcohol, cigarette, and marijuana use. *Addictive Behaviors* 26(6): 803–825.

Connor-Smith JK & Flachsbart C (2007) Relations between personality and coping: a meta-analysis. *Journal of Personality and Social Psychology* 93(6): 1080–1107.

Conrod PJ, Pihl RO, & Vassileva J (1998) Differential sensitivity to alcohol reinforcement in groups of men at risk for distinct alcoholism subtypes. *Alcohol: Clinical and Experimental Research* 22(3): 585–597.

Conrod PJ, Stewart SH, Pihl RO, Cote S, Fontaine V, & Dongier M (2000a) Efficacy of brief coping skills interventions that match different personality profiles of female substance abusers. *Psychology of Addictive Behaviors* 14(3): 231–242.

Conrod PJ, Pihl RO, Stewart SH, & Dongier M (2000b) Validation of a system of classifying female substance abusers on the basis of personality and motivational risk factors for substance abuse. *Psychology of Addictive Behaviors* 14(3): 243–256.

Conrod PJ, Stewart SH, Comeau N, & Maclean AM (2006) Efficacy of cognitive-behavioral interventions targeting personality risk factors for youth alcohol misuse. *Journal of Clinical Child and Adolescent Psychology* 35(4): 550–563.

Conrod PJ, Castellanos N, & Mackie C (2008) Personality-targeted interventions delay the growth of adolescent drinking and binge drinking. *Journal of Child Psychology and Psychiatry* 49(2): 181–190.

Conrod PJ, Castellanos-Ryan N, & Strang J (2010) Brief personality-targeted coping skills interventions and survival as a non-drug user over a 2-year period during adolescence. *Archives of General Psychiatry* 67(1): 85–93.

Conrod PJ, Castellanos-Ryan N, & Mackie CJ (2011) Long-term effects of a personality-targeted intervention to reduce alcohol use in adolescents. *Journal of Consulting and Clinical Psychology* 79(3): 296–306.

Conrod PJ, O'Leary-Barrett M, Newton N, Topper L, Castellanos-Ryan N, Mackie C, & Girard A (2013) Effectiveness of a selective, personality-targeted prevention program for adolescent alcohol use and misuse: a cluster randomized controlled trial. *JAMA Psychiatry* 70(3): 334–342.

Dishion TJ & Dodge KA (2005) Peer contagion in interventions for children and adolescents: moving towards an understanding of the ecology and dynamics of change. *Journal of Abnormal Child Psychology* 33(3): 395–400.

Emmers E, Bekkering GE, & Hannes K (2015) Prevention of alcohol and drug misuse in adolescents: an overview of systematic reviews. *Nordic Studies on Alcohol and Drugs* 32(2): 183–198.

Faggiano F, Galanti MR, Bohrn K, Burkhart G, Vigna-Taglianti F, Cuomo L, Fabiani L, Panella M, Perez T, Siliquini R, van der Kreeft P, Vassara M, & Wiborg G (2008) The effectiveness of a school-based substance abuse prevention program: EU-Dap cluster randomised controlled trial. *Preventive Medicine* 47(5): 537–543.

Faggiano F, Minozzi S, Versino E, & Buscemi D (2014) Universal school-based prevention for illicit drug use. *Cochrane Database Systematic Review* 12(CD003020).

Foxcroft DR & Tsertsvadze A (2011) Universal school-based prevention programs for alcohol misuse in young people. *Cochrane Database Systematic Review* 5(CD009113).

Foxcroft DR & Tsertsvadze A (2012) Universal alcohol misuse prevention programmes for children and adolescents: Cochrane Systematic Reviews. *Perspectives in Public Health* 132(3): 128–134.

Gottfredson DC & Wilson DB (2003) Characteristics of effective school-based substance abuse prevention. *Prevention Science* 4(1): 27–38.

Grant BF, Stinson FS, & Harford TC (2001) Age at onset of alcohol use and DSM-IV alcohol abuse and dependence: a 12-year follow-up. *Journal of Substance Abuse* 13(4): 493–504.

Hennessy EA & Tanner-Smith EE (2015) Effectiveness of brief school-based interventions for adolescents: a meta-analysis of alcohol use prevention programs. *Prevention Science* 16(3): 463–474.

Hussong AM, Jones DJ, Stein GL, Baucom DH, & Boeding S (2011) An internalizing pathway to alcohol use and disorder. *Psychology of Addictive Behaviors* 25(3): 390–404.

Kazdin AE & Nock MK (2003) Delineating mechanisms of change in child and adolescent therapy: methodological issues and research recommendations. *Journal of Child Psychology and Psychiatry* 44(8): 1116–1129.

Krank M, Stewart SH, O'Connor R, Woicik PB, Wall AM, & Conrod PJ (2011) Structural, concurrent, and predictive validity of the Substance Use Risk Profile Scale in early adolescence. *Addictive Behaviors* 36(1–2): 37–46.

Krueger RF, McGue M, & Iacono WG (2001) The higher-order structure of common DSM mental disorders: internalization, externalization, and their connections to personality. *Personality and Individual Differences* 30(7): 1245–1259.

Krueger RF, Hicks BM, Patrick CJ, Carlson SR, Iacono WG, & McGue M (2002) Etiologic connections among substance dependence, antisocial behavior, and personality: modeling the externalizing spectrum. *Journal of Abnormal Psychology* 111(3): 411–424.

Lammers J, Goossens F, Conrod P, Engels R, Wiers RW, & Kleinjan M (2015) Effectiveness of a selective intervention program targeting personality risk factors for alcohol misuse among young adolescents: results of a cluster randomized controlled trial. *Addiction* 110(7): 1101–1109.

Laucht M, Becker K, Blomeyer D, & Schmidt MH (2007) Novelty seeking involved in mediating the association between the dopamine D4 receptor gene exon III polymorphism and heavy drinking in male adolescents: results from a high-risk community sample. *Biological Psychiatry* 61(1): 87–92.

Le Bon O, Basiaux P, Streel E, Tecco J, Hanak C, Hansenne M, Ansseau M, Pelc I, Verbanck P, & Dupont S (2004) Personality profile and drug of choice: a multivariate analysis using Cloninger's TCI on heroin addicts, alcoholics, and a random population group. *Drug and Alcohol Dependency* 73(2): 175–182.

Leyton M, Boileau I, Benkelfat C, Diksic M, Baker G, & Dagher A (2002) Amphetamine-induced increases in extracellular dopamine, drug wanting, and novelty seeking: a PET/[11C]raclopride study in healthy men. *Neuropsychopharmacology* 27(6): 1027–1035.

Lynch AD, Coley RL, Sims J, Lombardi CM, & Mahalik JR (2015) Direct and interactive effects of parent, friend, and schoolmate drinking on alcohol use trajectories. *Psychology & Health* 1-36. DOI: 10.1080/08870446.2015.1040017.

Mackinnon SP, Kehayes IL, Clark R, Sherry SB, & Stewart SH (2014) Testing the four-factor model of personality vulnerability to alcohol misuse: a three-wave, one-year longitudinal study. *Psychology of Addictive Behaviors* 28(4): 1000–1012.

Mahu IT, Doucet C, O'Leary-Barrett M, & Conrod, PJ (2015) Can cannabis use be prevented by targeting personality risk in schools? 24-month outcome of the Adventure trial on cannabis use: a cluster randomized controlled trial. *Addiction* 110(10): 1625–1633.

Maierová E, Charvát M, Miovský M, & Šťastná L (2015) Preventure: adaptation and pilot implementation of a targeted brief intervention in the Czech setting – process evaluation study. *Adiktologie* 15(1).

Newton NC, Teesson M, Barrett EL, Slade T, & Conrod PJ (2012) The CAP study, evaluation of integrated universal and selective prevention strategies for youth alcohol misuse: study protocol of a cluster randomized controlled trial. *BMC Psychiatry* 12(118) doi:10.1186/1471-244X-12-118 (accessed 01/06/2015).

O'Leary-Barrett M, Mackie CJ, Castellanos-Ryan N, Al-Khudhairy N, & Conrod PJ (2010) Personality-targeted interventions delay uptake of drinking and decrease risk of alcohol-related problems when delivered by teachers. *Journal of the American Academy of Child & Adolescent Psychiatry* 49(9): 954–963.e951.

O'Leary-Barrett M, Topper L, Al-Khudhairy N, Pihl RO, Castellanos-Ryan N, Mackie CJ, & Conrod PJ (2013) Two-year impact of personality-targeted, teacher-delivered interventions on youth internalizing and externalizing problems: a cluster-randomized trial. *Journal of the American Academy of Child & Adolescent Psychiatry* 52(9), 911–920.

O'Leary-Barrett M, Castellanos-Ryan N, Pihl RO, & Conrod PJ (under revision) Mechanisms of Personality-Targeted Intervention Effects on Adolescent Alcohol Misuse, Internalising and Externalising Symptoms. Available from the author: maeve.oleary-barrett@mail.mcgill.ca.

Pape H (2012) Young people's overestimation of peer substance use: an exaggerated phenomenon? *Addiction* 107(5): 878–884.

Salvo N, Bennett K, Cheung A, Chen Y, Rice M, Rush B, Bullock H, Bowlby A, & the Evidence on Tap Concurrent Disorders Collaborative Team (2012) Prevention of substance use in children/adolescents with mental disorders: a systematic review. *Journal of the Canadian Academy of Child & Adolescent Psychiatry* 21(4): 245–252.

Sloboda Z, Stephens RC, Stephens PC, Grey SF, Teasdale B, Hawthorne RD, Williams J, & Marquette JF (2009) The Adolescent Substance Abuse Prevention Study: a randomized field trial of a universal substance abuse prevention program. *Drug and Alcohol Dependency* 102(1–3): 1–10.

Spoth R, Trudeau L, Guyll M, Shin C, & Redmond C (2009) Universal intervention effects on substance use among young adults mediated by delayed adolescent substance initiation.*Journal of Consulting and Clinical Psychology* 77(4): 620–632.

Spoth R, Trudeau L, Redmond C, & Shin C (2014) Replication RCT of early universal prevention effects on young adult substance misuse. *Journal of Consulting and Clinical Psychology* 82(6): 949–963.

Stephens PC, Sloboda Z, Grey S, Stephens R, Hammond A, Hawthorne R, Teasdale B, & Williams J (2009) Is the receptivity of substance abuse prevention programming affected by students' perceptions of the instructor? *Health Education & Behavior* 36(4): 724–745.

Stewart SH & Kushner MG (2001) Introduction to the Special Issue on 'Anxiety sensitivity and addictive behaviors'. *Addictive Behaviors* 26(6): 775–785.

Stiles WB, Hill CE, & Elliott R (2014) Looking both ways. *Psychotherapy Research* 25(3): 282–293.

Tanner-Smith EE & Lipsey MW (2015) Brief alcohol interventions for adolescents and young adults: a systematic review and meta-analysis. *Journal of Substance Abuse Treatment* 51: 1–18.

Werch CE & Owen DM (2002) Iatrogenic effects of alcohol and drug prevention programs. *Journal of Studies on Alcohol* 63(5): 581–590.

Willenbring ML (2013) Gaps in clinical prevention and treatment for alcohol use disorders: costs, consequences, and strategies. *Alcohol Research* 35(2): 238–243.

Woicik PA, Stewart SH, Pihl RO, & Conrod PJ (2009) The Substance Use Risk Profile Scale: a scale measuring traits linked to reinforcement-specific substance use profiles. *Addictive Behaviors* 34(12): 1042–1055.

Young JE & Beck AT (1980) *Cognitive Therapy Scale: Rating Manual.* Bala Cynwyd, PA: Beck Institute for Cognitive Therapy and Research.

Part IV

Action for policy and practice

Chapter 8

Reducing deaths from opiate overdose

Take-home naloxone

Rebecca McDonald, Rhian Hills, Carole Hunter, Kirsten Horsburgh, Andrew McAuley, Rosie Mundt-Leach, Sarah Small and John Strang

Introduction

Naloxone is an opioid antagonist, a medication used to counter the effects of opioid overdose. It blocks the opioid receptors in the brain and reverses opioid-induced respiratory depression. Serious side effects from naloxone are very rare. This chapter makes the case for the provision of take-home naloxone (THN) in a wide range of community and residential rehab settings. In November 2014, the World Health Organisation (WHO) released new guidelines, recommending that THN should be made available to all opioid users at risk of witnessing an overdose, as well as their families, and to service providers in frequent contact with opioid users. In this chapter, we pay particular attention to the period following residential rehab, since we now know that this is a period of increased risk of overdose. Clients leaving rehab have lowered tolerance, which is likely to make them underestimate the health risks of a potential relapse. Rehab provides an important opportunity to educate clients and their families about overdose risk factors, how to recognise an overdose and how to administer naloxone for overdose reversal. The chapter contains three case studies of successful THN implementation in the UK, in Scotland, Wales and South London. It then concludes with the implementation plan for THN provision at Clouds House, a residential rehab facility in Wiltshire, England, which can serve as guide for other residential rehab services wishing to introduce THN.

Risk populations and intervention opportunities

In 2013, the number of drug overdose fatalities in England and Wales reached a five-year peak, with a total of 2,955 deaths registered for all substances. During 2013, compared to the previous year, there was an alarming 32 per cent increase in people who died from heroin or morphine overdose (ONS, 2013). European-wide data show that 78 per cent of overdose deaths are male and, between 2006 and 2013, there were decreasing numbers of deaths among younger drug users (8 per cent were under 25) and increasing numbers among older users. This reflects the ageing nature of Europe's opioid-using population, who are at greatest risk (EMCDDA, 2015a: 56).

From a physiological perspective, overdoses can be distinguished into sudden and slow onset. Sudden-onset catastrophic overdoses are characterised by a rapid drop in blood-oxygen levels and respiration rate. They typically occur after intravenous use of heroin and are fairly easy for bystanders to recognise. The need for intervention is usually immediately apparent and at times the needle is still found in the arm. By contrast, slow-onset insidious overdoses are induced by long-acting opioids such as methadone and can be difficult to detect. The overdose victim may appear to be sleeping, when in reality their respiratory rate is gradually declining, eventually resulting in coma.

Although a substantial minority of opiate overdoses are intentional, with research findings varying between 26 per cent (Best et al., 2000) and 17 per cent (Heale, Dietz and Fry, 2003), the great majority of these events are accidental. In almost every case there is an opportunity for intervention and a great many deaths from overdose are preventable. It is important to improve clients' awareness of risk situations, as even a single relapse could prove fatal for clients leaving residential rehab. There are several behavioural risk factors for overdose. Risk is increased when:

- heroin or other opioids are injected (especially intravenously), as compared to inhalation, snorting, or ingestion
- alcohol and other sedative drugs (e.g. benzodiazepines) are also consumed
- a person is using alone, with no one around to intervene
- tolerance is reduced.

Empirical evidence for reduced tolerance as a risk factor comes from post-mortem analyses, showing heroin overdose victims had lower morphine concentrations in the hair and blood than do currently living heroin users (Darke et al., 2002). Loss of tolerance makes clients leaving drug-free rehab particularly prone to fatal overdose. It is thus important for rehab clients with a history of opioid use to learn how to recognise the impaired breathing pattern of overdose. In addition to the identification of overdose signs, training should comprise pre-provision of a THN kit to at-risk individuals. Training should cover how to manage an overdose emergency situation, including how to administer naloxone. THN is likely to have the biggest impact in cases of accidental opioid overdoses when bystanders are already present. UK law allows any member of the general public to administer naloxone for the purpose of saving a life. Emphasis should also be put on calling an ambulance, putting the victim into the rescue position, rescue breathing and performing cardiopulmonary resuscitation (CPR).

The rationale for THN in a residential rehab setting

Return into the community after a stay in a drug-free institution is characterised by increased risk of overdose as periods of abstinence lead to a significant reduction in tolerance. The most striking example is the concentration of overdose deaths among prisoners on release (Merrall et al., 2010). A similar, though less intense concentration of overdose deaths can be seen among patients on completion of residential treatment. Strang and colleagues (2003) found that opioid-dependent patients who had successfully completed inpatient abstinence-based treatment were more likely to die of overdose than those who had failed to complete the programme. Similarly, larger studies in Italy (Davoli et al., 2007), England (Cornish et al., 2010), Norway (Ravndal and Amundsen, 2010) and Scotland (Merrall, Bird and Hutchinson, 2013) found that the first month following conclusion of treatment generally bears a high risk of overdose.

The 2014 WHO Guidelines

Since THN was first proposed (Strang et al., 1996) it has served as a low-threshold intervention to prevent fatal outcomes from opioid overdose. In November 2014 the WHO released new guidelines on the management of overdoses in the community, recommending that 'people likely to witness an opioid overdose should have access to naloxone and be instructed in its administration' (WHO, 2014: *x*). The guidelines' potential impact on clinical practice is large, since they establish THN provision as a new standard of care for all providers regardless of treatment orientation. Even abstinence-only residential rehab providers should thus offer THN kits to all clients with a history of opioid use, as it cannot be ruled out that they may witness or experience an overdose in the future.

THN has been well received by drug users and carers, and training programmes for drug users (Strang et al., 2008) and families (Williams, Marsden and Strang, 2014) have been shown to improve knowledge and confidence regarding overdose emergency management and naloxone administration. Peer-reviewed data on the effectiveness of THN exists from Canada, Germany, the US and the UK. In the US alone, the provision of THN kits to 152,283 individuals led to 26,463 overdose reversals between 1996 and mid-2014 (Wheeler et al., 2015). While no data from randomised-controlled trials are available to date, a quasi-experimental study in Massachusetts found that communities with THN schemes had significantly lower overdose mortality rates than those without (Walley et al., 2013). A systematic review of THN programmes concluded that 'training interventions complemented by take-home naloxone decrease overdose-related mortality' (EMCDDA, 2015b: 1).

Widening knowledge, competence and provision

The WHO guidelines represent a significant step towards the prevention of overdose deaths. Residential treatment providers have the opportunity to contribute towards a reduction of mortality by raising clients' awareness of the risk factors and signs of overdose and training them in the use of THN. Implementation and dissemination of THN can occur in three stages: training of staff members and clients is essential, which at a second stage can then be extended to clients' family members. At a third stage, funders and other stakeholders not immediately involved in clinical day-to-day proceedings can be made aware of the THN initiative. The following three cases illustrate examples of successful THN implementation.

The Scottish National Naloxone Programme

Scotland has a population of about 5 million, and an estimated 60,000 heroin or other opioid users. Drug-related death rates in Scotland are the highest in the UK and among the highest in Europe (Davies et al., 2010) and there has been a steady increase from 244 in 1996 to 526 in 2013 (Barnsdale, Gordon and McAuley, 2015). The majority of these deaths are accidental, involve opioids and are witnessed. Therefore, the majority are preventable, and this has prompted exploration of more radical and innovative prevention approaches. One such approach is the provision of THN.

Following recommendations in the academic literature, and pilot studies in the USA and Europe, the Scottish Advisory Committee on Drug Misuse (SACDM) recommended in 2005 that those in a position to administer naloxone should receive appropriate training to do so (SACDM, 2005). The 2005 amendment to the Medicines Act 1968 soon afterwards effectively facilitated implementation of naloxone training and distribution programmes in Scotland in a way proposed by Strang and colleagues (1996). Local pilots in 2006, 2007 and 2009 demonstrated feasibility of implementation within the Scottish context. These early adopters effectively laid the foundations for a national naloxone programme in Scotland, officially launched in April 2011, the first of its kind internationally (McAuley et al., 2012). Anyone with a history of opioid use and at risk of future opioid overdose is eligible to receive a supply of naloxone in Scotland. This includes both current and former drug users, those engaged with treatment and those not, and those who have recently completed a period of abstinence.

Training the workforce

Training in overdose management and emergency naloxone administration in Scotland has evolved over time (Watt et al., 2014). At the outset, a national naloxone training resource was created by the Scottish Drugs Forum (2015) which provides support to all local areas across Scotland. A 'train the trainer' model was utilised to enable staff from across a range of services to cascade naloxone training to service users, their families and carers. The programme has since developed to meet different local service and geographical needs and now incorporates group sessions and one-to-one interventions. More recently the programme has supported the implementation of local networks of peer volunteers (including in prisons) to help widen the reach of the intervention. This project focuses on equipping peer volunteers, and people who have previously experienced substance use problems, to become THN trainers and train drug users, their friends, families and even staff working directly with service users. Since its launch in 2012, the naloxone peer educator initiative has successfully recruited and trained over 120 volunteers.

Implementation

Training is also delivered by a range of staff including nurses, pharmacists, voluntary sector workers and peer trainers. This typically takes place in the community via substance misuse treatment services and community pharmacies. In addition, in all 15 prisons in Scotland, naloxone is promoted throughout the prisoners' sentence with referral to naloxone training taking place closer to release. Those who successfully complete the training session have a naloxone kit placed within their property upon release.

Naloxone is a prescription-only medicine, and a Patient Group Direction (Armstrong et al., 2001) is used for supply, mainly by nurses working directly with people who use drugs, and in some areas by pharmacists also. Family members or carers can be supplied with THN provided consent from the person at risk of overdose has been obtained. Services which may come into contact with those at risk of overdose (including health and non-health based services) can be supplied with naloxone for use in an emergency, a scheme which is legally endorsed by Lord Advocate's Guidelines. This is a uniquely Scottish exemption, and examples of services that have utilised this to store stocks of naloxone for use in an emergency include homeless hostels, residential and community rehabs, street outreach teams, supported accommodation, women's aid and community wardens.

Key findings

A total of 13,808 kits were issued in Scotland from 2011 to 2014 (ISD, 2014). The number has increased year on year since the programme began with the vast majority supplied in the community (82 per cent), mainly to the person at risk (88 per cent). Males (65 per cent) are more likely to have received a kit than females, in particular via prison supply. In addition, naloxone supplies in the community are increasingly reaching an older cohort with the proportion of recipients aged 35 years and over increasing from 43 per cent in 2011/12 to 56 per cent in 2013/14.

An analysis has been undertaken of opioid-related deaths occurring amongst prisoners on release (Bird, Parmar and Strang, 2014). The percentage of opioid-related deaths occurring within four weeks of release was 9.8 per cent during 2006–2010 (baseline period) compared to 6.3 per cent during 2011–2013. This 36 per cent reduction has been ascribed directly to the implementation of the national naloxone programme in Scotland. Moreover, this represents the first evidence of the effectiveness of a national programme in reducing mortality rates and provides support for other nations adopting similar population level approaches.

The Welsh National Naloxone Programme

Wales has a population of 3 million, with an estimated 17,598 heroin or other opioid users. Throughout the late 1990s and early 2000s information from the Office for National Statistics showed a rise in drug related-deaths in Wales. In 2005 the Advisory Panel on Substance Misuse which advises on the delivery of the Welsh substance misuse strategy agreed the development of guidance for collecting data on drug-related deaths in Wales. The guidance provided advice for developing multi-agency review groups to undertake reviews of drug-related deaths and included scrutiny of inquest records. This allowed the development of specific recommendations and provided a national overview of circumstances and factors contributing to death.

The Welsh Assembly Government (2008) strategy for tackling substance misuse commits to reducing the number of drug-related deaths and near-fatal drug poisonings. One of its key actions is the development of guidance and protocols to introduce naloxone. A THN demonstration project was launched in four community-based locations known to have the highest number of drug-related deaths. In the following months, these were expanded to four prison-based locations and a further two community sites. Following consultation, a National Working Group decided on the use of ampoules of naloxone, contained within a sealed kit. The use of the kit continues to be monitored, as well as alternative methods of administering naloxone. The key aims of the demonstration project were to:

- reduce drug-related deaths in Wales
- promote harm reduction by disseminating overdose information
- improve health and social care for drug users and their carers
- assist in monitoring overdose incidents
- enhance service provision for service users
- provide communication about the risks of drugs.

Training users and workforce

In order to ensure robust mechanisms were in place to oversee the implementation of THN, it was imperative to engage professionals on a multi-agency level to ensure buy-in. Therefore, a range of professionals became members of a national working group including police, paramedics, drug treatment agencies, health professionals and service users. This group identified three key elements that needed to be addressed to effectively implement and deliver THN:

1 appropriate training of individuals who may use naloxone
2 establishment of locally agreed protocols for supply and administration
3 robust data collection.

The aim of the training is to reduce the vulnerability of injecting drug users by:

- developing targeted first aid learning for injecting drug users, focusing on the key skills most likely to make a difference in crisis situations
- providing access to naloxone and education in its use
- emphasising the importance of service users and carers contacting the emergency services when naloxone has been given, to counter the risk of returning to an overdose state.

The main targets for training are all opiate drug users past and present, but especially people most at risk of overdose, such as those leaving prison, those in or due to leave residential detoxification or residential rehabilitation, homeless people, and those not in contact with mainstream services. Another main target is drug service staff, some of whom may witness overdoses, and to ensure they have a good understanding of overdose prevention so they can advise service users and attract people into training. During 2013–2014 nearly 1,500 individuals in Wales were trained in administration of THN, 81 per cent for the first time, and nearly 90 per cent were service users.

National rollout

A process and outcome evaluation of the demonstration project was carried out by the University of South Wales. Twenty-two recommendations were listed, with the main one being that the THN scheme be rolled out nationwide (Bennett and Holloway, 2011). Following the evaluation the Minister for Health announced national implementation with a target to complete rollout in twelve months, a target that was met five months ahead of schedule.

Data collection

During the demonstration project all data were collected manually and held within agencies. In 2010, Public Health Wales introduced the Harm Reduction Database in all statutory and voluntary sector needle and syringe programmes across Wales. Following the demonstration, it was decided that the database would be extended to add a module on THN to gather information about the distribution, use, harm reduction information and circumstances surrounding the overdose event. All previously collected data were back-populated on to the database.

Key findings

Between July 2009 and March 2014:

- 4,579 THN kits were issued in Wales. This includes 3,207 kits to new individuals and 1,372 kits as re-supply following use, loss or expiry of previous kits

- THN was reportedly used during 375 opioid-poisoning events
- 61 per cent of all reported opioid-poisoning events occurred within a private residence.

During 2013–2014:

- A total of 1,802 THN kits were issued (supplied and re-supplied) in Wales during 2013–2014, an increase of 75 per cent on the previous year
- THN was reportedly used in 160 opioid-poisoning events, for 152 users, as a result of which two fatalities were recorded.

Over the decade 2003–2013, 1,278 drug misuse deaths were recorded in Wales of which 41 per cent were from heroin or morphine. Between the years 2003 and 2010, heroin and morphine deaths increased by 75 per cent. However, this has been followed by a decline of 40 per cent since phased implementation of THN registries.

Up until 2012, methadone and buprenorphine deaths followed an upward trend, increasing more than threefold from the early 2000s. This highlights the importance of THN provision not only to those presenting as active users of heroin or morphine, but also individuals prescribed opioid-substitution treatment (Morgan and Smith, 2014).

It is important to ensure that sufficient information is collected to assist in the evaluation of how naloxone has helped individuals. A database is currently being developed which all areas will be expected to complete during and following training. This is also an opportunity to identify and respond to other critical risks of harm e.g. blood-borne viruses.

THN in an NHS addiction treatment service in South London

South London and Maudsley (SLaM) NHS addiction services provide community drug and alcohol services to five south London boroughs. SLaM services are staffed by multi-disciplinary teams of consultant addictions psychiatrists, nurses and drugs workers. Most teams have in-house psychology services, and all run on-site needle and syringe programmes as well as hepatitis clinics for vaccinations and blood-borne virus testing. The SLaM THN programme has evolved from being an innovative practice by early adopters in one or two teams to a routine intervention offered to all opiate-using service users on an opt-out basis. This expansion has been spurred by the introduction of a more suitable naloxone product and a general culture change within the SLaM treatment system that now regards THN as standard care.

The earliest implementation of THN within the service was in 2001 for patients leaving inpatient treatment after opiate detoxification. A more robust introduction in a community setting began in 2007 when the SLaM addiction service in

Greenwich, in conjunction with a naloxone research project at the Institute of Psychiatry, began providing THN minijet kits (400mcg) for service users at high risk of overdose. The research project involved provision of standardised training sessions for patients and carers and included administration of baseline and post-training measures to assess the impact of training. All key-workers were shown how to assemble the naloxone minijets and were asked to teach the service users on their own caseloads how to use the take-home kits in an emergency (a training-the-trainers' model). The introduction of THN provision by the Greenwich team, as well as the wider initiative, has been described elsewhere (e.g. Mundt-Leach et al., 2010; Mayet et al., 2011).

However, the minijet device was problematic for at least three reasons: it only contained a low dose of naloxone, training participants found assembly of the kit challenging, and it came in flimsy cardboard packaging that would open easily in a bag or pocket. As a result, there were concerns that take-home recipients might not carry the minijet on them, and many key-workers did not establish a routine of handing out the kits. These issues were resolved in 2008, when a new 2mg/2ml pre-filled syringe product became available in a sturdy plastic box, to which SLaM staff taped a hypodermic needle. It now became much more manageable for SLaM staff to demonstrate the product and persuade service users to carry it with them.

Within a few weeks the majority of patients had received THN kits and appropriate training in how to use them. Training also covered recognising the signs of an overdose, putting the overdose victim in recovery position, and the importance of calling the ambulance. Many patients were very knowledgeable in recognising signs and symptoms of overdose, but misconceptions around overdose management among users were common, e.g. the false belief that injecting stimulants was the most effective treatment to reverse opiate overdose (Beswick et al., 2002).

Early results

By January 2010, 15 patients reported having used their THN kits to reverse 24 overdoses. The initial reactions of the resuscitated overdose victims varied, as some failed to recognise that heroin had put them in a life-threatening condition. However, none of these overdose reversals involved aggression or adverse events. In order to promote a culture of positive reinforcement, the rescuers were congratulated for intervening in the overdose emergency and thanked for having potentially saved a life. In addition, their stories of overdose reversal (suitably anonymised) were displayed on posters and leaflets at the treatment service. Project staff reported a sense of enthusiasm and pride in having facilitated an overdose reversal and found that THN provision led to a more collaborative relationship between key-workers and their clients. To allow for the immediate replacement of used or lost kits a Patient Group Direction (PGD) was introduced which authorised nurses and key-workers to issue the kits without a doctor's presence or individual prescription.

New policy

In October 2014, SLaM policy on THN was changed from an opt-in to an opt-out system and THN was offered to all opioid users (including patients receiving opioid substitution treatment), not just high-risk injectors. Naloxone prescriptions for service users were now prepared ahead of appointments, and signed prescriptions were placed in the service users' script folders, so that kits could be issued without any time delays. The number of THN prescriptions issued increased from 47 in May 2008 to 417 in 2011 and 863 in April 2015.

SLaM addiction services have also enrolled patients who are not well established in the services' caseloads in order to make THN available to those in transient contact. Many are at high risk of overdose, such as those leaving prison, attending needle-exchange sites, dropping in and out of treatment, or with a history of sporadic opiate use. A small number of service users have been identified who frequently require replacement kits because of a disproportionately high number of overdose events in their lives. In addition to providing replacement kits, SLaM staff try to address the patients' level of risk with a thorough review of their treatment needs.

Barriers and future aims

Needless to say, overdose deaths have not entirely stopped because of this work. Multiple barriers to THN distribution persist. Firstly, there are still service users who opt out of THN provision. Common reasons given are that service users say they (1) don't inject, (2) feel stable, (3) don't need it, or (4) always use alone and would not have anyone to rescue them if they 'went over'. As part of quality assurance, patient notes of fatal overdose cases are now examined for evidence of naloxone being issued in the weeks before the death or being offered repeatedly if the patient initially refused. Secondly, colleagues in shared care teams report that THN distribution is logistically more difficult when kits have to be issued via prescription and prescription holders need to collect the kit at a community pharmacy (as opposed to kits being supplied directly to opiate users on-site). Thirdly, it has been a challenge to sustain the momentum after an initially exciting phase of THN distribution. Service users may need to be reminded to carry the naloxone kits on a day-to-day basis, and SLaM teams need to develop a systematic method for providing repeat kits. Future efforts will concentrate on maintaining registers of THN recipients and setting up alerts for staff to make renewed offers for those who have either rejected a kit or need a replacement in case of naloxone expiry.

THN in a rehab setting

The charity Action on Addiction provides two residential programmes for people seeking treatment for opioid dependence and other addictive behaviours: Clouds House, a facility for both men and women in Wiltshire; and Hope House, a south London-based centre for women only. As an early adopter among residential treatment providers in Britain, Clouds House recently announced the introduction of a take-home naloxone programme. No plans exist at Hope House so far, but a future rollout is being considered.

Clouds House has 38 beds, with on-site 24-hour nursing care, and offers first stage treatment with simultaneous detoxification. The typical length of stay in the residential programme is six weeks, though shorter and longer admissions have become more common in recent years when deemed appropriate. In 2014, 43 clients were admitted with a primary diagnosis of opioid use. In addition, about 40 per cent of clients admitted for alcohol or other substance use have a history of opioid use. The Clouds residential programme is intense, with daily interpersonal group therapy, supported by individual counselling sessions. In addition, clients have access to educational and creative workshops, such as art therapy, creative writing and mindfulness-based relapse prevention, along with wellness activities including yoga, massage, acupuncture and shiatsu (see chapter by Gregory in present volume). The treatment programme is based on the belief that recovery is possible and can be maintained with support from mutual aid and strengthening recovery capital (see chapter by Leighton in present volume). The overarching aim is to help clients achieve and sustain abstinence from drugs and alcohol or other addictive behaviours. Clients admitted for opioid use will attend local 12-Step self-help groups such as Narcotics Anonymous (NA) during their stay (see chapter by Kelly and Bergman in present volume).

To prepare clients for their lives after rehab, the Clouds House counselling team facilitates a series of relapse prevention workshops, and offers weekly after-care programmes in Wiltshire and London. After treatment, clients are advised to attend NA or other fellowship meetings near their home to help maintain their recovery. In recognition that opioid dependence is a chronic condition with a high risk of relapse, Clouds House is integrating training in overdose management and THN provision into their care agenda. While it is expected that clients who have undergone opiate detoxification will abstain following completion at Clouds House, they are trained in overdose risk factors and how to recognise an overdose, plus how to access emergency help and how to administer THN, in case it should ever prove necessary. The availability of naloxone is anticipated to raise awareness of the continuing risk of relapse. It also has a protective effect and potentially makes Clouds clients more likely to survive should they relapse and overdose and have someone close by who can administer naloxone. Importantly, THN also allows Clouds clients to become part of a population equipped with the skills to intervene, manage and possibly reverse someone's overdose.

A small number of Clouds clients already receive THN kits. Clients from West Sussex with a history of opioid use are given two take-home kits on discharge. West Sussex was keen to back the THN initiative to help support their agenda of reducing drug-related deaths. The new take-home initiative will expand naloxone provision to all Clouds clients with a history of opioid use on an opt-out basis, meaning that naloxone and overdose training will be presumed to be part of standard care, unless the client specifically decides that they do not wish to receive this.

Phased rollout

The clinical leadership at Clouds recognises that THN is an evidence-based practice and believes that relapse prevention and training in relapse management (including THN provision) can occur alongside abstinence as a central treatment goal. Despite this, the leadership team at Clouds is aware that there may be initial puzzlement or challenge when introducing THN as standard care. Staff who believe in abstinence-only as the treatment goal may view THN as at odds with the traditional focus of the Minnesota Model (see chapter by Kelly and Bergman in present volume). Moreover, staff may voice concerns that the availability of THN could create the illusion of a safety net and make clients more likely to relapse. However, there is no empirical evidence to support this concern (Strang et al., 1999; Doe-Simkins, et al., 2014). In order to build support for THN at the staff level, an implementation approach in two phases will be taken.

Implementation Phase 1

The first implementation phase will comprise a baseline assessment of perceived clinical need and attitudes towards THN. No actual THN provision will occur during this phase. All members of the care team will be asked to complete a questionnaire indicating knowledge of overdose risk factors as well as attitudes on the acceptability and perceived importance of THN. This will capture potential staff ambivalence which may impact implementation.

For all clients, regardless of the reason for referral, an overdose questionnaire will be included in the registration forms. The questionnaire will enquire into their history of opioid use, personal overdose experience and witnessed overdoses (nonfatal and fatal). In case of a history of opioid use, the questionnaire will also prompt clients to indicate their willingness to receive overdose management and naloxone training.

With the clients' consent, relevant family members or partners will be sent a mail survey to assess their interest in receiving information about naloxone as well as their willingness to attend training at Clouds House covering overdose emergency management and naloxone administration. At an operational level, the first implementation phase will be used to seek regulatory approval for a Patient-Group Direction for naloxone provision.

Implementation Phase 2

Phase 2 of implementation will focus on providing training to staff and clients in overdose prevention, overdose emergency management and THN administration. In addition, training will be offered to clients' family members. All members of the care team at Clouds House will receive training, which will also cover the operational aspects of THN, e.g. where naloxone stocks are stored at Clouds, how THN provision is documented in the clients' notes and who is authorised to dispense it. Training will also involve open discussion, where questions or concerns regarding THN can be addressed. After training, all care team members will repeat the questionnaire from Phase 1, in order to assess changes in overdose-related knowledge and attitudes.

After training all clients with a history of opioid use will receive THN at discharge on an opt-out basis. Where clients choose to opt out, the reason for non-participation will be documented in their records. Training will be offered as part of an existing relapse prevention class. Family members will be offered educational material on relapse prevention and overdose management as well as training sessions at Clouds House. Two family counsellors as well as a health care assistant are available as part of the clinical team at Clouds, and training can be facilitated on Sundays as part of family visits. The THN initiative can also be covered in the For Families newsletter, which was introduced in December 2014 with the aim of informing family members of current Action on Addiction events and initiatives.

Progress at Clouds House will be carefully monitored and lessons learnt will be documented to facilitate a later rollout at the Hope House residential treatment facility as well as at Action on Addiction-led community treatment initiatives. The experiences within Action on Addiction will also contribute to consideration of introduction of THN schemes in other residential rehabs in the UK and internationally.

Concluding comments

Traditionally, the worlds of THN and abstinence-based residential rehabilitation may have been viewed as clashing, but the WHO Guidelines and the recent rise in UK drug-related deaths demonstrate a clear need for action. It is the collective responsibility of drug treatment providers to equip clients with the knowledge and skills required to prevent relapse and death from overdose. The case studies from Scotland, Wales and England demonstrate that the implementation of THN is possible in different formats, and Action on Addiction will lead the residential rehab field in England by integrating THN into its routine care.

References

Armstrong EM, Jarvie A, Scott W and Robson G (2001) *Patient Group Directions*. Available at: http://www.sehd.scot.nhs.uk/mels/HDL2001_07.HTM (accessed 06/08/2015).

Barnsdale L, Gordon R and McAuley A (2015) *The National Drug-Related Deaths Database (Scotland) Report: Analysis of Deaths occurring in 2013*. National Health Service Scotland. Available at: http://www.isdscotland.org/Health-Topics/Drugs-and-Alcohol-Misuse/Publications/2015-04-28/2015-04-28-NDRDD-Report.pdf (accessed 06/08/2015).

Bennett T and Holloway K (2011) *Evaluation of the Take Home Naloxone Demonstration Project*. Merthyr Tydfil: Welsh Assembly Government. Available at: http://gov.wales/statistics-and-research/evaluation-take-home-naloxone-demonstration-project/?lang=en (accessed 10/08/2015).

Best D, Gossop M, Man L-H, Finch E, Greenwood J and Strang J (2000) Accidental and deliberate overdose among opiate addicts in methadone maintenance treatment: are deliberate overdoses systematically different? *Drug and Alcohol Review* 19(2): 213–216.

Beswick T, Best D, Bearn J, Rees S, Gossop M, Coomber R and Strang J (2002) From salt injection to naloxone: accuracy and myths in peer resuscitation methods for opiate overdose. *Journal of Drug Issues* 32(4): 1103–1114.

Bird SM, Parmar MK and Strang J (2014) Take-home naloxone to prevent fatalities from opiate-overdose: protocol for Scotland's public health policy evaluation, and a new measure to assess impact. *Drugs: Education, Prevention and Policy* 22(1): 66–76.

Cornish R, Macleod J, Strang J, Vickerman P and Hickman M (2010) Risk of death during and after opiate substitution treatment in primary care: prospective observational study in UK General Practice Research Database. *British Medical Journal* 341: c5475. Available at: http://www.bmj.com/content/341/bmj.c5475.long (accessed 07/08/2015).

Darke S, Hall W, Kaye S, Ross J and Duflou J (2002) Hair morphine concentrations of fatal heroin overdose cases and living heroin users. *Addiction* 97(8): 977–984.

Davies C, English L, Lodwick A, McVeigh J and Bellis MA (2010) *United Kingdom Drug Situation: Annual Report to the European Monitoring Centre for Drugs and Drug Addiction.* London: Department of Health.

Davoli M, Bargagli AM, Perucci CA, Schifano P, Belleudi V, Hickman M, Salamina G, Diecidue R, Vigna-Taglianti F, Faggiano F and the VEdeTTE Study Group (2007) Risk of fatal overdose during and after specialist drug treatment: the VEdeTTE study, a national multi-site prospective cohort study. *Addiction* 102(12): 1954–1959.

Doe-Simkins M, Quinn E, Xuan Z, Sorensen-Alawad A, Hackman H, Ozonoff A and Walley AY (2014) Overdose rescues by trained and untrained participants and change in opioid use among substance-using participants in overdose education and naloxone distribution programs: a retrospective cohort study. *BMC Public Health* 14(1): 297. Available at: http://dash.harvard.edu/bitstream/handle/1/12152856/4004504.pdf?sequence=1 (accessed 10/08/2015).

EMCDDA (2015a) *European Drug Report 2015: Trends and Developments.* Available at: http://www.emcdda.europa.eu/publications/edr/trends-developments/2015 (accessed 06/08/2015).

EMCDDA (2015b) *Preventing Fatal Overdoses: A Systematic Review of the Effectiveness of Take-Home Naloxone.* Available at: http://www.emcdda.europa.eu/publications/emcdda-papers/naloxone-effectiveness (accessed 06/08/2015).

Heale P, Dietze P and Fry C (2003) Intentional overdose among heroin overdose survivors. *Journal of Urban Health* 80(2): 230–237.

ISD – Information Services Division (2014) *National Naloxone Programme Scotland – Naloxone Kits Issued in 2013/14 and Trends in Opioid-Related Deaths.* Available at: http://www.isdscotland.org/Health-Topics/Drugs-and-Alcohol-Misuse/Publications/2014-10-28/2014-10-28-Naloxone-Report.pdf (accessed 07/08/2015.

McAuley A, Best D, Taylor A, Hunter C and Robertson R (2012) From evidence to policy: the Scottish national naloxone programme. *Drugs: Education, Prevention and Policy* 19(4): 309–319.

Mayet S, Manning V, Williams A, Loaring J and Strang J (2011) Impact of training for healthcare professionals on how to manage an opioid overdose with naloxone: effective, but dissemination is challenging. *International Journal of Drug Policy* 22(1): 9–15.

Merrall ELC, Bird SM and Hutchinson SJ (2013) A record-linkage study of drug related death and suicide after hospital discharge among drug-treatment clients in Scotland, 1996–2006. *Addiction* 108(2): 377–384.

Merrall ELC, Kariminia A, Binswanger IA, Hobbs MS, Farrell M, Marsden J, Hutchinson SJ and Bird SM (2010) Meta-analysis of drug-related deaths soon after release from prison. *Addiction* 105(9): 1545–1554.

Morgan G and Smith J (2014) *Harm Reduction Database Wales: Take Home Naloxone 2013–14*. Public Health Wales. Available at: http://www2.nphs.wales.nhs.uk:8080/substancemisusedocs.nsf/%28$all%29/ecf9e1d7909a8abc80257e0a0059e887/$file/naloxone%20report%202014%20final.pdf (accessed 07/08/2015).

Mundt-Leach R, Jackson S, Keaney F and Morinan A (2010) Citizen medics. *DrugLink* 24.

ONS – Office of National Statistics (2013) *Statistical Bulletin: Deaths Related to Drug Poisoning in England and Wales, 2013*. Available at: http://www.ons.gov.uk/ons/rel/subnational-health3/deaths-related-to-drug-poisoning/england-and-wales---2013/stb---deaths-related-to-drug-poisoning-in-england-and-wales--2013.html (accessed 07/08/2015).

Ravndal E and Amundsen EJ (2010) Mortality among drug users after discharge from inpatient treatment: an 8-year prospective study. *Drug and Alcohol Dependence* 108(1): 65–69.

SACDM – Scottish Advisory Committee on Drug Misuse (2005) *Working Group on Drug Related Deaths: Report and Recommendations*. Edinburgh: Scottish Executive.

Scottish Drugs Forum SD (2015) *Take Home Naloxone (THN) Overdose Intervention Training*. Availableat: http://www.sdf.org.uk/drug-related-deaths/take-home-naloxone-thn-overdose-intervention-training/ (accessed 07/08/2015).

Strang J, Darke S, Hall W, Farrell M and Ali R (1996) Heroin overdose: the case for take-home naloxone. *British Medical Journal* 312(7044): 1435–1436.

Strang J, Powis B, Best D, Vingoe L, Griffiths P, Taylor C, Welch S and Gossop M (1999) Preventing opiate overdose fatalities with take-home-naloxone: pre-launch study of possible impact and acceptability. *Addiction* 94(2): 199–204.

Strang J, McCambridge J, Best D, Beswick T, Bearn J, Rees S and Gossop M (2003) Loss of tolerance and overdose mortality after inpatient opiate detoxification: follow up study. *British Medical Journal* 326(7396): 959–960.

Strang J, Manning V, Mayet S, Best D, Titherington E, Santana L, Offor E and Semmler C (2008) Overdose training and take-home naloxone for opiate users: prospective cohort study of impact on knowledge and attitudes and subsequent management of overdoses. *Addiction* 103(10): 1648–1657.

Walley AY, Xuan Z, Hackman HH, Quinn E, Doe-Simkins M, Sorensen-Alawad A, Ruiz S and Ozonoff A (2013) Opioid overdose rates and implementation of overdose education and nasal naloxone distribution in Massachusetts: interrupted time series analysis. *British Medical Journal* 346 (f174).

Watt G, Jaquet S, Ellison S, Christie I and Nicholson J (2014) *Service Evaluation of Scotland's National Take-Home Naloxone Programme*. Edinburgh: Scottish Government. Available at: www.gov.scot/Resource/0045/00451251.pdf (accessed 07/08/2015).

Welsh Assembly Government (2008) *Working Together to Reduce Harm*. Available at: http://www2.nphs.wales.nhs.uk:8080/SubstanceMisuseDocs.nsf/($All)/6361D5806F16EEDD80257C5B005AC8AF/$File/Working%20Together%20to%20Reduce%20Harm%20-%20SM%20Strategy%202008-2018.pdf?OpenElement (accessed 08/08/2015).

Wheeler E, Jones TS, Gilbert MK and Davidson PJ (2015) Opioid overdose prevention programs providing naloxone to laypersons – United States 2014. *Centers for Disease Control and Prevention (CDC) Morbidity and Mortality Weekly Report*. Available at: http://www.cdc.gov/mmwr/preview/mmwrhtml/mm6423a2.htm (accessed 06/08/2015).

WHO (2014) *Community Management of Opioid Overdose*. Available at: http://apps.who.int/iris/bitstream/10665/137462/1/9789241548816_eng.pdf?ua=1&ua=1 (accessed 08/08/2015).

Williams AV, Marsden J and Strang J (2014) Training family members to manage heroin overdose and administer naloxone: randomized trial of effects on knowledge and attitudes. *Addiction* 109(2): 250–259.

Chapter 9

Management of alcohol use disorders in the UK

Ed Day and Mandip Jheeta

Introduction

Alcohol has been valued by humans for its psychoactive properties for thousands of years, and has held a central role in religious, cultural and social practices in most societies. However, as the production and distribution of alcohol has become increasingly sophisticated, the harms associated with consumption have become more apparent. In addition, a proportion of individuals develop an 'addiction' to alcohol, whereby their ability to control the frequency and extent of their consumption becomes eroded. Alcohol consumption can impact on both the incidence and course of many health conditions, and 5.9 per cent of all global deaths in 2012 were estimated to be attributable to alcohol (WHO, 2014). Despite an increasing understanding of the neurobiological and psychological processes involved in the development and maintenance of these problems (Volkow and Li, 2005; West, 2006), alcohol use disorders remain a heavily stigmatised problem.

Level of alcohol consumption

Accurate and reliable information about patterns of alcohol consumption is hard to obtain, and surveys report lower levels of consumption than would be expected from data on alcohol sales. People tend to consciously or unconsciously underestimate how much they consume, and measures of alcohol consumed away from licensed premises are particularly likely to be underestimated (Bellis et al., 2015). Interpretation of national figures is also complicated by the variety of influences on how much an individual drinks. For example, there are large regional differences between self-reported drinking levels, with the north-east and north-west of England consuming considerably more than London or the south-west (Health and Social Care Information Centre, 2014).

Alcoholic drinks are consumed by 85 per cent of the population of England. Although most (61 per cent men, 72 per cent women) either drink no alcohol or drink within the recommended levels, it is estimated that a quarter of the adult population of England drinks in a way that is potentially or actually harmful to their health. National statistics show an upwards trend in alcohol-related health problems. In 2012/13, there were an estimated 1,008,850 admissions related to alcohol consumption where an alcohol-related disease, injury or condition was the primary reason for hospital admission or a secondary diagnosis (Health and Social Care Information Centre, 2014).

The current advice (see www.nhs.uk/Change4Life/Pages/drink-less-alcohol.aspx) from the UK Department of Health is that in order to minimise the risk of health harms associated with drinking:

- Men and women are advised not to regularly drink more than 14 units a week.
- Spread your drinking over three days or more if you drink as much as 14 units a week.
- Pregnant women or women trying to conceive should not drink alcohol at all. If they do choose to drink they should not drink more than 1–2 units of alcohol once or twice a week and should not get drunk.
- Children should not drink alcohol at all, but if they do, they should be at least 15 years old, never drink more than once a week, be supervised by a parent or carer, and never exceed the recommended adult daily limits.

Calculating units of alcohol

A drink's alcohol content is usually expressed by the standard measure 'Alcohol by Volume' or ABV. This is a measure of the amount of pure alcohol as a percentage of the total volume of liquid in a drink, and is found on the labels of cans and bottles. For example, if a can of beer has a label reading '5% ABV' this means that 5 per cent of the volume of that drink is pure alcohol. The number of units in any drink can be calculated by multiplying the total volume (in ml) by its ABV and dividing the result by 1,000. For the number of units in a pint (568ml) of strong lager (ABV 5 per cent) the calculation is 568 by 5 divided by 1000, which comes to 2.84 units. Keeping track of units is important, as the increasing strength of many alcoholic drinks and larger glass sizes served in many bars mean that people are often drinking more alcohol than they realise. Units calculators are available, e.g. http://www.nhs.uk/Tools/Pages/Alcohol-unit-calculator.aspx.

Defining alcohol use disorders

Three categories of alcohol use disorder (AUD) have been defined, although more recently the UK Department of Health has renamed the first two groups below, based on weekly alcohol consumption and/or AUDIT score (see Figure 9.1 below).

- *Hazardous* drinking is a pattern of alcohol consumption in excess of the recommended levels above, but without experiencing harm. It may also be defined by a score of 8–15 on the AUDIT screening tool.
- *Harmful* drinking is a pattern of consumption in excess of the recommended levels and experiencing health-related harms. The damage may be physical (e.g. hepatitis), mental (e.g. depressive episodes secondary to heavy alcohol intake), or social (e.g. unemployment, domestic violence). This may also be defined by an AUDIT score of 16–19.
- *Alcohol dependence* is drinking above recommended levels whilst experiencing harm and symptoms of dependence. The term 'addiction' is not used in current classificatory systems due to its perceived pejorative connotations, but is most closely associated with the concept of dependence.

The International Classification of Disorders (ICD-10) criteria for a diagnosis of alcohol dependence are listed below (WHO, 1992). Dependence may exist at different levels of severity, and the concept is useful for determining treatment strategies and prognosis. However, the latest version of the *Diagnostic and Statistical Manual of Mental Disorders* (DSM-5) used in the USA has removed the category of dependence, preferring to describe a spectrum of alcohol use disorders of different severity (Hasin et al., 2013).

Categories of drinking

- Low risk: No amount of alcohol consumption can be called 'safe', but risks of harm are low if below UK Department of Health recommended levels (see above), and AUDIT score 7 or less.
- Increasing risk (hazardous): Regularly drinking more than 2–3 units a day (for both women and men), and AUDIT score 8–15.
- Higher risk (harmful): Regularly drinking more than 6 units per day (women) or more than 8 units per day (men). Or more than 35 units per week (women) and more than 50 units per week (men), and AUDIT score 16–19.
- Dependence: A definite diagnosis of dependence should be made only if there is an AUDIT score of 20 or more, and three or more of the following have been present together at the same time during the previous year:

  a a strong desire or sense of compulsion to drink alcohol (an essential characteristic)
  b difficulties in controlling drinking behaviour in terms of onset, termination, or levels of consumption
  c a physiological withdrawal state when drinking ceases or is reduced, evidenced by the characteristic alcohol withdrawal syndrome; or use of a closely related substance with the intention of relieving or avoiding withdrawal symptoms e.g. benzodiazepines

d evidence of tolerance, such that increased quantities of alcohol are required in order to achieve the effects originally produced by lesser amounts
e progressive neglect of alternative pleasures or interests because of alcohol consumption, increased amount of time necessary to obtain or drink alcohol or to recover from its effects
f persisting with drinking alcohol despite clear evidence of overtly harmful consequences, such as liver damage, depressive mood or impaired cognitive functioning.

It is estimated that 38 per cent of men and 16 per cent of women in England aged between 16 and 64 years have an alcohol use disorder as defined above, with 6 per cent of men and 2 per cent of women meeting the criteria for alcohol dependence (Drummond et al., 2005). In terms of numbers it is therefore clear that most alcohol-related problems occur in hazardous and harmful drinkers rather than people with alcohol dependence. From a public health perspective, secondary prevention aims to detect health problems at an early stage and intervene to produce positive changes in behaviours. This has been called the 'prevention paradox', i.e. the greatest impact at a population level is likely to come from reducing (not necessarily stopping) consumption in hazardous and harmful drinkers rather than focusing on the heaviest, dependent drinkers. Most hazardous and harmful drinkers are unaware of their alcohol-related risk or harm, and so some form of screening is required to detect them. There is a strong evidence base supporting the effectiveness of screening and brief interventions for people who are drinking at risky levels but who are not actively seeking treatment for alcohol problems (NICE, 2010a).

As the level of daily and weekly alcohol consumption goes up, so the risk of physical, psychological and social problems increases. Therefore strategies that reduce average consumption across the whole population by a small amount produce considerable health benefits. Increasing the cost of alcohol relative to earnings has been consistently associated with reduction in alcohol-related harm (Alcohol and Public Policy Group, 2010), and a minimum cost for a unit of alcohol has been under consideration in the UK (Rice and Drummond, 2012).

Causes of alcohol use disorders

There is no single theory or model that comprehensively explains addiction. There is general consensus that addiction is a 'biopsychosocial phenomenon', i.e. it is best understood by looking at the interaction between biological, psychological and social factors. This complex and dynamic interplay partly explains why not everyone who drinks or experiments with alcohol will develop problematic use.

Biological factors

Alcohol has reinforcing properties through its pleasurable and anxiolytic effects. At a molecular level, dopamine and the mesolimbic pathway in the brain seem to be crucial for reward, reinforcement and subsequent substance misuse problems (Volkow and Li, 2005). Children of parents with alcohol problems have an increased risk of developing an AUD. Genetic factors account for approximately 50 per cent of the aetiology of AUDs, with the rest being attributable to environmental factors or their interaction with genetic factors (Goldman, Oroszi and Ducci, 2005). Genetic findings have not yet led to new or targeted substance misuse treatments.

Psychological factors

Using substances to cope with or enhance emotions and associated thoughts and behaviours is a key aspect of substance use (Mitcheson et al., 2010). Conditioning theories may explain why certain cues (e.g. the sight or smell of a favourite drink) can trigger cravings for alcohol, leading to relapse after a period of abstinence. Adverse life events may also trigger excessive drinking and so may predispose to AUDs. People who are alcohol dependent report much higher levels of childhood abuse and neglect, particularly sexual abuse, and have a significantly greater risk of having an antisocial personality disorder or other psychiatric disorders than people in the general population (Regier et al., 1990).

Social factors

Both the development and maintenance of AUDs invariably happen in a social context. Social learning theory is important, as people learn from families and peers through a process of modelling patterns of drinking, beliefs about the effects of alcohol, coping skills and self-efficacy. Environmental factors include affordability and availability of alcohol, high consumption rates in the general population, social pressure to drink, and religious or culturally related attitudes towards alcohol.

When trying to help a person with an AUD it is important to consider the different biopsychosocial factors that are likely to be contributing. It has often been argued that interventions that do not take note of the social content of substance use are likely to be ineffective. As explained later, a decision to change and a degree of motivation to implement that decision are seen as essential for change to happen.

Problems associated with alcohol consumption

Alcohol is associated with a wide range of problems, and a more detailed review can be found in chapter 2 of the National Institute for Health and Care Excellence (NICE), Clinical Practice Guideline 115 (www.nice.org.uk/CG115).

Physical health problems

The mortality rate of heavy drinkers is at least twice that of the normal population. No organ system in the body remains unaffected by the direct toxic effects of chronic alcohol consumption, and many of these effects are compounded by dietary insufficiency associated with the 'empty calories' of alcohol (for a detailed review see Day and Khurmi, 2012). Alcohol-related hypertension occurs in up to 25 per cent of those drinking at a harmful level. Other conditions associated with AUDs include stroke, obesity, alcoholic liver disease (including fatty liver, hepatitis and cirrhosis), various cancers, aspiration pneumonia, pancreatitis, cognitive deficits, alcohol-related brain damage, epileptic seizures, peripheral neuropathy, foetal alcohol syndrome and sexual dysfunction. Intoxication with alcohol also increases the risk of soft-tissue injuries, fractures, head injuries and other trauma.

Mental health problems

Alcohol is strongly associated with depression, anxiety, nicotine dependence, other drug misuse, self-harm and suicide. One UK study found that 85 per cent of patients attending specialist alcohol treatment services had a psychiatric disorder in addition to alcohol dependence, while one-quarter of patients of community mental health teams reported harmful levels of alcohol use (Weaver et al., 2003). Such comorbidity or 'dual diagnosis' of mental illness and substance misuse should be considered the norm rather than the exception, though it is often unrecognised and associated with poorer outcomes. Comorbidity is likely to vary by area and population groups, and existing care provisions have often been criticised as inadequate (Gerada, Chawla and Day, 2013). The relationship between alcohol or drug use and symptoms of mental health disorders is often complex. Alcohol use can be the cause, consequence or mimicker of symptoms such as low mood or tiredness, and it is often hard to completely separate all parts of a person's presentation. Heavy drinking can contribute to non-compliance, interaction and reduced efficacy of medical and other treatments. Therefore, seeking and recognising comorbidity is important.

Social problems

Alcohol is often implicated in relationship breakdown, domestic violence and poor parenting, including child neglect and abuse. Up to 60 per cent of cases of child protection cases involve alcohol and an estimated 1 million children are affected by parental alcohol misuse (Prime Minister's Strategy Unit, 2004). Alcohol also contributes to absenteeism from work, financial problems, accidents in the workplace and decline in work performance. Harmful use of alcohol can also lead to job loss, and nearly 2 per cent of all working age claimants of Incapacity Benefit in England in 2007 (40,000 people) had a diagnosis of 'alcoholism' (Deacon et al., 2007). Alcohol also contributes to unsafe sex, unplanned pregnancy and homelessness, and is associated with significant and long-term stressful impacts on family members. Though hard to calculate, the cost to society of alcohol in England has been estimated to be at least £21 billion per year (HM Government, 2012).

Antisocial behaviour

Crime, especially violent crime, is associated with alcohol, mainly through its disinhibiting effect on behaviour. Criminal damage, domestic violence, sexual assaults, burglary, theft, robbery and homicide are all associated with alcohol consumption, and it is estimated that half of those who commit assault and two-thirds who murder are drunk at the time. An international estimate of AUDs amongst prisoners was 18–30 per cent for males and 10–24 per cent for females, both much higher than in the general population (Fazel, Bains and Doll, 2006). Even higher rates (two-thirds of males and half of females) are reported in young offenders in the year before prison. Despite this high prevalence, treatment in prisons for AUDs has often been seen as neglected when compared to treatment for drug misuse.

Identifying and diagnosing alcohol use disorders

NICE recommends that NHS professionals should carry out alcohol screening as part of routine practice (NICE, 2010a). If screening everyone is not feasible, the focus should be on groups with an increased risk of harm from alcohol e.g. people with relevant physical problems (e.g. hypertension, gastrointestinal or liver problems) or mental health conditions (e.g. anxiety or depression), at risk of self-harm, or who regularly experience accidents or minor trauma. All health care professionals should feel comfortable and confident in raising the topic of alcohol consumption in a consultation.

The most cost-effective way of screening for AUDs is through questionnaires. The Alcohol Use Disorders Identification Test, (AUDIT, Figure 9.1), consists of 10 questions about drinking frequency and intensity, experience of alcohol-related problems and signs of possible dependence (Babor et al., 2001), and is considered the 'gold standard' screening questionnaire for detecting hazardous and harmful drinkers (NICE, 2010a). Briefer versions are available (e.g. AUDIT-C, AUDIT-PC, FAST) which may be more suited to particular settings. The AUDIT score can guide the decision whether to offer the patient a 'brief intervention' or to make a referral for specialist services. This may be supplemented by the use of a Drinks Diary in order to calculate the weekly alcohol consumption in units. Biochemical measures such as liver function tests are not useful for screening, but may be used to assess the severity and progress of an established alcohol-related problem, or as part of a hospital assessment (Drummond, Ghodse and Chengappa, 2007).

ALCOHOL USE DISORDERS IDENTIFICATION TEST (AUDIT)

1. How often do you have a drink containing alcohol?

(0) Never
(1) Monthly or less
(2) 2 to 4 times a month
(3) 2 to 3 times a week
(4) 4 or more times a week

2. How many units of alcohol do you have on a typical day when you are drinking?

(0) 1 or 2
(1) 3 or 4
(2) 5 or 6
(3) 7, 8 or 9
(4) 10 or more

3. How often do you have 6 or more units if female, or 8 or more units if male, on a single occasion in the last year?

(0) Never
(1) Less than monthly
(2) Monthly
(3) Weekly
(4) Daily or almost daily

4. How often during the last year have you found that you were not able to stop drinking once you had started?

(0) Never
(1) Less than monthly
(2) Monthly
(3) Weekly
(4) Daily or almost daily

5. How often during the last year have you failed to do what was normally expected from you because of drinking?

6. How often during the last year have you needed a first drink in the morning to get yourself going after a heavy drinking session?

(0) Never
(1) Less than monthly
(2) Monthly
(3) Weekly
(4) Daily or almost daily

7. How often during the last year have you had a feeling of guilt or remorse after drinking?

(0) Never
(1) Less than monthly
(2) Monthly
(3) Weekly
(4) Daily or almost daily

8. How often during the last year have you been unable to remember what happened the night before because you had been drinking?

(0) Never
(1) Less than monthly
(2) Monthly
(3) Weekly
(4) Daily or almost daily

9. Have you or someone else been injured as a result of your drinking?

(0) No
(2) Yes, but not in the last year
(4) Yes, during the last year

10. Has a relative or friend, doctor or another health worker been concerned about your drinking or suggested that you cut down?

(0) Never (1) Less than monthly (2) Monthly (3) Weekly (4) Daily or almost daily	(0) No (2) Yes, but not in the last year (4) Yes, during the last year
TOTAL SCORE:	

Figure 9.1 The AUDIT questionnaire

Brief interventions

Treatment interventions for AUDs do not need to be of long duration to be effective (Heather, 1995) and a few minutes of advice about moderating alcohol consumption has been shown to be an effective strategy in hazardous and harmful drinkers in various settings (Jackson et al., 2010). A large body of international research evidence indicates that 1 in 8 people drinking at hazardous or harmful levels who receive structured brief advice will reduce their drinking to within lower risk levels (NICE, 2010a). Raising the issue of alcohol consumption with patients can meet with a range of attitudes, including indifference, confusion about what is or is not healthy, and possibly defensiveness and irritability. The clinician should ensure that they are aware of the facts about alcohol consumption and health-related harms in order to accurately convey the risks of drinking to the patient. It is important to avoid stigmatising terms like 'alcoholic', but, instead, to emphasise the point that there is increased risk with increased consumption, and to suggest cutting down to a lower risk level rather than stopping. However, the clinician should also be able to detect alcohol dependence and refer on for specialist help. The process is described below and summarised in Figure 9.2.

Stage 1: raise the issue

It may be easiest to embed questions about alcohol in a general enquiry about lifestyle factors e.g. smoking, diet and exercise. Ask the first three questions on the AUDIT questionnaire (Figure 9.1) and score the answers (known as AUDIT-C). A score of 5 or more suggests a high likelihood that the person is drinking at an increasing risk or hazardous level, and the full AUDIT questionnaire should be administered.

Stage 2: administer and score the 10-item AUDIT questionnaire

A score of 7 or less should be fed back in a positive manner e.g. reiterate the sensible drinking guidelines and point out that people who exceed these levels increase their chances of alcohol-related health problems, whilst congratulating them for adhering to guidance. A score between 8 and 19 suggests that the individual's drinking pattern is in the hazardous or harmful band, and the clinician should move to stage 3.

Stage 3: deliver structured brief advice

Use an open-ended 'transitional' question such as 'how important is it for you to change your drinking?', possibly accompanied by a simple 'readiness ruler' i.e. asking the individual to rate between 1 and 10 how confident they feel in making changes, followed by asking what would have to happen to make the number go up. A structured episode of brief advice may only last 5–10 minutes, and is best guided by a structured advice tool (such as available at www.alcohollearningcentre.org.uk/alcoholeLearning/learning/IBA/Module4_v2/pdf/structured_advice_tool.pdf). This makes use of the FRAMES structure for brief interventions (Feedback, Responsibility, Advice, Menu, Empathy, Self-efficacy) (Miller and Sanchez, 1993). The leaflet provides material to use for three of these elements: Feedback on the patient's level of drinking when compared to others, the common effects of drinking, and the potential benefits of reduction; a Menu of options to support the attainment of their preferred drinking goal; and Advice on units and limits.

The clinician should be firm enough to ensure that the individual realises that it is their own responsibility to make the change (restating the need to reduce risk and encouraging the patient to begin now), whilst also showing empathy (e.g. 'it can be very difficult to make these changes if everyone around you is drinking heavily') and aiming to boost their confidence and self-efficacy ('You mentioned you were going to drink a non-alcoholic drink first when you get home in the evening. That sounds like an excellent start'). Ideally the individual should be offered a follow-up appointment to assess their progress in reducing their alcohol consumption.

An 'extended brief intervention' places greater emphasis on exploring the pros and cons of change and formulating a specific action plan. This approach is often based on the principles of motivational interviewing (Rollnick et al., 2010) and again is best guided by a structured leaflet such as the one available at:

http://www.alcohollearningcentre.org.uk/alcoholeLearning/learning/IBA/Module5_v2/extended_intervention_worksheet.pdf. A patient should be referred for more specialist alcohol assessment and intervention if they ask for such help, are already exhibiting significant alcohol-related harm, have an AUDIT score of more than 20 or exhibit the features of the dependence syndrome.

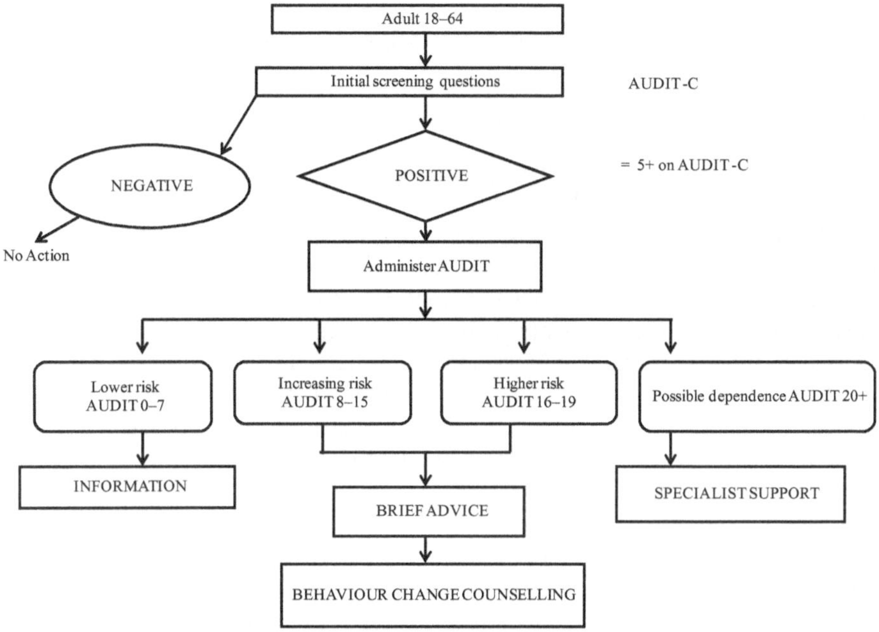

Figure 9.2 Managing alcohol use disorders

Treatment of alcohol dependence

People with a moderate to severe level of alcohol dependence benefit from more intensive specialist help (NICE, 2010a). Abstinence is the preferred goal for many such individuals, particularly for those whose organs have already been damaged through alcohol use, or for those who have previously attempted to cut down their drinking without success. In considering the correct level of treatment intensity it is important to consider risks, capacity to consent to treatment, the experience and outcome of previous episodes of treatment, motivation for change, and other existing problems including harm to others.

Current provision in the UK is a mix of brief interventions provided by GPs, NHS and non-statutory specialist community alcohol services, a few inpatient units providing assisted alcohol withdrawal and a declining number of (mostly non-statutory or private) residential rehabilitation centres (National Collaborating Centre for Mental Health, 2011). A system of case management should form part of routine care in specialist agencies, and includes the coordination of assessment, interventions and monitoring of progress, and coordination with other agencies (Department of Health, 2006). Initial assessment must determine key issues such as the pattern and nature of alcohol consumption (using a drink diary and AUDIT), the need for urgent treatment including medically assisted withdrawal, any associated risks to self or others and the presence of alcohol-related problems or co-morbidities. The Severity of Alcohol Dependence Questionnaire (SADQ) is a useful tool for quantifying the degree of dependence (Stockwell, Murphy and Hodgson, 1983).

Medically assisted withdrawal

The alcohol withdrawal syndrome includes a wide range of symptoms, the most severe of which are potentially life-threatening. About six to eight hours after an abrupt reduction in alcohol intake most people experience hyperactivity, anxiety, tremor, sweating, nausea and retching, increased heart rate, high blood pressure and mildly raised temperature. These symptoms usually peak over 10–30 hours, and subside by 40–50 hours. More seriously, seizures may occur in the first 12–48 hours but rarely after this. Auditory and visual hallucinations, characteristically frightening, may develop in the first 48 hours and last for up to six days. Delirium tremens occurs in up to 5 per cent, and usually starts 48–72 hours after stopping drinking. Major symptoms include coarse tremor, agitation, fever, rapid heart rate, profound confusion, delusions and hallucinations.

Minor degrees of alcohol withdrawal are common, and can be managed with information, reassurance, adequate fluid intake and diet. Moderate to severe alcohol withdrawal symptoms often require sedation to prevent exhaustion and injury. Long-acting benzodiazepines (chlordiazepoxide or diazepam) are the drug of choice for managing them. Rating scales such as the Clinical Institute Withdrawal Assessment for Alcohol (CIWA-Ar) can be used to measure the severity of the withdrawal symptoms and more accurately adjust the dose (Sullivan et al., 1989). The use of such a 'symptom-triggered' regimen is only recommended if trained staff are available e.g. in an inpatient setting (NICE, 2010b).

Psychosocial interventions

Interventions based on psychological or social processes of change are a mainstay of treatment for alcohol dependence. Evidence-based treatments include:

- Motivational interviewing (MI). This uses a guiding style to engage with patients, elicit and reinforce their strengths and goals, and evoke their own motivational statements for change in their drinking patterns. It has been shown to promote behaviour change in many healthcare settings and lead to better outcomes for patients (Rollnick et al., 2010). MI has been incorporated into a manual-based intervention which has been shown to be effective in large research trials in the USA (Project Match, 1997) and the UK (UKATT, 2005).
- Cognitive behavioural therapy (CBT). Cognitive techniques (e.g. identifying and challenging negative thinking) and behavioural 'experiments' are used to help achieve specific goals e.g. cutting down or stopping drinking. 'Relapse Prevention' is one example of an individual- or group-based CBT programme which may include identifying high-risk situations and triggers

for craving, developing strategies to avoid such situations, enhancing skills to manage cravings and painful emotions without using alcohol, learning to cope with lapses, and increasing pleasurable sober activities and relationships (Wanigaratne et al., 1990).

- Contingency Management. Operant conditioning theory suggests that some consequences strengthen behaviour, whilst others weaken it. The Community Reinforcement Approach is based on the principle that individuals have their own positive reinforcers in their environment, which maintain either their drinking or non-drinking behaviours. By altering these reinforcement contingencies (and involving the client's social network in this process), the individual can make changes in their lifestyle that will support abstinence from alcohol (Meyers and Smith, 1995).
- Family and social interventions. Utilisation of social support for change is a powerful tool, and this may come from sexual partners, family members or friends. Family-focused interventions can be broadly grouped into three areas: (1) working with family members to encourage people with AUDs into treatment; (2) involving family members in the treatment of people with AUD; and (3) treatment of family members in their own right (Copello, Velleman and Templeton, 2005; Copello et al., 2009).
- Mutual self-help approaches: Alcoholics Anonymous (AA) is a self-help fellowship that provides support, friendship and a structured programme. The 12 Steps of AA lay out a process that individuals are recommended to follow, based on the belief that alcohol dependence is a disease and can be treated by lifelong abstinence. Manual-driven 12 Step facilitation approaches guide professionals through the process of effectively linking their patients to AA meetings, with the aim of patients maintaining abstinence whilst in treatment and sustaining gains made after treatment concludes. Other mutual-help groups such as SMART Recovery are also increasingly available in the UK.

Although research suggests that such treatments lead to improved outcomes when compared to no treatment at all, the evidence favouring one type of psychological intervention over another is less clear. Other factors such as therapist characteristics and service variables are also important (Miller and Moyers, 2015). There is wide variation in the uptake and implementation of psychological approaches in the UK (National Collaborating Centre for Mental Health, 2011), and most practice involves an eclectic approach that combines strategies from various psychological approaches that typically lasts 12 weeks. Psychological treatments can also be used to help people experiencing harmful alcohol use or dependence to address coexisting problems such as anxiety and depression.

Relapse prevention medication

Acamprosate and the opioid-antagonist naltrexone are both effective in increasing the time to first drink and to relapse in people with alcohol dependence who have achieved abstinence (National Collaborating Centre for Mental Health, 2011). Both should only be used in combination with an individual psychological intervention, started as soon as possible after withdrawal, and may be prescribed for six months or more depending on perceived benefit. Disulfiram works by interfering with the metabolism of alcohol, and leads to an unpleasant set of symptoms, including hypertension and a throbbing headache. It should be used with caution in pregnancy, severe mental illness, stroke, heart disease or hypertension. Nalmefene is licensed for use in adults with alcohol dependence who continue to drink more than 7.5 units/day in men and 5 units/day in women, but who do not have physical withdrawal symptoms and do not need immediate medically assisted withdrawal.

Conclusions

Problems relating to alcohol occur across the full spectrum of levels of consumption, and may be physical, psychological or social in nature. At one extreme there is a small but significant proportion of people who develop alcohol dependence and may require both intensive and extensive support. However, on a population level huge reductions in the harm caused by alcohol could be made if everyone was encouraged to drink a little less. All health and social care professionals should be able to screen for potential alcohol use disorders, deliver brief advice and refer on to specialist services where appropriate. The evidence base for treatment of alcohol use disorders has developed over the past 30 years, and clinicians should be positive and optimistic that meaningful change in drinking behaviours can be achieved. Prompt referral to the right level of support and treatment may prevent future problems.

Useful resources

Public Health England Alcohol Learning Resources. Available at: www.alcohollearningcentre.org.uk/.

Resources for People with Alcohol Use Disorders. Available at: www.nhs.uk/Change4Life/Pages/drink-less-alcohol.aspx.

Mutual Aid Organizations. Available at: www.alcoholics-anonymous.org.uk/; www.smartrecovery.org.uk/.

Help to find alcohol treatment. Available at: www.alcoholconcern.org.uk/concerned-about-alcohol/alcohol-services.

Adfam, a Charity Aiming to Improve Support for Families Affected by Drug and Alcohol Problems: Available at: www.adfam.org.uk/.

References

Alcohol and Public Policy Group (2010) Alcohol: No Ordinary Commodity – a summary of the second edition. *Addiction* 105(5): 772.

Babor TF, Higgins-Biddle JC, Saunders JB and Monteiro MG (2001) *AUDIT: The Alcohol Use Disorder Identification Test. Guidelines for Use in Primary Care.* Geneva: World

Health Organization. Available at: http://apps.who.int/iris/bitstream/10665/67205/1/WHO_MSD_MSB_01.6a.pdf (accessed 27/08/2015).

Bellis MA, Hughes K, Jones L, Morleo M, Nicholls J, McCoy E, Webster J and Sumnall H (2015) Holidays, celebrations, and commiserations: measuring drinking during feasting and fasting to improve national and individual estimates of alcohol consumption. *BMC Medicine* 13: 113. Available at: http://www.biomedcentral.com/content/pdf/s12916-015-0337-0.pdf (accessed 20/07/2015).

Copello A, Velleman R and Templeton L (2005) Family interventions in the treatment of alcohol and drug problems. *Drug and Alcohol Review* 24(4): 369–385.

Copello A, Templeton L, Orford J, Velleman R, Patel A, Moore L, MacLeod J and Godfrey C (2009) The relative efficacy of two levels of a primary care intervention for family members affected by the addiction problem of a close relative: a randomized trial. *Addiction* 104(1): 49–58.

Day E and Khurmi S (2012) Alcohol. In: Cormac I and Gray D (eds) *Essentials of Physical Health in Psychiatry*. London: RCPsych Publications, 301–315.

Deacon L, Hughes S, Tocque K and Bellis MA (2007) *Indications of Public Health in English Regions: 8. Alcohol*. York: Association of Public Health Observatories.

Department of Health (2006) *Models of Care for Alcohol Misusers (MoCAM)*. London: National Treatment Agency for Substance Misuse.

Drummond C, Ghodse H and Chengappa S (2007) Use of investigations in the diagnosis and management of alcohol use disorders. In: Day E (ed.) *Clinical Topics in Addiction*. London: RCPsych Publications, 113–129.

Drummond DC, Oyefeso N, Phillips T, Cheeta S, DeLuca P, Perryman K et al. (2005) *Alcohol Needs Assessment Research Project: The 2004 National Alcohol Needs Assessment for England*. London: Department of Health.

Fazel S, Bains P and Doll H (2006) Substance abuse and dependence in prisoners: a systematic review. *Addiction* 101(2): 181–191.

Gerada C, Chawla R and Day E (2013) Drug misuse and co-morbid illness: 'dual diagnosis'. In: Wright N, Gerada C and Sheard L (eds) *RCGP Guide to the Management of Substance Misuse in Primary Care* 2nd edn. London: Royal College of General Practitioners, 407–426.

Goldman D, Oroszi G and Ducci F (2005) The genetics of addictions: uncovering the genes. *Nature Review Genetics* 6: 521–532.

Hasin DS, O'Brien CP, Auriacombe M, Borges G, Bucholz K, Budney A et al. (2013) DSM-5 criteria for substance use disorders: recommendations and rationale. *American Journal of Psychiatry* 170(8): 834–851.

Health and Social Care Information Centre (2014) *Statistics on Alcohol: England, 2014*. Available at: http://www.hscic.gov.uk/catalogue/PUB14184/alc-eng-2014-rep.pdf (accessed 20/07/2015).

Heather N (1995) Brief intervention strategies. In: Hester RK and Miller WR (eds) *Handbook of Alcoholism Treatment Approaches: Effective Alternatives*. Boston: Allyn & Bacon.

HM Government (2012) *The Government's Alcohol Strategy*. Available at: https://www.gov.uk/government/uploads/system/uploads/attachment_data/file/224075/alcohol-strategy.pdf (accessed 20/07/2015).

Jackson R, Johnson M, Campbell F, Messina J, Guillaume L, Meier P, Goyder E, Chilcott J and Payne N (2010) *Screening and Brief Intervention for Prevention and Early Identification of Alcohol Use Disorder in Adults and Young People*. Sheffield: University of Sheffield, School of Health and Related Research (ScHARR) Public Health Collaborating Centre.

Meyers RJ and Smith JE (1995) *Clinical Guide to Alcohol Treatment: The Community Reinforcement Approach*. New York: The Guilford Press.

Miller WR and Moyers TB (2015) The forest and the trees: relational and specific factors in addiction treatment. *Addiction* 110(3): 401–413.

Miller WR and Sanchez VC (1993) Motivating young adults for treatment and lifestyle change. In: Howard G (ed.) *Issues in Alcohol Use and Misuse by Young Adults*. Notre Dame, IN: University of Notre Dame Press, 55–82.

Mitcheson L, Maslin J, Meynen T, Morrison T, Hill R and Wanigaratne S (2010) *Applied Cognitive and Behavioural Approaches to the Treatment of Addiction: A Practical Treatment Guide*. Chichester: Wiley-Blackwell.

National Collaborating Centre for Mental Health (2011) *Alcohol-Use Disorders: The NICE Guideline on Diagnosis, Assessment and Management of Harmful Drinking and Alcohol Dependence*. London: The British Psychological Society and The Royal College of Psychiatrists.

NICE (2010a) *Alcohol-use Disorders: Preventing Harmful Drinking. NICE Public Health Guidance*. National Institute for Health and Clinical Excellence. Available at: https://www.nice.org.uk/guidance/ph24/resources/guidance-alcoholuse-disorders-preventing-harmful-drinking-pdf (accessed 20/07/2015).

NICE (2010b) *Alcohol-Use Disorders: Diagnosis and Clinical Management of Alcohol-Related Physical Complications*. Clinical Guideline 100. Available at: https://www.nice.org.uk/guidance/cg100/resources/guidance-alcoholuse-disorders-diagnosis-and-clinical-management-of-alcoholrelated-physical-complications-pdf (accessed 20/07/2015).

Prime Minister's Strategy Unit (2004) *Alcohol Harm Reduction Strategy for England*. London: Cabinet Office.

Project MATCH Research Group (1997) Matching alcoholism treatments to client heterogeneity: Project MATCH post treatment drinking outcomes. *Journal of Studies on Alcohol* 58(1): 7–29.

Regier DA, Farmer ME, Rae DS, Locke BZ, Keith SJ, Judd LL and Goodwin FK (1990) Comorbidity of mental disorders with alcohol and other drug abuse. Results from the epidemiologic catchment area (ECA) study. *JAMA* 264(19): 2511–2518.

Rice P and Drummond C (2012) The price of a drink: the potential of alcohol minimum unit pricing as a public health measure in the UK. *British Journal of Psychiatry* 201(3): 169–171.

Rollnick S, Butler CC, Kinnersley P, Gregory J and Mash B (2010) Motivational interviewing. *British Medical Journal* 340: 1242–1245.

Stockwell T, Murphy D and Hodgson R (1983) The Severity of Alcohol Dependence Questionnaire: its use, reliability and validity. *British Journal of Addiction* 78(2): 145–155.

Sullivan JT, Sykora K, Schneiderman J, Naranjo CA, Sellers EM (1989) Assessment of alcohol withdrawal: the revised Clinical Institute Withdrawal Assessment for Alcohol Scale (CIWA-Ar). *British Journal of Addiction* 84(11): 1353–1357.

UKATT Research Team (2005) Effectiveness of treatment for alcohol problems: findings of the randomised UK Alcohol Treatment Trial (UKATT). *British Medical Journal* 331(7516): 541–544.

Volkow N and Li T-K (2005) The neuroscience of addiction. *Nature Neuroscience* 8(11): 1429–1430.

Wanigaratne S, Wallace W, Pullin J, Keaney F and Farmer R (1990) *Relapse Prevention for Addictive Behaviours*. Oxford: Blackwell Science.

Weaver T, Madden P, Charles V, Stimson G, Renton A, Tyrer P, Barnes T, Bench C, Middleton H, Wright N, Paterson S, Shanahan W, Seivewright N and Ford C (2003) Comorbidity of substance misuse and mental illness in community mental health and substance misuse services. *British Journal of Psychiatry* 183: 304–313.

West R (2006) *Theory of Addiction*. Oxford: Blackwell Publishing.

WHO (2014) *Global Status Report on Alcohol and Health 2014*. Geneva: World Health Organization.

WHO (1992) *The ICD-10 Classification of Mental and Behavioural Disorders*. Geneva: World Health Organization.

Chapter 10

New drugs, old responses?

Willm Mistral

Background

International policy responses to a perceived threat from the use of psychotropic substances other than alcohol began in the early twentieth century with the 1909 Shanghai Opium Commission, the Hague Conference of 1911 and the Opium Convention of 1912. A range of international treaties and conventions followed, and the 1988 United Nations Convention against Illicit Traffic in Narcotic Drugs and Psychotropic Substances made it mandatory for every signatory country to 'adopt such measures as may be necessary to establish as criminal offences under its domestic law' all non-authorised activities related to the production, sale, transport, distribution, possession, etc. of a range of restricted substances (United Nations, 2013a: 127). The reason given for this was that the parties to the convention were:

> Deeply concerned by the magnitude of and rising trend in the illicit production of, demand for and traffic in narcotic drugs and psychotropic substances, which pose a serious threat to the health and welfare of human beings and adversely affect the economic, cultural and political foundations of society.
>
> (United Nations, 2013: 123)

Until the 1980s most governments' policy responses to psychoactive drug use had been focused on a relatively stable set of substances and their direct derivatives, mainly opiates, cocaine, cannabis and hallucinogens such as LSD and psilocybin. However, since that time a major new phenomenon has arisen: the increasing availability of new herbal and synthetic psychoactive substances which came to be known as 'legal highs', 'designer drugs' or 'new psychoactive substances'. The term 'new' in this context did not initially refer to newly invented, but rather newly used (or misused, depending on one's point of view).

Emergence of new designer drugs

New 'designer' drugs are substances intended for recreational use which are derivatives of other drugs, manufactured so as to circumvent existing legal restrictions (Buchanan and Brown, 1988). Many of the new designer drugs that have risen to prominence contain synthetic cannabinoids or synthetic cathinones. Synthetic cannabinoids are functionally similar to the active principle of cannabis, and cathinone derivatives are reported to have similar effects to that of cocaine, amphetamines or MDMA. These substances are sold under a variety of names which regularly change as new combinations of compounds are introduced. The marketing of these new drugs has been a massive internet phenomenon, but they have also been sold in specialist 'head shops' or 'smart shops' where they are often labelled as 'incense' or 'bath salts' or for various purposes other than human consumption (Reuter, 2011). Of course the vast majority of these new psychoactive substances are intended as legal replacements for controlled drugs, and have rapidly become a popular form of recreational substance use, especially amongst young adults.

Many of the early 'new' drugs were first created many years previously and were related to amphetamine and MDMA. MDMA (or Ecstasy as it became known), which combines some properties of both stimulants and hallucinogens, was originally developed in 1912 but largely forgotten until the late 1970s when it emerged as the drug of choice at 'raves' across the Western world. Although Ecstasy was made illegal in the UK in 1977 and in the USA in 1985, it proved to be the 'tip of an iceberg' as rapidly increasing numbers of newly developed drugs designed to fall outside the remit of existing laws became available.

Monitoring availability

In the European Union the appearance of these new drugs raised concerns about possible health risks, and also about problems arising for international law enforcement if such substances were controlled in some countries but not in others. This led, in 1997, to the Council of the European Union adopting a three-step approach. The first was exchange of information and an early-warning system; the second was risk assessment; and third was a procedure for bringing specific new synthetic drugs under control (European Monitoring Centre for Drugs and Drug Addiction, 2007). Since 1997 the European Monitoring Centre for Drugs and Drug Addiction (EMCDDA) and Europol, the law enforcement agency of the European Union (EU), have played central roles in the European response to new psychoactive substances. These two agencies, with support from their wider networks, have operated the world's only regional early warning system for an ever-increasing influx of new psychoactive substances. As these substances are not easily detected by conventional drug screening methods, monitors obtain many of them via test-purchases in specialist shops and on the internet. In 2013, the EMCDDA identified 651 websites selling 'legal highs' to Europeans (EMCDDA, 2014).

Wastewater analysis

The monitoring process for drug use is becoming increasingly sophisticated. In May 2013 the EMCDDA organised the first international multidisciplinary conference on detecting drug residues in wastewater, with a session focused on the potential of sewage water analysis for identifying and monitoring population-level trends in usage of new substances. This is a rapidly developing scientific discipline, and advances in analytical chemistry have made it possible to identify drugs in the urinary excretions of entire communities. Data from wastewater analysis carried out in a recent Europe-wide study demonstrated relatively high concentrations of amphetamine in samples from several cities in the north and northwest of Europe, while the highest levels of methamphetamine were found in cities of the Czech Republic and Slovakia (EMCDDA, 2014). While this method does not provide detailed data on individual consumption, its ability to provide estimates of drug consumption in a given population makes it a useful complement to existing methods for studying drug use trends in Europe (Velleman, 2013).

Levels of use

During 2010, 41 new substances were reported for the first time within the EU, increasing to 49 in 2011, to 74 in 2012 and to 81 in 2013, including new synthetic opioids. Many of the new substances are apparently produced in bulk outside the EU (e.g. China and India) and imported into individual member states, where they are processed, packaged and sold. Across Europe, reliable, albeit limited, information suggests that prevalence of use remains low. An estimated 1.3 million young adults (15 to 34 years) used ecstasy in the previous year (1.0 per cent of this age group), with national estimates ranging from under 0.1 per cent to 3.1 per cent, and with most countries reporting stable or declining trends in ecstasy use between 2007 and 2012 (EMCDDA, 2014). In England and Wales the most recent survey (2012/13) returned an estimated past-year use of mephedrone among adults (16 to 59 years) of 0.5 per cent. This marked a decrease from 1.1 per cent in 2011/12 and 1.4 per cent in 2010/11. Results from a survey of regular clubbers in the United Kingdom also show a decrease in use of mephedrone, from 19.5 per cent in 2011 to 13.8 per cent in 2012 (EMCDDA, 2014).

Stogner and Miller (2013) report that in the US, despite many high-profile media stories, the only evidence of extensive use of synthetic cathinones was during a peak period in 2011, when poison control centres were receiving about 600 calls per month about 'bath salts'. In the period from November 2012 to May 2013, however, calls to poison centres regarding 'bath salts' dropped to an average of 88 per month (American Association of Poison Control Centers, 2013a). In comparison, calls to poison centres during the same time period regarding synthetic marijuana averaged 229 calls per month (American Association of Poison Control Centers, 2013b). The news media, however, continued to imply that use of 'bath salts' was rampant among adolescents and young adults (Stogner and Miller, 2013), warranting stricter regulation and enforcement.

Levels of risk

A recent review of the literature (Cottencin, Rolland and Karila, 2014) demonstrates that new drugs appear on the market as soon as previous compounds are banned, and this is especially true of synthetic cathinones. Consumers of these new stimulant drugs seem to use them as replacements for illegal cocaine or amphetamines. The absence of legal risk, the ease of obtaining the drugs and their low cost are very attractive to consumers. However, because a substance is advertised as legal does not necessarily make it legal or, importantly, safe.

Positive effects of synthetic cathinones reported by users include increased energy, empathy, openness and increased libido. On the negative side, cardiac, psychiatric and neurological signs and symptoms are the most common adverse effects reported by users who require medical care (Prosser and Nelson, 2011). Nevertheless, a number of scientists believe that the addictive potential of these substances appears significant and that people exposed to high doses can experience life-threatening medical complications (Baumann, 2014). Cannabinoids and synthetic cathinones have been associated with seizures, renal failure and death (Khullar, Jain and Sattari, 2014). Cathinone use has also been associated with short-term circulatory issues, hallucinations, psychosis and violence (Coppola and Mondola, 2012), as well as long-term cognitive dysfunction, emotional instability and kidney damage (Durham, 2011). However, the most common reported adverse effects from synthetic cathinones include nasal irritation, hypertension, tachycardia and psychiatric symptoms. Although a small number of cathinone-related deaths have been reported, these events are rare, and most of these individuals had a history of polysubstance use, resulting in difficulty determining whether 'bath salts' were the direct cause of the adverse events or whether the effects were exacerbated by other substances. Much of the literature consists of case reports and cross-sectional studies, which are not the highest level of evidence (Fass, Fass and Garcia, 2012). However, a number of scientists argue that the current available evidence demonstrates the existence of a public health emergency (e.g. Baumann, 2014; Fass, Fass and Garcia, 2012).

Reports of deaths and acute intoxications are central to the work of the early warning system in Europe. However, only a few countries have robust monitoring systems for drug-related emergencies, and standardised reporting does not take place at an EU level. This represents a blind spot in Europe's surveillance of emerging health threats, and makes it difficult to determine the importance of reports of severe reactions to synthetic compounds (EMCDDA, 2014).

Drugs legislation

The Single Convention on Narcotic Drugs of 1961, as amended by the 1972 Protocol (United Nations, 2013b) is an international treaty by which drugs are classified according to four Schedules. These Schedules affect the level of control exercised on the use of each drug. Schedule 1 is applied to substances considered to have no currently accepted medical use and a high potential for abuse (German, Fleckenstein and Hanson, 2014). As Hughes and Winstock (2012) remind us, the United Nations Drugs Conventions make clear that any unauthorised trade in psychoactive substances should be a criminal offence. As criminal offences should be precise, drugs legislation has hitherto covered specific substances, as opposed to whole classes of chemicals. National drug laws in Europe control more than 600 named substances or plants (Hughes and Winstock, 2012). Thus, when a new drug is synthesised it is unaccountable under existing legislation. In theory drugs are only added to the list of controlled substances as evidence accrues of risks to public health or the economic, cultural and political foundations of society (United Nations, 2013: 123).

However, as newly synthesised drugs have only a brief history of human consumption, little or no data exist as to their psychopharmacological or toxicological properties, nor of any negative impact on public health or the fabric of society. The process of testing and gathering relevant data is time-consuming and expensive, and can easily take over a year, while new psychoactive substances are appearing at a rate of more than one a week. So policy decisions regarding them are often made without sufficient scientific evidence being available. Rapid legal processes have been introduced in some countries, including placing substances under temporary controls, or fast-tracking the consultation period to placing them under permanent control (Velleman, 2013). This means that long before there is sufficient evidence as to whether or not the substance is dangerous, legislators appear to be swayed by perceived public opinion, or 'moral panics' (Cohen, 1972) created by lurid reports in the popular 'news' media, of deaths or even boisterous behaviour related to use of specific substances. One example of the latter is that following media reports of the association of MDMA (ecstasy) and the free party, rave and dance scene from the late 1980s onwards, the UK Criminal Justice and Public Order Act 1994 contained several sections designed to suppress these forms of free dance gatherings (Stevens and Measham, 2014).

Responding to public concern about a perceived drug problem via criminal sanctions is often the quickest way for politicians to demonstrate that they are 'doing something' (Krajewski, 2012). However, the decision to prohibit should not be taken lightly, and despite the difficulties in collecting valid scientific data to determine the health consequences of use of new drugs, this process is preferable to allowing a civil servant to make such a decision without public scrutiny (Reuter, 2012). The rush to criminalise behaviours can mean over-riding the principle that such sanctions should only be applied where there is no other way of addressing a problem and, if applied, the level of sanction should be proportionate to a clearly identified threat to individuals or society.

Nevertheless the history of drug policy over the last 100 years has generally involved increasingly punitive criminal sanctions, and this process appears to be continuing with reaction to the influx of new synthetic drugs (Krajewski, 2012). Stevens and Measham (2014) also argue that historic analyses demonstrate that there is in general a ratcheting-up process whereby all substances labelled as drugs are likely to face ever tighter controls. The fact that, from time to time, there is a reduction of control over one drug does not undermine the essential direction of travel. Despite the fact that cannabis remains illegal under US Federal law, twenty-three states and the District of Columbia allow some degree of medical use of marijuana, fourteen states have taken steps to decriminalise it to some degree, and very recently four states have legalised and taxed retail of the drug for recreational use.

The approach taken to drug policy by most governments has been very ably summarised by MacCoun and Reuter (2008) who listed what they describe as eight implicit, but not publicly acknowledged, rules underpinning drug policy in the US and, by extension, much of the western world:

1 Evidence that a drug impairs human capacities is always believable and important.
2 Our best estimate of a drug's harm is not the average estimate but the most severe yet obtained.
3 Evidence that an illicit drug could have benefits may not be collected.
4 Treatment requires evidence of both effectiveness and cost-effectiveness.
5 Evidence regarding prevention is always welcome, but it will not gain much funding.
6 Law enforcement and interdiction require no evidence at all: they are assumed to be effective and appropriate.
7 Evidence against enforcement creates a presumption that the researcher is a liberal.
8 Evidence for harm reduction creates a presumption the researcher approves of drug use.

One additional implicit rule was added two years later:

9 Scientific research on drugs cannot motivate a change from tough law to lenient law, but it can motivate a change in the opposite direction (MacCoun, 2010).

Thus, as Stevens and Measham (2014) argue, the history of drug policy demonstrates that decisions about the control of substances do not follow from dispassionate consideration of scientific evidence and relative levels of harm. Instead, consistent patterns of bias are discernible. Politicians believe that they cannot be seen as 'weak' when it comes to protecting the public from the dangers believed inherent in the use of certain drugs, or from the users of these drugs. This being the case, scientific evidence and expert opinion can be, and are, disregarded if they do not favour the application of tougher controls on whatever substances have come to the attention of a government.

Unlooked-for consequences

The rush to legislate, in effect to ban any production, possession or use of any particular substance and its analogues, can be seen to have a number of negative, unlooked-for consequences. As noted above, the justification for the illegality of many drugs is that they are harmful and that criminal sanctions are necessary to prevent or reduce harm. However, a number of researchers argue that, paradoxically, harms may be increased by making these drugs illegal (e.g. Nutt, 2013, 2014). Baumann (2014) makes the point that, although banning synthetic cathinones may seem a viable law enforcement strategy, this hinders the research that is crucial to understanding the pharmacology and toxicology of cathinone analogues. This argument is echoed by other researchers who believe that, although there are dangers attached to the use of synthetic cathinones, classifying them as Schedule 1 substances without the necessary supporting research is problematic.

Absence of an accepted medical use is a major distinction between Schedule 1 (no accepted medical use) and Schedule 2 (accepted medical use). However, possible medical uses will not be discovered unless research is undertaken before a drug is classified as Schedule 1, as a very limited number of laboratories and institutions have the necessary licence to work with Schedule 1 drugs. This means research into the effects of these drugs and ways to treat dependence or toxicity is severely restricted. It is thought that synthetic cathinones may be a useful alternative to amphetamines in treating disorders such as attention deficit hyperactivity disorder (ADHD) or treatment-resistant depression, but without appropriate research the necessary evidence cannot be obtained (German, Fleckenstein and Hanson, 2014). This contention has been repeatedly and forcefully argued in the UK by David Nutt, former chairman of the Advisory Council on the Misuse of Drugs (ACMD), a body set up to consider available evidence and then advise the UK government on drug classification. He was dismissed from this post following repeated clashes with government ministers over issues of drug harm and scheduling. Nutt (2013, 2014) argues that the classification system is, in many instances, irrational and unscientific. For example, in the UK scientists need to obtain a Schedule 1 licence to undertake research with cannabis or MDMA, but not with heroin or cocaine. This is exactly the opposite of what would be expected from assessments of the relative harmfulness of these drugs. In the UK a licence to work with Schedule 1 drugs costs around £6,000 in fees and related expenses and takes about a year to issue. Obtaining the banned drugs for legitimate research is also difficult and expensive, as there are almost no production facilities that have the necessary licences for holding and dispensing Schedule 1 drugs. As research grants are bounded by both financial and time limits these factors alone put almost insurmountable barriers in the way of any scientific investigation.

Moreover, for recreational drug users, the harms that derive from increased legal controls may greatly exceed the harms of the drugs themselves. If a drug is banned, this may encourage the use of new, unknown and possibly more dangerous synthetic compounds, and this situation worsens as more so-called 'legal highs' are banned. Arrests and imprisonment for drug offences destroy individual lives and families, and there is no scientific evidence that the health or social harm caused by drugs such as cannabis or ecstasy justify such penalties (Nutt, 2013, 2014). The nadir of this approach has been the so-called 'war on drugs' declared by US President Nixon in 1971, which has been not only a spectacular failure in terms of reducing the production, distribution and consumption of drugs, but has been astonishingly expensive to operate, destructive of individual lives, discriminatory against particular ethnic groups, and counterproductive in that it has led to a vast expansion of organised crime (Report of the Global Commission on Drug Policy, 2011). The Drug Policy Alliance (2014) reports that the US annual expenditure for the war on drugs is more than $51,000,000,000 (51 billion dollars). In the US, during 2012, 1.55 million people were arrested on nonviolent drug charges, and the number of people charged with possession of marijuana was 658,231. Of those incarcerated in state prisons for drug offences, black or Hispanic people make up 61 per cent, although these groups comprise about 30 per cent of the population and use and sell drugs at similar rates to white people. America has 5 per cent of the world population, but 25 per cent of the total world prison population, with convictions in 1998 for drug offences accounting for 59 per cent of the federal prison population, up from 25 per cent in 1980. Although the UK, Canada and Australia have similar levels of drug problems relative to the US, incarceration rates of drug users in these countries are about one quarter of US rates.

The paucity of treatment in US prisons for drug addiction has become an extension of a moral crusade of the 'war on drugs' as legitimate questions of how best to minimise harm are subordinated to a policy of zero tolerance (Drucker, 2014). For example, the Centers for Disease Control and Prevention found that syringe exchange programmes lower HIV incidence among injecting drug users by 80 per cent, yet the US federal government provides no financial support for these programmes, as Congress reinstated prohibition of any federal assistance in 2011 (Drug Policy Alliance, 2014). Similarly, in the US, it is argued that zero tolerance and criminalisation is counterproductive, as it simply creates a market for new, unregulated and possibly more harmful synthetic compounds (Perrone, Helgesen and Fischer, 2013).

Thus, as Griffiths, Evans-Brown and Sedefov (2013) point out, the model on which drug policies have been based appears to be in need of complete reconfiguration as it fails to meet the challenges posed by a global market place which reacts rapidly to legal challenges by simply producing new substances. They go on to say that policy makers, practitioners and researchers need access to reliable evidence about new drugs, their usage and the dangers they may pose, in order to take appropriate measures to minimise harm. Alongside early warning systems it is essential that multi-disciplinary research and analysis, coupled with the debate that these often bring, continue to inform policy responses (Griffiths, Evans-Brown and Sedefov, 2013).

Other ways

Although drug control policies were founded ostensibly on public health principles, they have in the main been applied via the criminal justice system. However, the Report of the Global Commission on Drug Policy (2011) has acknowledged that criminalisation of users has failed as an effective way to protect individual or public health, and has called on governments to move beyond simple punitive ways of disabling the market. To address this, Hughes and Winstock (2012) propose three alternative solutions which they believe are already available across Europe, which require only minimal extra legislation, do not criminalise users and have already stopped the open trade of various harmful substances.

The first option is to allow unrestricted sale, subject to the range of consumer protection and food safety laws that already exist to control the sale of legal goods. Producers and distributors are bound by these laws to ensure that their product is safe and fit for purpose. If new psychoactive substances were regulated like any other commodity, they would have to be marketed and labelled in such a way as to clearly declare potential health effects, which would, ideally, include information on dosing, precautions and contraindications.

A second option is restricted marketing and sale, whereby there may be age limits set for purchase, and sales outlets subject to specific licensing. This method is currently used to control the sale of alcohol, tobacco and some other volatile substances. In the Netherlands, this level of control applies to cannabis sales via 'coffeeshops', and includes rules such as no advertising, no hard drugs, no disturbance, no sales to anyone under 18 years and restricted amounts per transaction. Breaching these regulations could result in a fine, loss of licence, or a prison sentence.

A third option is to restrict marketing and sale by classifying these drugs as requiring medical supervision. Once a substance is declared to be subject to medicine laws, a marketing authorisation is required before it can be sold. The terms of the marketing authorisation may be varied as required, and one control technique would be to declare that a new psychoactive substance is a medicinal product, but not issue a marketing authorisation. This approach has already been used by a number of European countries for specific substances. Finland and the Netherlands applied this control with mephedrone. In the United Kingdom and Germany, open sale of 'spice' which contains a range of synthetic cannabinoid agonists with no history of medical use, was rapidly controlled under medicines legislation, before being banned under drug control laws. Interestingly in Austria, medicines legislation was chosen specifically to avoid criminalising users of spice and, as the open sale of these products stopped soon afterwards, there has been no move to apply drugs legislation.

Hughes and Winstock (2012) argue that the above alternatives to criminalisation would facilitate rapid control of the marketing of new substances without penalising possession for consumption. However, Sheridan, Atmore and Russell (2012) respond that although use of existing consumer or medicines legislation may appear convenient, it is not fit for the purpose proposed. Using medicines legislation to control new psychoactive substances debases the integrity of the law by falsely labelling substances as 'medicinal products' when most have never claimed to have any medicinal benefit. Also, and importantly, while the legislative alternatives offered by Hughes and Winstock might remove new psychoactive substances from open commercial markets, they could drive users to the illicit market and potentially more harmful alternatives.

However, the New Zealand government recently announced its intention to introduce a regulated retail regime for 'legal highs'. Manufacturers and distributors of new psychoactive substances will have to demonstrate that the product poses a 'low risk of harm' in order to gain approval from a regulatory body in advance of sale (Ministry of Health, 2012). There is to be strict controls over availability and advertising of approved substances and, following a transition period, all unapproved 'legal highs' will become illegal. Although this represents a more nuanced response to drug control than the default prohibition response it leaves a number of uncertainties. One of these is whether the regulatory framework will be able to withstand pressure from this new industry once it develops the capacity to promote its own interests. Governments have had a very mixed record of success with regard to the control of alcohol and tobacco use, and related health and social harms (Sheridan, Atmore and Russell, 2012; Wilkins et al., 2013).

A different policy approach was instigated in Portugal with the 1999 National Strategy for the Fight against Drugs which laid the foundations for current drug policy in that country. This strategy included a set of 13 options to guide public action: reinforce international cooperation; decriminalise (but still prohibit) drug use; focus on primary prevention; assure access to treatment; extend harm reduction interventions; promote social reintegration; develop treatment and harm reduction in prisons; develop treatment as an alternative to prison; increase research and training; develop evaluation methodologies; simplify interdepartmental coordination; reinforce the fight against drug trafficking and money laundering; and double public investment to finance the national strategy.

In Portugal, decriminalisation retains the recognition that drug possession is illegal, but removes criminal penalties in most cases, the offence being dealt with by an administrative procedure. If a person is caught in possession of not more than 10 daily doses of a drug, and the police have no evidence of a supply offence, the drug will be seized. The case is then passed to a local Commission for the Dissuasion of Drug Abuse, composed of three members appointed by the Ministries of Justice and Health, and a small team of practitioners who meet the offender and evaluate the situation. Based on this evaluation the Commission rules on the offence, aiming to treat any addiction and rehabilitate the person using the most appropriate interventions. Options include warnings, banning from certain places or from meeting certain people, obligation of visits to a defined place, removal of professional licence or firearms licence. Sanctioning by fine is also an option (though not for addicts) but is not the main objective. Users found in possession of more than 10 daily doses will be prosecuted in court for a criminal offence. The EMCDDA (2011) reports that drug use prevalence rates in Portugal have not increased, that the policy appears internally consistent and responds to drug problems in a pragmatic and innovative way. This is not always the case in much modern drug policy.

The UK Home Office recently produced a report (Home Office, 2014) stating there was no obvious relationship between the toughness of a country's enforcement against drug possession and the levels of drug use in that country. Trend data from Portugal show that although levels of drug use rose between 2001 and 2007, use of most drugs has since fallen to below 2001 levels. One clear change in Portugal since 2001 has been a considerable improvement in the health of drug users, with significant reductions in new diagnoses of HIV and AIDS, and overall drug-related deaths stable since 2001.

In contrast to Portugal, Sweden has a very tough drug policy, with three categories of offences. Very 'minor' offences can be punished by fines or up to six months' imprisonment, 'ordinary' offences can result in three years' imprisonment, and 'serious' offences up to ten years. However, in stark contrast with Portugal, the number of drug-related deaths in Sweden more than doubled between 2004 and 2012. The drug-induced mortality rate among adults (aged 15–64) in Portugal was 4.2 per million, compared with 62.6 deaths per million in Sweden, the latter being 3.66 times the European average of 17.1 deaths per million (EMCDDA, 2013).

Conclusions

Throughout the twentieth century there was a drive to demonise drug users, to criminalise their activities, and to constantly enact new laws and statutes in an attempt to restrict drug use. This approach has not only failed to reduce the use of these substances but has caused enormous collateral damage in terms of individual lives blighted by damaged health, incarceration and criminal records, an explosion of international criminal organisations, undue and unnecessary restrictions on scientific research and possible development of new medicines, and an enormous waste of public monies.

In the twenty-first century in many countries this approach appears to be continuing to underpin policy decisions with regard to new psychoactive substances. Nevertheless, a major rethink of international drug policies is underway, with ever-more insistent calls for an end to the 'war on drugs', and the reallocation of resources on the basis of principles of harm reduction, expanded access to healthcare, minimisation of problematic consumption and the impact of the illicit market, rigorously monitored experimentation in regulatory approaches, and an unwavering commitment to principles of human rights (LSE Expert Group, 2014). This chapter has cited a number of proposals and approaches which exemplify these principles. Although the new regulatory approach proposed by the government of New Zealand has not yet been put to the test, the decriminalisation policies enacted in Portugal can be seen as a successful, public-service and humane way to mitigate health and social problems which can arise from excessive use of psychoactive substances, whether these be new or old.

References

American Association of Poison Control Centers (2013a) *Bath Salts Data*. Available at: https://aapcc.s3.amazonaws.com/files/library/Bath_Salts_Data_for_Website_5.31.2013.pdf (accessed 01/04/2015).

American Association of Poison Control Centers (2013b) *Synthetic Marijuana Data*. Available at: https://aapcc.s3.amazonaws.com/files/library/Synthetic_Marijuana_Data_for_Website_5.31.2013.pdf (accessed 01/04/2015).

Baumann MH (2014) Awash in a sea of 'bath salts': implications for biomedical research and public health. *Addiction* 109(10): 1577–1579.

Buchanan JF and Brown CR (1988) 'Designer drugs': A problem in clinical toxicology. *Medical Toxicology and Adverse Drug Experience* 3(1): 1–17.

Cohen S (1972) *Folk Devils and Moral Panics*. London: MacGibbon & Kee.

Coppola M and Mondola R (2012) Synthetic cathinones: chemistry, pharmacology and toxicology of a new class of designer drugs of abuse marketed as 'bath salts' or 'plant food'. *Toxicology Letters* 211(2): 144–149.

Cottencin O, Rolland B and Karila L (2014) New designer drugs (synthetic cannabinoids and synthetic cathinones): review of literature. *Current Pharmaceutical Design* 20(25): 4106–4111.

Drucker E (2014) Mass incarceration as a global policy dilemma: limiting disaster and evaluating alternatives. In: *Report of the LSE Expert Group on the Economics of Drug Policy, Ending the Drug Wars*. London: London School of Economics.

Drug Policy Alliance (2014) *Drug War Statistics*. Available at: http://www.drugpolicy.org/drug-war-statistics (accessed 01/04/2015).

Durham M (2011) Ivory wave: the next mephedrone? *Emergency Medicine Journal* 28(12): 1059–1060.

EMCDDA (2007) *Early-warning System on New Psychoactive Substances. Operating Guidelines*. Luxembourg: European Monitoring Centre for Drugs and Drug Addiction.

EMCDDA (2011) *Drug Policy Profiles: Portugal*. Luxembourg: Publications Office of the European Union.

EMCDDA (2013) *Country Overview: Sweden*. Available at: http://www.emcdda.europa.eu/publications/country-overviews/se#gps (accessed 01/04/2015).

EMCDDA (2014) *European Drug Report. Trends and Developments*. Luxembourg: European Monitoring Centre for Drugs and Drug Addiction.

Fass JA, Fass AD and Garcia AS (2012) Synthetic cathinones (bath salts): legal status and patterns of abuse. *Annals of Pharmacotherapy* 46(3): 436–441.

German CL, Fleckenstein AE and Hanson GR (2014) Bath salts and synthetic cathinones: an emerging designer drug phenomenon. *Life Sciences* 97(1): 2–8.

Griffiths P, Evans-Brown M and Sedefov R (2013) Getting up to speed with the public health and regulatory challenges posed by new psychoactive substances in the information age. *Addiction* 108(10): 1700–1703.

Home Office (2014) *Drugs: International Comparators*. London: Home Office.

Hughes B and Winstock AR (2012) Controlling new drugs under marketing regulations. *Addiction* 107(11): 1894–1899.

Khullar V, Jain A and Sattari M (2014) Emergence of new classes of recreational drugs – synthetic cannabinoids and cathinones. *Journal of General Internal Medicine* 29(8): 1200–1204.

Krajewski K (2012) Against excess. *Addiction* 107(11): 1900.

LSE Expert Group (2014) *Ending the Drug Wars: Report of the LSE Expert Group on the Economics of Drug Policy*. London: London School of Economics.

MacCoun RJ (2010) The implicit rules of evidence-based policy analysis, updated. *Addiction* 105(8): 1335–1336.

MacCoun RJ and Reuter P (2008) The implicit rules of evidence-based drug policy: a US perspective. *International Journal of Drug Policy* 19(3): 231–232.

Ministry of Health (2012) *Regulatory Impact Statement – New Regulatory Regime for Psychoactive Substances*. Available at: http://www.health.govt.nz/about-ministry/legislation-and-regulation/regulatory-impact-statements/new-regulatory-regime-psychoactive-substances (accessed 09/04/2015).

Nutt D (2013) How current drug laws impede research and clinical treatments. In: Mistral W (ed.) *Emerging Perspectives on Substance Misuse*. Chichester: Wiley Blackwell.

Nutt D (2014) Mind-altering drugs and research: from presumptive prejudice to a Neuroscientific Enlightenment? *EMBO reports* 15(3): 208–211.

Perrone D, Helgesen RD and Fischer RG (2013) United States drug prohibition and legal highs: how drug testing may lead cannabis users to Spice. *Drugs: Education, Prevention and Policy* 20(3): 216–224.

Prosser JM and Nelson LS (2011) The toxicology of bath salts: a review of synthetic cathinones. *Journal of Medical Toxicology* 8(1): 33–42.

Report of the Global Commission on Drug Policy (2011) *War on Drugs*. Available at: http://www.globalcommissionondrugs.org/wp-content/themes/gcdp_v1/pdf/Global_Commission_Report_English.pdf (accessed 15/12/2015).

Reuter P (2011) *Options for Regulating New Psychoactive Drugs: A Review of Recent Experiences*. UK Drug Policy Commission. Available at: http://www.ukdpc.org.uk/publication/options-regulating-new-psychoactive-drugs-a-review-recent-experience/ (accessed 09/04/2015).

Reuter P (2012) The dangerous charms of the unknown. *Addiction* 107(11): 1902–1903.

Sheridan J, Atmore B and Russell B (2012) New Zealand to establish fit for purpose regulation for new psychoactive substances. *Addiction* 107(11): 1901–1902.

Stevens A and Measham F (2014) The 'drug policy ratchet': why do sanctions for new psychoactive drugs typically only go up? *Addiction* 109(8): 1226–1232.

Stogner JM and Miller BL (2013) Investigating the 'bath salt' panic: The rarity of synthetic cathinone use among students in the USA. *Drug and Alcohol Review* 32(5): 545–549.

United Nations (2009) *World Drug Report 2009*. New York: United Nations, 167–168.

United Nations (2013a) United Nations Convention against Illicit Traffic in Narcotic Drugs and Psychotropic Substances 1988. *The International Drug Control Conventions*, ebook. Available at: https://www.unodc.org/unodc/en/treaties/illicit-trafficking.html (accessed 09/04/2015).

United Nations (2013b) The International Drug Control Conventions Schedules of the Single Convention on Narcotic Drugs of 1961 as amended by the 1972 Protocol, as at 25 September 2013. Available at: https://www.unodc.org/documents/commissions/CND/Int_Drug_Control_Conventions/1961_Schedules/ST-CND-1-Add1_E.pdf

Velleman R (2013) Changing perspectives on problematic drug use. In: Mistral W (ed.) *Emerging Perspectives on Substance Misuse*. Wiley Blackwell: Chichester.

Wilkins C, Sheridan J, Adams P, Russell B, Ram S and Newcombe D (2013) The new psychoactive substances regime in New Zealand: a different approach to regulation. *Journal of Psychopharmacology* 27(7): 584–589.

Chapter 11

Improving addiction workforce skills

Devin Ashwood and Jane Rowley

Introduction

Alcohol and drug misuse continues to be a destructive and expensive societal problem impacting on individuals, their family and friends as well as the wider community (HSCIC, 2014). It is possible, however, to reduce this harm and expense. It has been estimated, in the UK, that for every pound spent on drug treatment services £2.50 is saved in crime, health and other social costs (National Audit Office, 2010). To realise and improve upon these kinds of savings however, treatment must be as effective as possible.

In line with many professions in the social sector who work with those at the margins of society, addiction treatment has historically been underfunded, given low priority and impacted by the political discourse dominant at the time. The issue of underfunding was in part addressed by the establishment of a National Treatment Agency for Substance Misuse (NTA) in 2001. This special health authority, responsible for improving the capacity and outcomes of drug treatment in the UK, was given a remit to respond to both the public health and criminal justice agendas around problematic drug use (NTA, 2013). A few years later, the 2008 UK National Drug Strategy (HM Government, 2008) supported a move towards a more holistic, recovery-focused agenda. This broader approach with its focus on the benefits of psychosocial interventions signalled a fundamental shift in paradigm from short treatment journeys and prescribing substitute medication to individually focused care. This approach requires additional skills and time and the 2008 strategy clearly asserted that 'Developing a competent substance misuse workforce, including both generic and specialist practitioners, is crucial to ensuring a high standard of service delivery' (HM Government, 2008: 47).

The 2010 drug strategy (HM Government, 2010), although helpfully embracing the concept of integrated community supported recovery, in practice entrusted ensuring a 'high standard of service delivery' to competitive tendering and payment by results. While these policies may appear economically sound, the present authors' experience of supervising students and workers in this environment has shown that agencies who have to re-tender every few years are in a constant state of upheaval and uncertainty, working toward short-term targets in an environment that potentially rewards collection of fraudulent statistics. Staff in these organisations may experience the effect of insufficient longer-term investments in workforce training (Sheridan, Barnard and Webster, 2011) and their loss of professional development opportunities becomes a loss to their clients and wider society. A recent study exploring the effectiveness of payment-by-results has shown significantly poorer outcomes for providers piloting this system compared with the old system of providers being rewarded for clinical quality. In the first year of the 'Payment by Results for Drugs Recovery' scheme in England, linking payments to outcomes increased the proportion of service users declining to continue with treatment and reduced the probability of completing drug misuse treatment (Mason et al., 2015).

At the time the 2008 drug strategy was released, Professor Neil McKeganey (2008) argued that we trust that a doctor, lawyer or social worker will have a university-level education and be regulated by a professional body. The addiction field is equally as complex as the above professions and requires as much professional knowledge and regulation. However, those seeking help with drink or drug problems are likely to be seen by someone with no relevant university-level qualification, who may have only entered the field very recently and whose practice could be subject to inconsistent supervision and regulation. For many, recovery from drug dependency can make the difference between life and death, so the consequences of poor professional practice can be of critical importance.

McKeganey (2008) highlighted one of the main problems in the field as a lack of a career structure. While other professions allow for a lifetime of career development, encourage training and reward expertise, the choices for a drug worker to move on in their career are either to continue working at street level for low pay or, if they are lucky, manage a treatment agency, which is still likely to attract a relatively poor salary and offer limited, if any, further career prospects. Little wonder many do not stay in the field for very long.

Evolution of workforce development

Creating a dedicated, well-trained, highly qualified addiction professional is a complex undertaking. Addressing the complexity of issues arising from addiction requires a range of skills and experience and, above all, sufficient empathy and compassion to relate to people who are often in the most vulnerable periods of their lives. Historically, in the UK, addictions treatment has been shared between the health and criminal justice sectors. Arising from this, a key challenge in workforce development is preparing people to straddle an ideological dichotomy which is evident in many drug treatment agencies. To work therapeutically in response to the health needs of an individual, whilst also being responsible for implementing punitive measures when necessary, requires a broad skillset. One response to this was the introduction, in 2002, of National Occupational Standards later known as Drug and Alcohol National Occupational Standards (DANOS). This resulted, for a relatively short period between 2002 and 2008, in a wide variety of training courses being in demand. However, achieving a standardised workforce qualification within this field, where skills are drawn from different disciplines, is not a simple task. Although this movement towards accreditation was a step in the right direction, it relied on the subjective assessment of ethics and competence of different organisations involved in delivering training and suffered from variations in standards and lack of quality monitoring. In 2008 DANOS was repackaged as guidelines for services rather than an issue impacting on treatment commissioning. It is beyond the scope of this chapter to look at this in more detail, but what DANOS achieved was to highlight the difficulties of workforce development in the sector.

In 2009 training organisations collaborated with the National Treatment Agency to consider how best to develop workforce skills (Skills Consortium, 2010) and in 2010 a conceptual model was endorsed as a framework for effective treatment and this formed the basis of an online resource now managed by three organisations as a skills hub for practitioners (Drink and Drugs Net, 2014). This is home to the DANOS guidelines and a database of qualifications serving the sector. However, there remains a challenge in how organisations respond to the training needs of staff and volunteers, particularly with how training is funded and how it translates into improvements in practice.

The need for professional training

If we are to address the above issues and comply with guidelines to offer treatments delivered by 'trained and competent staff' (NICE, 2011: 1.3.2.1) we will need to develop sophisticated treatment and community recovery support systems for some of the most disadvantaged clients, with complex needs, that professionals are likely to meet. It is essential there is a long-term commitment, where government policy, treatment commissioners, regulatory and professional bodies demand and develop educational standards and professional career pathways comparable to those of nurses, doctors, social workers or any other professionals working at a similar level of complexity and with equal importance to the individuals affected and wider society.

Whilst a varied and flexible range of skills is necessary to respond to the complex range of needs presented by people seeking help and treatment, it becomes problematic when we attempt to map the qualifications and, more specifically, to standardise them. This attempt to develop quality by standardisation, again important in the professionalisation of the sector, does not easily lend itself to maintaining diversity in recruitment to the field. If we acknowledge the fact that people having problems with drugs or alcohol are not a homogeneous group, we need to embed this in our approaches to workforce development. We need practitioners who are not only diverse in background, skills, experience and understanding but who are also committed to personal and professional development, and in a position to undertake a course of study which represents a serious financial as well as emotional investment.

While short, workshop-based courses in substance misuse psychosocial interventions may show skill improvement immediately after training, this is not evidenced in the longer term (Carroll and Rounsaville, 2007). It has also been observed that no matter what addiction therapists claim to be doing in treatment sessions, their actual practice often bears little resemblance to their stated model (Miller, 2007). Therefore, more extended courses with protracted tutor contact, supervision and feedback are needed for sustained practice change in the workforce (Walters et al., 2005).

CATS at Action on Addiction

In the UK there are now numerous formal qualifications on offer for people who wish to work in the drugs field, with some providers offering higher education degrees. Training within the higher education (HE) system includes the benefits of funding for students and inbuilt standardised quality systems which offer the potential for transferable skills and additional credibility for practitioners. Training to HE level may also contribute to retaining the workforce, in a sector traditionally serviced by charity and voluntary organisations with scant funding for staff development.

One example of efforts to address the longstanding skills deficit has come from the Centre for Addiction Treatment Studies (CATS) supported by the charity Action on Addiction. This will now be described as an important example of the kinds of training needed to prepare addiction professionals to work in treatment settings. CATS, in partnership with the University of Bath, England, offers both a Foundation Degree and an Honours Degree in Addiction Counselling as well as continuing professional development (CPD) courses.

Training pathways in working therapeutically with addictions need to be directed at two main kinds of student: those entering the field as a new career and those already working in substance misuse settings who wish to develop their skills. For those seeking a new career who have the time and who are willing to take on student loans, there are accredited full-time degree courses such as those found at CATS. However, the financial barriers to entering such courses are high and individuals drawn to them are of necessity highly motivated, often having a personal connection to addiction that inspires them to pursue a career helping those affected.

While the course described below is of a high quality and achieves excellent student satisfaction, it is only able to be delivered with such standards to small cohorts with the support of charity funding from Action on Addiction. This is not a model that can easily be replicated, and there is therefore a need for high-quality, but lower-cost, part-time CPD courses that allow students to study while working. These not only help those already in the field to increase their skill level, but also help people not able or willing to take on large student loans to develop the skills necessary to pursue a career as an addiction specialist.

At CATS the teaching team is drawn from experienced professionals with continued practice and expertise in their field. All CATS training has an integral element of professional practice. Students either complete extended work placements throughout the course or are already employed in the field. This work experience is fundamental to the training, offering the opportunity to apply theory to practice, and to attain an academic qualification whilst also gaining work experience. The work-based learning is designed to enable students to situate the academic teaching in specific practice contexts, having a keen appreciation of the tensions inherent in agencies delivering treatment within the shifting demands of commissioning and treatment focus.

Elements of CATS training

The CATS Foundation Degree begins by contextualising the field of practice. Individual and societal problems associated with substance misuse and the responses societies have made to these are explored and students have an opportunity to compare harm reduction and abstinence-focused interventions as well as governmental policies that range in emphasis from tolerance, legalisation and therapy to those focusing on criminalisation and punishment. Understanding the role of a drug or alcohol worker within its historical and political context allows prejudices and assumptions to be questioned and the student to develop a critical awareness of the context within which they work.

Students go on to study a range of evidence-based and theoretically informed approaches, all underpinned with a person-centred model of counselling. In their first year, students receive training in assessment and treatment planning, diversity issues, motivational interviewing and interpersonal group therapy all while undergoing a structured programme of personal and professional development in a work placement. In their second year, students are introduced to harm reduction and 12-Step programmes as well as cognitive behavioural and family-oriented approaches to treatment. Issues encountered in working with dually diagnosed mental health and substance use problems are explored and students are also introduced to research methods so they can conduct their own research project in the work place. Those going on to the Honours year stay in a work placement and engage in a more in-depth research project and also develop their understanding and skills in key therapeutic group interventions and one-to-one motivational and cognitive behavioural approaches. In addition, Honours year students, being those most likely to rise up in their field, are given training in supervision and management. This training encourages students to be critically self-aware and to exercise judgement in a professional context. Students are taught how to generate knowledge using research methods that are situated in the context of practice whilst at the same time developing evidence-based skills as a practitioner and disseminating their findings into specific practice settings.

Relational model

The unifying principle that links together the Foundation and Honours degree training offered at CATS is a relational model. Attachment theory, inspired and developed by John Bowlby (1907–1990), has arguably been the single most influential body of work to straddle the fields of child development, social work and therapy. It proposes that for our survival we are innately programmed to form attachments with others. Dunbar (1993) argues convincingly that species intelligence and brain size are directly functionally related to their social tendency. The importance of human relationships has also been emphasised by Yalom and Leszcz (2005) who point out that humans have always lived in groups sharing persistent and intense relationships and this has been a powerful evolutionary force. For these reasons, any attempt to support recovery from addiction must promote adaptive social relationships for the individual and implement treatment which takes account of the systemic nature of a client's social environment.

Time and again, it has been shown that the therapeutic relationship makes substantial and consistent difference to therapy outcome, independently of the model being offered. In their wide ranging review of the literature Norcross and Wampold (2011) offer empirically founded recommendations that training and ongoing professional education should be encouraged to maximise therapist capacity in the areas of:

- developing a therapeutic alliance (for individual, youth and family therapy)
- developing group cohesiveness (in group therapy)
- developing empathy
- collecting and responding to feedback
- consensual goal setting
- working collaboratively, and
- holding the client in positive regard.

Models of treatment

It is further recommended by Norcross and Wampold (2011) that the therapeutic relationship be available in conjunction with evidence-based treatments tailored to individual clients. The National Institute for Health and Clinical Excellence (NICE) recommends evidence-based psychosocial treatments for differing substance misuse problems that include motivational, cognitive-behavioural and socially focused interventions (NICE, 2007, 2011). Contingency management, by rewarding clean urine tests with vouchers for example, is one of just two psychosocial therapies recommended by NICE to treat illicit substance use. However, its systematic implementation has been practically non-existent due to social, financial and ethical considerations (Weaver et al., 2007), and it also fails to evidence outcomes much beyond the period of contingency (Benishek et al., 2014). Part of the failure of contingency management to deliver is that it changes very little for the person, relying on operant conditioning to increase motivation for abstinence for the brief period while rewards are available. In this sense, it is about as far away from treating the whole person in their systemic context as one can get. More effective and recovery sustaining treatment requires a holistic understanding and systemic approach.

Towards recovery

Granfield and Cloud (2001) have argued that the elements that provide capacity to achieve and sustain recovery from addiction can be classified into four components: social capital, physical capital, human capital and cultural capital. Social capital resources come from interactions with individuals and groups in society. Physical capital, for example financial resources, may allow access to private detoxification programmes. Problem-solving ability, which can be important on the recovery journey, is one important aspect of human capital (and additionally, we posit, so is the ability to reflect). An example of cultural capital includes values and beliefs that are associated with social conformity (De Clercq and Voronov, 2009).

Recovery capital has emerged as an organising concept for the elements in a person's life that provide the capacity to achieve and sustain recovery from addiction. It coincides with the shift in principles that underpin intervention from pathological theories toward a sustained recovery paradigm (White, 2007). Recovery capital specifically refers to the broad range of resources and strengths that individuals in addiction recovery particularly need to have or to acquire (White and Cloud, 2008; Best and Laudet, 2010). It is closely related to social capital as it explores the resources people require to make sustained behavioural change in the context of addiction recovery. The concept of recovery capital is not new, but is embedded in biopsychosocial approaches to addiction, such as Zinberg (1984). His model of drug, set and setting have formed the foundation for approaches which combine recognition that the nature of the drug, the person taking it, and their environment have a specific impact on the person's reaction and ability to cease use and maintain recovery.

Effective and promising interventions such as motivational interviewing (Miller and Rollnick, 2012), couples and family work (O'Farrell and Fals-Stewart, 2000; Copello, Velleman and Templeton, 2005), interpersonal group therapy (Yalom and Leszcz, 2005), cognitive therapy (Beck et al., 2011), mutual aid facilitation (Kaskutas et al., 2009) and mindfulness-based relapse prevention (Bowen, Chawla and Marlatt, 2010) can complement each other and all have the potential to develop different aspects of recovery capital. For example, learning to identify and stay with difficult sensations through mindfulness training can develop human recovery capital by facilitating greater toleration of negative emotions, and this in turn can make engaging in challenging interpersonal family and other situations easier and more productive. Developing interpersonal awareness and confidence in an interpersonal therapy group can facilitate active involvement in mutual aid groups and access to services, thereby improving social and community recovery capital. Resultant increases in self-efficacy, motivation, confidence and interpersonal skills are likely to put people into the best possible situation to improve their physical recovery capital.

Developing a workforce that has an appreciation of these therapeutic interventions and how they can be tailored to complement each other in an individualised treatment plan can be accomplished on a HE degree course. However, it is not necessary that every addiction worker be an expert in all the therapeutic modalities mentioned, and those motivated to specialise can develop expertise through continuing professional development on supervised training pathways. Agencies that recruit diversely skilled, specialist and experienced staff who enable them to address social, physical, human and cultural capital are likely to offer the best service to their clients.

Research and reflexive understanding

An important aspect of the training at CATS is the introduction of research methods at Foundation degree level. Notwithstanding some notable exceptions, there has been a paucity of practitioner research in the addiction field as well as little that has a focus on the service user voice. Equipping more practitioners with an understanding of the evidence base through initial explorations of research methods will contribute to ongoing study and further development of that evidence base. The emphasis of training in this sector needs to be on the therapeutic relationship and therapeutic models, in the context of a reflective practice that persists through the lifetime of a career. Norcross and Wampold's (2011) extensive review of the efficacious aspects of therapies highlighted the importance of adapting them to clients' needs depending on resistance/reactance, preferences, culture, religion/spirituality and possibly also stages of change and coping style. Practitioners are trained at CATS to be responsive to the changing needs of both their clients and themselves. Being able to adapt a therapy and approach to the specific needs of a client at a particular time in their process requires critically self-aware and informed therapists. Hence, the importance of focusing on reflection and reflexive practice is a focus throughout CATS training, and especially when conducting research projects. Schon (1983) highlights the way experiential learning is a necessary aspect of learning and how this aspect of reflection is developed through research skills:

> Even when (the worker) makes conscious use of research-based theory and techniques, he is dependent on tacit recognition, judgements and skilful performances.
>
> (Schon, 1983: 50)

The aim at CATS is to provide practitioners with the resources they need to work with others and develop an appreciation of their own need for continuous professional development. It is intended that students develop critical awareness, an understanding of how to systematically generate knowledge, and the flexibility to think on their feet in response to the unique scenarios they will face with individuals in treatment. Engaging in research as well as work-based, reflective assignments supports practitioners in training to gain skills not only of reflection but also reflexivity. While development of reflective practitioner skills is essential to training, at CATS students are encouraged to explore beyond reflection and into a reflexive style of practice which enables them to collaborate with colleagues and service users in a self-aware way, to develop meaningful support for their clients' sustained recovery.

Skilful interpretation of evidence, its application in interventions, and developing a workforce that has its focus in reflexive, professional practice are crucial to developing the field into one with a career structure and opportunities for advancement. By placing value on the role of the practitioner researcher, graduates begin to consider how academic understanding can integrate into treatment communities and structures that may have previously been overly reliant on ideological standpoints or tradition. It is this academic, reflective and integrative aspect of a drug and alcohol practitioner's work that will best prepare them to support diverse clients to develop sustained recovery.

Challenges facing addictions students

Entering education as an adult is not without its challenges, but often there is an added layer of complexity for addiction workers. They are asked to work in unfamiliar settings, often with an integrated workforce, developing relationships with practitioners drawn from health and criminal justice fields, as well as working in both the statutory and the wider social sectors. Also, they may be supervised by workers who are not themselves supported in their own professional development, and this can create tension and confusion.

The experience of addiction for the majority of students at CATS is personal, and typically half have prior personal experience of addiction and recovery, with the vast majority being impacted by addiction in the family. They are driven to explore and respond to the issues recovery presents whilst also managing their own history, values and beliefs. We cannot underestimate the challenges inherent in balancing one's own values and beliefs about the efficacy of specific treatment regimes, models, approaches and theories whilst at the same time learning to offer a broad response to the individualised needs of others. This uniquely personal aspect offers a complex layer to learning which adds to the inherent challenges of studying as an adult, working in placement and managing one's family and personal life. Historical, personal circumstances related to their motivation for choosing this area of work often mean that many students have experienced long periods of instability and low employment; they therefore often enter higher education older and with fewer social and financial resources. Many students arrive redefining their identities as a person in recovery, offering support to others with similar experiences, with a personal recovery narrative which needs to be both acknowledged and also identified as being not the only way forward for other people.

The impact of student debt also cannot be underestimated. Higher education in the UK has been significantly affected in recent years by the government's response to financial deficit. Employers who previously felt able to support their staff by paying part-time tuition fees of £673 per year have stopped funding HE training as this cost has increased up to £3000. To compound the problem, mature students who already have a degree or equivalent qualification are disqualified from obtaining the loans offered to non-graduates. As fees have gone up, there has been a 40 per cent reported drop nationally in part-time HE students (Universities UK, 2013) and the numbers of part-time students accessing the University of Bath's part-time Foundation Degree in Addiction Counselling have dropped to the point that the university have closed this programme.

The average student debt in England in 2000 was just £2690 (Student Loans Company, 2014). It has been estimated that the 2012 funding reforms will leave students who need to take out their full loan entitlement with £44,035 to repay after graduation (Crawford and Jin, 2014). To have confidence in repaying debts, people need to know how their career might develop, but this is impacted by changing and reinterpreted strategies and commissioning frameworks. Recently the policy move from drug worker to recovery worker discourse has underpinned attempts to integrate services, developed treatment hubs staffed by people from several different services, but has resulted in fewer paid roles in each area.

This is not a high-income profession for most, and it may be seen as a vocation rather than a career by many. To supplement low salaries and part-time or short contracts, addiction counsellors frequently have the added pressure of working to establish private practice in the field. The challenges presented by working with often disenfranchised, socially excluded people are high. As with all therapeutic work, it can be chaotic and compassion fatigue or burnout is common. As well as high workloads and low pay, poor supervision is often reported. Work in the field may not sound like an enticing prospect, but the need is not going away and the passion stimulated by helping others ensures that people keep putting themselves forward.

Addiction counsellors deserve a professional career structure with consistency in salary levels across the sector. We ask a great deal of practitioners in training, we ask them to take on responsibility for continued learning, we ask that they work to improve life for themselves, the beneficiaries of their support, their colleagues and ultimately the wider community. There are many stakeholders in the process of recovery: these individuals and the communities they live in are invested in their work, though they may never meet everyone involved. In the wings there are parents, partners, children and friends asking, 'How was your counselling', 'What's happening with your treatment' and hoping that the ones they love are being supported by experts, by practitioners who are consciously competent, updating their knowledge, skills and experience continuously. These practitioners cannot deliver this without support and overall some recognition of the valuable work they undertake. The stakes are high, the salaries are low, with average starting salaries of £19,000, and a senior worker after some years can only expect to achieve £28,000. Perhaps, in comparison to the probation service where salaries start at £28,000 (National Careers Service, 2012) it is understandable that the focus remains on criminal justice interventions and not prevention, despite the recent move towards 'full recovery'.

Deciding to engage in higher education training in this field, and following it through, takes dedication and discipline and involves significant personal development for many students. However, the efforts put in often bear fruit, as graduates from the Honours Degree in Addiction Counselling at the University of Bath receive a disproportionate number of First Class awards and the field and wider society benefit as a result of their efforts. The challenges highlighted above indicate the importance of making access to practice-changing training pathways as accessible and affordable as possible.

Conclusion

The need for professionally trained staff in the addiction sector is accepted but the question of how this is funded is not. Funding for substance misuse treatment as with almost all statutorily funded services is going through a period of contraction. The combination of this with a presiding philosophy that free market economics are the best guarantee of quality has led to a climate of competitive tendering to provide services and performance-related payment. While it may be argued that this stimulates efficiency, there is concern that services which may appear efficient on paper may not be investing in the long-term future of the field by offering their workforce robust practice-developing training pathways. The relatively high turnover in workers, stimulated in part by the lack of a clear career progression, is likely to exacerbate this problem as the training and experience held by these workers is lost as they move into different areas.

Despite the challenges faced, there are good-quality courses available to offer a range of evidence-based and theoretically informed interventions, as well as passionate people looking to be of help in this field who are willing to take these courses. However, unless there is a political decision taken at the highest levels to raise the status of substance misuse treatment professionals to be on a par with other vital professions with similar complexity and consequences for society, it is likely that high-quality treatment from a well-trained workforce will only be available to those paying privately or through the postcode lottery of services supported by charities such as Action on Addiction.

References

Beck AT, Wright FD, Newman CF and Liese BS (2011) *Cognitive Therapy Of Substance Abuse*. New York: Guilford Press.

Benishek LA, Dugosh KL, Kirby KC, Matejkowski J, Clements NT, Seymour BL and Festinger DS (2014) Prize-based contingency management for the treatment of substance abusers: a meta-analysis. *Addiction* 109(9): 1426–1436.

Best D and Laudet AB (2010) *The Potential Of Recovery Capital*. London: Royal Society for the Arts. Available at: https://www.google.co.uk/search?q=The+potential+of+recovery+capital.+London:+Royal+Society+for+the+Arts.&ie=utf-8&oe=utf-8&gws_rd=cr&ei=FlFLVfX8JKW67gb1kYG4Bg (accessed 07/05/2015).

Bowen S, Chawla N and Marlatt GA (2010) *Mindfulness-based Relapse Prevention for Addictive Behaviors: A Clinician's Guide*. New York: Guilford Press.

Carroll KM and Rounsaville BJ (2007) A vision of the next generation of behavioral therapies research in the addictions. *Addiction* 102(6): 850–862.

Copello AG, Velleman RD and Templeton LJ (2005) Family interventions in the treatment of alcohol and drug problems. *Drug and Alcohol Review* 24(4): 369–385.

Crawford C and Jin W (2014) *Payback Time? Student Debt and Loan Repayments: What Will the 2012 Reforms Mean for Graduates?* IFS Report R93. The Institute of Fiscal Studies. Available at: http://www.ifs.org.uk/comms/r93.pdf (accessed 07/05/2015).

De Clercq D and Voronov M (2009) The role of cultural and symbolic capital in entrepreneurs' ability to meet expectations about conformity and innovation. *Journal of Small Business Management* 47(3): 398–420. Available at: http://ssrn.com/abstract=1417664 (accessed 07/05/2015).

Drink and Drugs Net (2014) *Workforce Development: DANOS*. Available at: http://www.drinkanddrugs.net/workforcedevelopment/danos.php (accessed 07/05/2015).

Dunbar RI (1993) Coevolution of neocortical size, group size and language in humans. *Behavioral and Brain Sciences* 16(4): 681–694.

Granfield R and Cloud W (2001) Social context and 'natural recovery': the role of social capital in the resolution of drug-associated problems. *Substance Use and Misuse* 36(11): 1543–1570.

HSCIC – Health and Social Care Information Centre (2014) *Statistics on Alcohol: England, 2014*. Available at: http://www.hscic.gov.uk/catalogue/PUB14184 (accessed 06/05/2015).

HM Government (2008) *Drugs: Protecting Families and Communities: The 2008 Drug Strategy* 1st edn. London: HM Government. Available at: http://webarchive.nationalarchives.gov.uk/20100413151441/drugs.homeoffice.gov.uk/publication-search/drug-strategy/drug-strategy-2008.html (accessed 06/05/2015).

HM Government (2010) *Drug Strategy 2010: Reducing Demand, Restricting Supply, Building Recovery. Supporting People to Live a Drug Free Life*. London: HM Government. Available at: https://www.gov.uk/government/publications/drug-strategy-2010–2 (accessed 06/05/2015).

Kaskutas LA, Subbaraman MS, Witbrodt J and Zemore SE (2009) Effectiveness of making Alcoholics Anonymous easier: a group format 12-step facilitation approach. *Journal of Substance Abuse Treatment* 37(3): 228–239.

McKeganey N (2008) Up to the job? *Drink and Drug News*. March 10, 13.

Mason T, Sutton M, Whittaker W, McSweeney T, Millar T, Donmall M, Jones A and Pierce M (2015) The impact of paying treatment providers for outcomes: difference-in-differences analysis of the 'payment by results for drugs recovery' pilot. *Addiction* 110(7): 1120–1128.

Miller WR (2007) Bring addiction treatment out of the closet. *Addiction* 102(6): 863.

Miller WR and Rollnick S (2012) *Motivational Interviewing: Helping People Change* 3rd edn. New York: Guilford Press.

National Audit Office (2010) *Tackling Problem Drug Use*. Available at: http://www.nao.org.uk/report/tackling-problem-drug-use (accessed 06/05/2015).

National Careers Service (2012) *Probation Officer Job Information*. Available at: https://nationalcareersservice.direct.gov.uk/advice/planning/jobprofiles/Pages/ProbationOfficer.aspx (accessed 06/05/2015).

NICE (2007) *Drug Misuse – Psychosocial Interventions* (update). Available at: http://www.nice.org.uk/guidance/cg51 (accessed: 07/05/2015).

NICE (2011) *Alcohol-use Disorders: Diagnosis, Assessment and Management of Harmful Drinking and Alcohol Dependence*. Available at: http://www.nice.org.uk/guidance/cg115/chapter/1-recommendations (accessed 01/05/2015).

Norcross JC and Wampold BE (2011) Evidence-based therapy relationships: research conclusions and clinical practices. *Psychotherapy* 48(1): 98.

NTA – National Treatment Agency (2013) *About Us*. Available at: http://www.nta.nhs.uk/about.aspx (accessed 07/05/2015).

O'Farrell TJ and Fals-Stewart W (2000) Behavioral couples therapy for alcoholism and drug abuse. *Journal of Substance Abuse Treatment* 18(1): 51–54.

Schon DA (1983) *The Reflective Practitioner: How Professionals Think in Action*. London: Temple Smith.

Sheridan J, Barnard M and Webster S (2011) Influences on the provision of drug services in England: the experiences and views of front line treatment workers. *Health and Social Care in the Community* 19(4): 403–411.

Skills Consortium (2010) *About Us*. Available at: http://www.skillsconsortium.org.uk/about.aspx (accessed 07/05/2015).

Student Loans Company (2014) *Statistical First Release, Student Loans in England, Financial Year 2013–14*. Glasgow: The Student Loans Company. Available at: http://www.slc.co.uk/media/775303/slcsfr012014.pdf (accessed 07/05/2015).

Universities UK (2013) *The Power of Part-Time, Review of Part-Time and Mature Higher Education*. London: Universities UK. Available at: http://www.universitiesuk.ac.uk/highereducation/Documents/2013/PowerOfPartTime.pdf (accessed 07/05/2015).

Walters ST, Matson SA, Baer JS and Ziedonis DM (2005) Effectiveness of workshop training for psychosocial addiction treatments: a systematic review. *Journal of Substance Abuse Treatment* 29(4): 283–293.

Weaver T, Hart J, Fehler J, Metrebian N, D'Agostino T and Benn P (2007) *Are Contingency Management Principles Being Implemented in Drug Treatment in England?* London: National Treatment Agency for Substance Misuse.

White W (2007) The new recovery advocacy movement in America. *Addiction* 102(5): 696–703.

White W and Cloud W (2008) Recovery capital: a primer for addiction professionals. *Counselor* 9: 22–27.

Yalom ID and Leszcz M (2005) *The Theory and Practice of Group Psychotherapy* 5th edn. New York: Basic Books.

Zinberg N (1984) *Drug, Set and Setting: The Basis for Controlled Intoxicant Use*. Boston: Yale University Press.

Chapter 12

Reducing alcohol-related harm among young people

Willm Mistral

The problem

Globally, harmful use of alcohol causes approximately 3.3 million deaths every year (5.9 per cent of all deaths) and 5.1 per cent of the global burden of disease (WHO, 2014: vii). The percentage of alcohol-attributable deaths among males is higher than among females, an indicator of the difference in drinking patterns both in volume consumed and in number of heavy drinking occasions (WHO, 2014: 8). Worldwide the prevalent trend is towards a growth in recorded alcohol consumption, driven mainly by increases in China and India in line with economic development. In contrast, there has been a decrease in per capita consumption in parts of Africa, the Americas, and notably in Europe where it has fallen from 12.2 litres of pure alcohol annually in 2005 to 10.9 litres in 2010 (WHO, 2014: 42). Nevertheless, alcohol consumption in Europe still remains much higher than the global average of 6.2 litres per annum, and it also has the highest fractions of alcohol-attributable death and disease.

Across the European Union, Anderson and Baumberg (2006) report that the impact of alcohol is very wide ranging, including 17,000 deaths per year from road traffic accidents (1 in 3); 27,000 accidental deaths; 2,000 homicides (4 in 10); 10,000 suicides (1 in 6); 45,000 deaths from liver cirrhosis; 50,000 cancer deaths; 17,000 deaths from neuropsychiatric conditions; as well as 200,000 episodes of depression. Young people account for a disproportionate number of the deaths, with over 10 per cent of youth female mortality and about 25 per cent of youth male mortality due to alcohol (Foxcroft and Tsertsvadze, 2012).

It has been estimated that, worldwide, 4 per cent of 11 year olds, 8 per cent of 13 year olds, and 21 per cent of 15 year olds drink alcohol weekly; 14 per cent of 15 year olds have been drunk at least once by the age of 13; and 32 per cent of 15 year olds have been drunk at least twice (Currie et al., 2012). Young people aged 10–24 years represent 27 per cent of the world population, and children and adolescents (as well as elderly people) are typically more vulnerable to alcohol-related harm from a given volume of alcohol than other age groups. Early initiation of alcohol use (before 14 years of age) is a predictor of impaired health status because it is associated with increased risk for alcohol dependence at a later age (WHO, 2014: 7).

Although disability or disease from major risk factors is generally low in early adolescence, rates rise sharply in later adolescence and early adulthood, especially in males, for road traffic accidents, psychological problems, unsafe sex and alcohol use (Gore et al., 2011). All these factors have been shown to be linked. Also in this age group, homicides, suicides, falls and other accidents are all strongly associated with alcohol consumption.

Because about 80 per cent of deaths among young adults are due to these causes, as opposed to cancer, infectious disease or other causes, interventions that change the ways and the extent to which young people consume alcohol have the potential to substantially affect the mortality rate of this population (Carpenter and Dobkin, 2011).

Modes of intervention

Although the primary focus of the present chapter is on initiatives to reduce alcohol-related harm among young people, it includes interventions aimed at the wider population which may have a particular resonance with regard to young people. Kumpfer (1999) classifies approaches to reducing alcohol-related harm as *Universal*, *Selective* or *Indicated*. *Universal* approaches target a large group or population, many of whom may not exhibit individual risk factors, with interventions aiming to delay or prevent use or harm. *Selective* approaches target sub-groups considered at high risk (e.g. children from troubled families, or with a poor academic record). *Indicated* interventions are designed to prevent or reduce harm among those who already show signs of problematic behaviour (e.g. binge drinking) or show indications of other serious disorders (e.g. depression) that increase their chances of developing a problem with alcohol.

Overview of interventions

The European Commission, in preparing a comprehensive population-wide strategy, commissioned a report on the social, health and economic burden of alcohol for European citizens, and on initiatives that could be effective in reducing alcohol-related harm. The report (Anderson and Baumberg, 2006) offers a synthesis of published systematic reviews, meta-analyses, and individual papers, as well as analyses of data made available by the European Commission and the World Health Organization. Anderson and Baumberg (2006) group alcohol policies under several headings, including:

1 policies to support education, communication, training and public awareness
2 policies to reduce drink-driving
3 policies to regulate the alcohol market.

School-based programmes

School-based alcohol programmes have been classified as *educational-informational* or *psychosocial*, although of course the latter also involves dissemination of information. Purely *informational* interventions aim to raise awareness and increase knowledge of the potential dangers of alcohol; while *psychosocial* interventions aim to develop psychological and social skills in young people so they are less likely to be influenced by other people or circumstances to misuse alcohol, or develop problems related to alcohol or other drug use.

All young people need to be informed about the harm that can result from misuse of alcohol, and the reach of school-based educational programmes can be high because of captive audiences. Nevertheless, a great deal of research over many years has shown that although school-based *information* programmes can increase knowledge and apparently change attitudes, alcohol use remains largely unaffected (Paglia and Room, 1999; Foxcroft et al., 2003; Anderson and Baumberg, 2006).

A number of systematic reviews have concluded that there is only limited positive evidence supporting *universal* school-based programmes (e.g. Foxcroft and Tsertsvadze, 2011; Faggiano et al., 2014). Some programmes have actually shown negative effects, one example being the Take Charge of Your Life intervention, presented by Drug Abuse Resistance Education (DARE) police officers. Analysis of data from 17,320 students involved in this intervention showed increased alcohol and cigarette use over five years, relative to a control group, among youth who had reported not using these substances at baseline (Sloboda et al., 2009).

There are, nevertheless, *some* universal programmes shown to be effective in reducing the incidence of drunkenness and binge drinking. *Psychosocial* interventions aiming to enhance the social skills of young people, including several *universal multi-component* interventions which engage the wider family, appear to show more effect in reducing problematic alcohol use. Foxcroft and Tsertsvadze (2012), in a major review of school-based prevention programmes, demonstrated that those based on psychosocial or developmental approaches such as the Life Skills Training programme (Botvin et al., 2001); Unplugged (Faggiano et al., 2010); and the Good Behaviour Game (Kellam, Reid and Balster, 2008) were more likely to report positive results. These programmes generally teach alcohol and drug resistance skills and norms against drinking and drug use, and are designed to develop personal and social skills to resist social pressure to use alcohol or other drugs. However, many of these interventions take up a comparatively large amount of time and resources and can prove difficult to implement in school settings.

A recent review of 185 studies (Hennessy and Tanner-Smith, 2015; Tanner-Smith and Lipsey, 2015) indicated that some brief alcohol interventions, less than five hours in duration, can reduce alcohol-related problems in adolescents and college-age students. Individually delivered interventions were consistently effective and showed significant reductions in adolescents' alcohol use, but group-delivered brief interventions showed no effect on average. The authors suggest that group-delivered brief interventions might yield better outcomes with more careful implementation, monitoring and feedback to providers to ensure fidelity to the model being implemented. Other very important moderators of programme effectiveness are staff training, experience and the ability to build relationships with youth (Dishion and Dodge, 2005).

In any case, interactive and personalised approaches offer the greatest promise, particularly those programmes using motivational enhancement techniques. These modalities focus on enhancing participants' motivations to self-evaluate and self-regulate their behaviour, and often involve goal-setting or contracting and decisional balance exercises. Educational, or informational, prevention modalities, in contrast, tend to be less interactive, and are typically didactic presentations focused on providing information about alcohol-related harm.

One brief psychosocial *selective* approach, the Preventure programme, has been showing very positive results. Preventure is based on the finding that four personality traits (hopelessness, anxiety-sensitivity, impulsivity and sensation seeking) are associated with particular motivational pathways to substance misuse, as well as a risk of specific mental health problems (Conrod et al., 2013). A brief personality questionnaire, the Substance Use Risk Profile Scale, is used to identify high-risk young people, and they receive an intervention in small groups tailored to their personality profile. The Preventure approach is described in detail in a separate chapter in this volume (Young People and Substance Misuse: the power of personality, O'Leary-Barrett and Conrod).

Warning labels

Many health researchers and policy makers advocate mandated warning labels on alcoholic beverages, and the alcohol industry has claimed great kudos for implementing this (see https://responsibilitydeal.dh.gov.uk/henry-ashworth-new-year-message/). However, a systematic review of the literature has demonstrated that although the introduction of warning labels is associated with increased recognition of the label messages, little change is shown in beliefs about the risks of alcohol use or of participation in risky alcohol-related behaviours (Scholes-Balog, Heerde and Hemphill, 2012). Alcohol warning labels, in comparison with warnings on tobacco products, are far more modest in design, prominence, impact or integration with broader campaigns, and this may be a factor in the lack of supporting evidence. Nevertheless, even in the absence of strong evidence of impact, consumers have a right to information about risks, especially if that information is in close proximity to the time and place of consumption (Wilkinson et al., 2009).

However, it has been suggested that in the case of pregnant women an unintended consequence of alcohol warning labels can be to increase their anxiety, feelings of guilt and blame by reinforcing beliefs about personal responsibility. There can be a failure on the part of harm-reduction advocates to acknowledge the systemic and social circumstances that may influence women to consume alcohol while pregnant, especially those women subject to historical, multigenerational influences (Bell, Zizzo and Racine, 2015).

Social marketing

Social marketing seeks to use marketing concepts to influence behaviours that benefit individuals and communities, in contrast with commercial marketing which has the primary aim of increasing financial profit.

Alcohol-related social marketing campaigns usually focus on the hazards of driving under the influence of alcohol, or other risks associated with excessive consumption of alcohol, and usually encourage 'responsible drinking'. These campaigns are often intended to be relevant to young people, and are mainly distributed through drinking venues, magazines, television, radio, billboards, newspaper and magazine advertisements. However, both the quality and quantity of these messages have been assessed as poor in comparison with the high-quality pro-drinking advertisements that frequently appear, and the former are considered an ineffective antidote to the latter (Anderson and Baumberg, 2006). In the UK, the Government has entered into a 'Responsibility Deal' with alcohol suppliers wherein the alcohol companies agreed to improve labelling, and pledged to encourage responsible drinking and not to put alcohol adverts on outdoor poster sites within 100 metres of schools. They have also pledged to support DrinkAware, an organisation which provides information promoting non-harmful drinking as well as to provide funds for educational interventions in schools. However, it has been pointed out (e.g. Hastings and Angus, 2011; Sheron et al., 2012) that the primary aim of the alcohol industry is to deliver profit, which in a competitive marketplace is achieved by maximising consumption, and so there is a fundamental though unmentioned conflict of interest at the very heart of this initiative.

These researchers argue that the principal beneficiaries of apparently public-spirited campaigns run by alcohol companies are the companies themselves, and that social marketing controlled by a corporation will always transmute into commercial marketing. Nevertheless, despite the fallibility of public informational campaigns, this does not mean that commercial marketers cannot make some contribution to achievement of social good. The intention to remind people of danger may be being met to some extent and, as long as it does no harm, can represent a benefit.

It has been argued that the internet and social media are shifting how social marketing campaigns should be operationalised, as the old one-way communication model is not compatible with the way people interact in online environments (Lefebvre, 2007). The findings from a meta-analysis assessing online intervention design features (Cugelman, Thelwall and Dawes, 2011) suggest it is feasible to target individual-level behaviour change, which may be scaled-up to achieve population-level health benefits. Great attention should be paid to the quality of these interventions as the potential online audience has a multitude of other postings vying for its attention. Recently Twitter has presented a new channel for both commercial and social marketing. In a study by Burton, Dadich and Soboleva (2013), six Twitter accounts of organisations promoting safe drinking or abstinence were compared with six accounts maintained by alcohol companies. The researchers found that the Twitter accounts of alcohol companies were followed by more people, more likely to be forwarded to others, and more likely to be associated with positive stimuli, all these suggesting greater influence than pro-health Twitter messages. Again this demonstrates the skill and influence of commercial marketers as compared with much social marketing.

Nevertheless, mass media social marketing may be useful in reinforcing community awareness of the problems created by alcohol use, and in mobilising public support for prevention approaches that have demonstrated effectiveness, including drink-driving countermeasures and regulation of drinking environments.

Drink-driving

Of the drink-driving policies discussed below some are *universal* (applied to the whole population) some are *selective* (applied to young people) and some are *indicated* (applied to individuals already known to drink-drive). As young people have less driving experience and account for a high number of road accidents, all three types of applications are relevant to this group.

Increased minimum legal drinking age

Almost all studies designed specifically for the purpose show a minimum legal drinking age of 21 years reduces drinking, problematic drinking, drinking and driving, and alcohol-related crashes among young people (e.g. McCartt, Hellinga and Kirley, 2010). Nonetheless, across much of the world the minimum age is 18 years.

Lower legal driving BAC limits

In 2001, the European Commission adopted a recommendation urging member states to prescribe two different blood alcohol concentration (BAC) limits for drivers. The standard BAC limit for all motor vehicle drivers was to be one not exceeding 0.05 per cent. In addition, a BAC limit of 0.02 per cent was recommended for inexperienced drivers, motorcyclists, drivers of lorries weighing more than 3.5 tonnes or carrying dangerous goods, and any passenger vehicle with over eight passenger seats. According to estimates by the European Commission, 25 per cent of all road deaths across the EU are alcohol-related, which means that, in 2010, 6,500 deaths would have been prevented if all drivers had obeyed the law on drink driving (Podda, 2012). In the UK, Scotland has opted for a 0.05 per cent limit while the remainder of the UK, despite calls for a reduction, especially for young drivers, has a legal BAC limit set at 0.08 per cent.

In the US the BAC limit is also 0.08 per cent, and motor vehicle accidents are the leading cause of death and injury for US teenagers. Per mile driven, drivers aged 16 to 19 are nearly three times more likely than drivers aged 20 and older to be in a fatal crash. Despite this, the number of alcohol-related traffic deaths among 16 to 20 year-olds decreased from 5,244 in 1982 to 1,987 in 2008. This appears to be in large measure because of the introduction of a legal drinking age of 21 years and zero tolerance laws leading to licence suspension. Although the percentage of US high school students who drink and drive has decreased by more than half since 1991, it is still one in ten (Centers for Disease Control and Prevention, 2012), and alcohol is involved in 37 per cent of all traffic deaths among persons aged 16 to 20 (NIH, 2013).

A meta-analysis of data from 1982 to 2000 across nine studies in different US states showed that reduction of alcohol-related motor fatalities was greater in states that had frequent sobriety checkpoints and licence suspension laws (Tippetts et al., 2005). In Australia, BAC reductions from 0.08 per cent to 0.05 per cent are reported as having reduced serious crashes by 7–15 per cent (Anderson and Baumberg, 2006) although it appears that effectiveness can reduce over time as drivers gradually realise that their chances of detection are not very high. Doran et al. (2008) calculate that, in Australia, random breath testing of drivers, when combined with other interventions to reduce alcohol-related problems, is cost effective, but if taken alone it requires a lot of police resources and therefore becomes expensive.

There are two types of driver sobriety checks: random and selective breath testing. Both types generally are accompanied by news media efforts to publicise both the enforcement activity and the consequences of driving with a BAC above the legal limit. An EU recommendation states that all member states should adopt random breath tests, with each driver exposed to a statistically real probability of being checked at least once every three years (Janitzek, 2008). Random breath checks are used in Australia and several European countries and any motorist at any time may be required to take a test, with refusal equivalent to failing. In the UK, and in many states of the US, police must have a valid reason to demand a breath test. Currently in the UK, for police to be able to require a breath test, a driver must have either committed a traffic offence, been involved in an accident to which the police were called, or given the police grounds to suspect they had consumed alcohol above the legal limit, e.g. by driving erratically or walking unsteadily before getting into the car.

Designated driver campaigns

Designated driver campaigns require that either the driver abstain from all alcohol or maintain a blood alcohol content at less than the legal limit (Anderson and Baumberg, 2006). In Europe, a designated driver programme targeted at young drivers (the BOB campaign) originated in Belgium in 1996, and fourteen countries participated in 2006, the most recent year it was run at a European level. Many countries still run this campaign at a national level and local initiatives also promote the concept. The designated driver idea appears sound, although there is no solid evidence for an effective impact.

Alcohol ignition locks

An alcohol ignition lock requires a driver to provide a breath sample every time an attempt is made to start the vehicle. Alcohol ignition interlocks are gaining acceptance, with legislation and programmes in countries such as the US, Canada and Australia and feasibility studies in the European Union. A systematic review of research evidence (Willis, Lybrand and Bellamy, 2004) found that recidivism was lower while the device was installed in the vehicle, but the benefit disappeared once it was removed. This finding has been supported in later studies (e.g. Elder et al., 2011).

Brief interventions in primary care

Primary healthcare settings are seen as ideal for early detection and prevention of alcohol-related problems because of the level of contact with the general population and the frequency with which higher-risk drinkers present. A review of systematic reviews across 56 trials (O'Donnell et al., 2014) supports the effectiveness of brief interventions in primary healthcare. However, much of the evidence centres on middle-aged men, and there is a knowledge gap regarding the effectiveness of brief alcohol interventions with pregnant women, older and younger drinkers, or those from ethnic minority groups. There is also no consensus on the optimum length, frequency and necessary content of brief intervention required to maintain a long-term effect.

Control of the alcohol market

Restricting advertising

The alcohol industry, like the tobacco industry, generally argues that advertising does not target young people nor increase consumption, but simply promotes product switching or brand loyalty. However a US study (Chung et al., 2010) demonstrated that almost all cable tv alcohol advertisements appeared in time slots with audiences of up to 30 per cent underage viewers. At these times each percentage point increase in adolescent viewers was associated with 7 per cent more beer, 15 per cent more spirits, and 22 per cent more alcopop advertisements. A German study of 3415 students, mean age 12.5 years from 29 schools, showed evidence for an independent, specific relationship between higher exposure to alcohol advertisements and multiple measures of alcohol use, including current and binge drinking (Morgenstern et al., 2011). In Australia a study of 1113 adolescents aged 12–17 found that exposure to alcohol advertisements was strongly associated with drinking patterns (Jones and Magee, 2011). Although some attempts have been made to control the time and content of these advertisements, the alcohol industry generally finds ways to circumvent any restrictions.

Outlet density and opening times

The link between higher outlet density and alcohol-related harms is reasonably well established (Livingston, 2011). A large Canadian study found a clear increase in overall consumption of alcohol when the number of off-licence outlets increased by a third (Stockwell et al., 2011). These harms include not only alcohol-related health problems but also local levels of public disturbance, related road traffic accidents, self-reported injuries, child neglect and domestic violence. Nevertheless in recent years planning restrictions for alcohol outlets have been relaxed in many countries.

Regulation of alcohol price

The impact of price changes on alcohol consumption and related harm has been more extensively investigated than any other potential alcohol policy measure. A wide range of research has found that increasing the price of alcohol reduces alcohol consumption levels among young people, with the greatest impact on more frequent and heavier drinkers. Alcohol price increases are also associated with a reduction in road traffic accidents and fatalities among people of all ages, but particularly for younger drivers (Anderson and Baumberg, 2006).

Other research has demonstrated that general price increases to all alcohol products in the on- and off-licence trade tend to result in a range of positive outcomes. Targeted price increases on low-priced alcohol disproportionately affect harmful drinkers and 11–18 year olds, but lead to smaller changes in overall consumption, as only part of the market is covered. A 10 per cent general price rise in all categories of alcohol results in a reduction in weekly consumption by 11–18 year olds of –5.3 per cent, and by 18–24 year old hazardous drinkers of –6.0 per cent. As prices increase, alcohol-attributable hospital admissions and deaths reduce, and there are reductions in violent crime, criminal damage and theft, robbery and other crimes (Meier et al., 2008). An earlier report from the Academy of Medical Sciences (2004) estimated that a 10 per cent rise in the price of alcohol would lead to a drop of 5.0 per cent for male victims and 7.1 per cent for female victims of homicide; and a drop of 28.8 per cent for male and 37.4 per cent for female deaths from alcohol-involved causes.

Moderate drinkers are affected in only very small ways by the price increase policy both in terms of their consumption of alcohol and their spending. In 2006, the Advisory Council for the Misuse of Drugs (2006) recommended that the UK Government should progressively raise the excise duty on alcohol. Increased taxes on alcohol are, seemingly, an attractive instrument of alcohol policy because they can be used both to generate government revenue and to reduce alcohol-related harm if they are passed on to the retail price (Alcohol and Public Policy Group, 2010: 772). Nevertheless, in England in 2015 the chancellor of the exchequer cut the duty on spirits and cider by 2 per cent and lowered the duty on beer for the third year in a row. It would seem that the most effective harm-reduction policy is not always politically acceptable.

Barriers to effective alcohol control interventions

Governments have difficulties in applying effective policies to control alcohol-related harm. Alcohol is not an ordinary commodity, and good policy must balance the positive and negative effects of this unusual product. On the one hand there is its capacity for contributing to employment, earnings, corporate profits and public pleasure, and on the other the so-called 'acceptable level' of its harms (Davidson, 2013). Early in the twentieth century, at a time when the level of harm appeared unacceptable, major controls including total prohibition of the manufacture and sale of alcohol were applied in many countries including the US, Canada, Iceland, Finland and Norway, as well as both czarist Russia and the Soviet Union. Many of these laws were repealed after a few years as they proved difficult or impossible to police, encouraged organised criminal activity, and had massive unintended negative economic affects.

The importance of the alcohol industry to many national economies cannot be overstated. In the European Union (EU) in 2013, spirits and liqueurs dominated the basket of exported products with a value of 10 billion euros, and wines and vermouth closely followed with 9.1 billion euros of export sales. Together these accounted for 14 per cent of EU exports (MAP, 2014). The brewing sector is also of major importance to the EU economy. In 2012, it was responsible for 2 million jobs, and the production and sale of beer generated 53 billion euros revenue for EU governments (Berkhout et al., 2013). In the UK, in 2012, the wine and spirit industry directly or indirectly supported over £40 billion of economic activity (WSTA, 2013). The alcohol beverage industry is also a major contributor to the US economy, responsible for over $400 billion in total economic activity in 2010, generating over 3.9 million jobs for US workers and nearly $90 billion in wages (Distilled Spirits Council, 2015).

The obvious economic importance of the alcohol industry means that despite alcohol-related impacts on health and social order, many governments are loath to confront the risk to jobs and tax revenues inherent in curtailing alcohol sales. As Vogel (2002: 5) argues:

> it is obviously not feasible to deny regulatory approval or restrict any or all commercial activities that might pose risks to consumers . . . a literal application of the precautionary principle would impose unacceptably high economic costs as well as unnecessarily restrict many potentially beneficial commercial activities . . . Accordingly, governments must make often difficult choices.

Another factor supporting the increasing availability of alcohol is the neo-liberal free market ideology underpinning most governments in the developed world, which militates against state alcohol monopolies, increases in taxation or any other restrictions on the sale or profits of this product. So, despite the many well-documented health, social and economic costs arising from excessive alcohol consumption, this generally remains low on the public policy agenda while many lesser health risks are given a higher priority.

Despite the fact that considerable efforts have been made over a number of years to persuade general practitioners to apply brief alcohol harm-reduction interventions, most have yet to do so. Barriers include a lack of time, training and resources, as well as a belief that patients will not take advice to change drinking behaviour; and a fear of offending patients by discussing alcohol (O'Donnell et al., 2014).

Conclusion

Research indicates that information-based interventions, whether provided in schools or via social marketing, although increasing knowledge, have not demonstrated effectiveness in reducing alcohol-related harm. There is, however, good evidence to support targeted *selective* or *indicated* psychosocial interventions in schools or with families.

The most effective policy measures in reducing alcohol-related harm among young people, and the associated costs to wider society, are those that increase the retail price of alcohol, restrict its availability, increase restrictions on novice drivers and provide brief advice interventions in the primary care setting. Applying a range of policies in a complementary manner to restructure the total environment in relation to alcohol consumption has been assessed as most effective in reducing alcohol-related problems for young people as well as the rest of society.

References

Academy of Medical Sciences (2004) *Calling Time: The nation's drinking as a major public health issue*. Available at: http://www.acmedsci.ac.uk/policy/policy/calling-time-the-nations-drinking-as-a-major-health-issue/ (accessed 13/07/2015).

Advisory Council for the Misuse of Drugs (2006) *Pathways to Problems: Hazardous use of tobacco, alcohol and other drugs by young people in the UK and its implications for policy*. Advisory Council for the Misuse of Drugs. Available at: https://www.gov.uk/government/uploads/system/uploads/attachment_data/file/119053/Pathwaystoproblems.pdf (accessed 13/07/2015).

Alcohol and Public Policy Group (2010) Alcohol: No Ordinary Commodity – A summary of the second edition. *Addiction* 105(5): 772.

Anderson P and Baumberg B (2006) *Alcohol in Europe: A public health perspective. A report for the European Commission*. London: Institute of Alcohol Studies.

Bell E, Zizzo N and Racine E (2015) Caution! warning labels about alcohol and pregnancy: unintended consequences and questionable effectiveness. *The American Journal of Bioethics* 15(3): 18–20.

Berkhout B, Bertling L, Bleeker Y, de Wit W, Kruis G, Stokkel R and Theuws R (2013) *The Contribution Made by Beer to the European Economy*. Amsterdam: Brewers of Europe. Available at: http://www.ey.com/Publication/vwLUAssets/EY_-_The_Contribution_made_by_Beer_to_the_European_Economy/$FILE/EY-The-Contribution-made-by-Beer-to-the-European-Economy.pdf (accessed 13/07/2015).

Botvin GJ, Griffin KW, Diaz T and Ifill-Williams M (2001) Preventing binge drinking during early adolescence: one- and two-year follow-up of a school-based preventive intervention. *Psychology of Addictive Behaviors* 15(4): 360–365.

Burton S, Dadich A and Soboleva A (2013) Competing voices: marketing and counter-marketing alcohol on Twitter. *Journal of Nonprofit and Public Sector Marketing* 25(2): 186–209.

Carpenter C and Dobkin C (2011) The minimum legal drinking age and public health. *Journal of Economic Perspectives* 25(2): 133–156.

Centers for Disease Control and Prevention (2012) *Teen Drinking and Driving*. Available at: http://www.cdc.gov/vitalsigns/teendrinkinganddriving/index.html (accessed 13/07/2015).

Chung PJ, Garfield CF, Elliott MN, Ostroff J, Ross C, Jernigan DH, Vestal KD and Schuster MA (2010) Association between adolescent viewership and alcohol advertising on cable television. *American Journal of Public Health* 100(3): 555–563.

Conrod PJ, O'Leary-Barrett M, Newton N, Topper L, Castellanos-Ryan N, Mackie C and Girard A (2013) Effectiveness of a selective, personality-targeted prevention program for adolescent alcohol use and misuse: a cluster randomized controlled trial. *JAMA Psychiatry* 70(3): 334–342.

Cugelman B, Thelwall M and Dawes P (2011) Online interventions for social marketing health behavior change campaigns: a meta-analysis of psychological architectures and adherence factors. *Journal of Medical Internet Research* 13(1): e17. Available at: http://www.ncbi.nlm.nih.gov/pmc/articles/PMC3221338/ (accessed 13/07/2015).

Currie C, Zanotti C, Morgan A, Currie D, de Looze M, Roberts C and Barnekow V (2012) *Social Determinants of Health and Well-Being among Young People. Health behaviour in school-aged children (HBSC) study: International report from the 2009–2010 survey (Health Policy for Children and Adolescents, No. 6)*. Copenhagen: WHO Regional Office for Europe.

Davidson R (2013) Formulating effective alcohol policy: not as simple as it sounds. In: Mistral W (ed.) *Emerging Perspectives on Substance Misuse*. Abingdon: Wiley Blackwell, 23–39.

Dishion TJ and Dodge KA (2005) Peer contagion in interventions for children and adolescents: moving towards an understanding of the ecology and dynamics of change. *Journal of Abnormal Child Psychology* 33(3): 395–400.

Distilled Spirits Council (2015) *Economic Contributions of the Distilled Spirits Industry*. Distilled Spirits Council of the United States. Available at: http://www.discus.org/economics/ (accessed 13/07/2015).

Doran C, Vos T, Cobiac L, Hall W, Asamoah I, Wallace A, Naidoo S, Byrnes J, Fowler G and Arnett K (2008) *Identifying Cost-Effective Interventions to Reduce the Burden of Harm Associated with Alcohol Misuse in Australia*. Report for the Alcohol Education Rehabilitation Foundation, Australia.

Elder RW, Voas R, Beirness D, Shults RA, Sleet DA, Nichols JL, Compton R and Task Force on Community Preventive Services (2011) Effectiveness of ignition interlocks for preventing alcohol-impaired driving and alcohol-related crashes: a community guide systematic review. *American Journal of Preventive Medicine* 40(3): 362–376.

Faggiano F, Vigna-Taglianti F, Burkhart G, Bohrn K, Cuomo L, Gregori D et al. (2010) The effectiveness of a school-based substance abuse prevention program: 18-month follow-up of the EU-Dap cluster randomised controlled trial. *Drug and Alcohol Dependence* 108(1–2): 56–64.

Faggiano F, Minozzi S, Versino E and Buscemi D (2014) Universal School-based Prevention for Illicit Drug Use (Review) The Cochrane Library. Available at: http://onlinelibrary.wiley.com/doi/10.1002/14651858.CD003020.pub3/pdf/standard (accessed 13/07/2015).

Foxcroft DR and Tsertsvadze A (2012) Universal Alcohol Misuse Prevention Programmes for Children and Adolescents: Cochrane Systematic Reviews. *Perspectives in Public Health* 132(3): 128–134.

Foxcroft DR, Ireland D, Lister-Sharp DJ, Lowe G and Breen R (2003) Longer-term primary prevention for alcohol misuse in young people: a systematic review. *Addiction* 98(4): 397–411.

Gore FM, Bloem PJN, Patton GC, Ferguson J, Joseph V, Coffey C, Sawyer SM and Mathers CD (2011) Global burden of disease in young people aged 10–24 years: a systematic analysis. *The Lancet*. Available at: http://www.thelancet.com/journals/lancet/article/PIIS0140-6736%2811%2960512-6/abstract (accessed 13/07/2015).

Hastings G and Angus K (2011) When is social marketing not social marketing? *Journal of Social Marketing* 1(1): 45–53.

Hennessy EA and Tanner-Smith EE (2015) Effectiveness of brief school-based interventions for adolescents: a meta-analysis of alcohol use prevention programs. *Prevention Science* 16(3): 463–474.

Jones SC and Magee CA (2011) Exposure to alcohol advertising and alcohol consumption among Australian adolescents. *Alcohol and Alcoholism* 46(5): 630–637.

Kellam S, Reid J and Balster RL (2008) Effects of a universal classroom behavior program in first and second grades on young adult outcomes. *Drug and Alcohol Dependence* 95(Suppl 1): S5–S28.

Kumpfer KL (1999) *Strengthening America's Families: Exemplary parenting and family strategies for delinquency prevention*. US Department of Justice, Office of Juvenile Justice and Delinquency Prevention. Available at: http://www.strengtheningfamilies.org/html/literature_review_1999.pdf (accessed 13/07/2015).

Janitzek T (2008) *Drink Driving: Young drivers and recidivist offenders*. European Transport Safety Council. Available at: http://www.etsc.be/documents/ETS_004-08.pdf (accessed 13/07/2015).

Lefebvre C (2007) The new technology: the consumer as participant rather than target audience. *Social Marketing Quarterly* 3(3): 31–42.

Livingston M (2011) A longitudinal analysis of alcohol outlet density and domestic violence. *Addiction* 106(5), 919–925.

McCartt AT, Hellinga LA and Kirley BB (2010) The effects of minimum legal drinking age 21 laws on alcohol-related driving in the United States. *Journal of Safety Research* 41(2): 173–181.

MAP (2014) *Monitoring Agri-trade Policy Agricultural Trade in 2013: EU gains in commodity exports*. European Commission. Available at: http://ec.europa.eu/agriculture/trade-analysis/map/2014-1_en.pdf (accessed 13/07/2015).

Meier P, Brennan A, Purshouse R, Taylor K, Rafia R, Booth A, O'Reilly D, Stockwell T, Sutton A, Wilkinson A and Wong R (2008) *Independent Review of the Effects of Alcohol Pricing and Promotion: Part B, Modelling the potential impact of pricing and promotion policies for alcohol in England*. Report for Department of Health Policy Research Programme. Sheffield, UK: University of Sheffield.

Morgenstern M, Isensee B, Sargent JD and Hanewinkel R (2011) Exposure to alcohol advertising and teen drinking. *Preventive Medicine* 52(2): 146–151.

NIH (2013) *Alcohol-related Traffic Deaths*. US Department of Health and Human Services. Available at: http://report.nih.gov/nihfactsheets/ViewFactSheet.aspx?csid=24 (accessed 13/07/2015).

O'Donnell A, Anderson P, Newbury-Birch D, Schulte B, Schmidt C, Reimer J and Kaner E (2014) The impact of brief alcohol interventions in primary healthcare: a systematic review of reviews. *Alcohol and Alcoholism* 49(1): 66–78.

Paglia A and Room R (1999) Preventing substance use problems among youth: a literature review and recommendations. *Journal of Primary Prevention* 20(1): 3–50.

Podda F (2012) *Drink Driving: Towards zero tolerance.* European Traffic Safety Council. Available at: http://archive.etsc.eu/documents/Drink_Driving_Towards_Zero_Tolerance.pdf (accessed 13/07/2015).

Scholes-Balog KE, Heerde JA and Hemphill SA (2012) Alcohol warning labels: unlikely to affect alcohol-related beliefs and behaviours in adolescents. *Australian and New Zealand Journal of Public Health* 36(6): 524–529.

Sheron N, Gilmore I, Parsons C, Hawkey C and Rhodes J (2012) Projections of alcohol-related deaths in England and Wales – tragic toll or potential prize? *The Lancet* 379(9817): 687–688.

Sloboda Z, Stephens RC, Stephens PC, Grey SF, Teasdale B, Hawthorne RD, Williams J and Marquette JF (2009) The Adolescent Substance Abuse Prevention Study: a randomized field trial of a universal substance abuse prevention program. *Drug and Alcohol Dependency* 102(1–3): 1–10.

Stockwell T, Zhao J, Macdonald S, Vallance K, Gruenewald P, Ponicki W, Holder H and Treno A (2011) Impact on alcohol-related mortality of a rapid rise in the density of private liquor outlets in British Columbia: a local area multi-level analysis. *Addiction* 106(4): 768–776.

Tanner-Smith EE and Lipsey MW (2015) Brief alcohol interventions for adolescents and young adults: a systematic review and meta-analysis. *Journal of Substance Abuse Treatment* 51: 1–18.

Tippetts AS, Voas RB, Fell JC and Nichols JL (2005) A meta-analysis of .08 BAC laws in 19 jurisdictions in the United States. *Accident Analysis and Prevention* 37(1): 149–161.

Vogel D (2002) *The Politics of Risk Regulation in Europe and the United States.* Prepared for publication in *The Yearbook of European Environmental Law*, Volume 3 (2003) Available at: http://faculty.haas.berkeley.edu/vogel/uk%20oct.pdf (accessed 13/07/2015).

WHO (2014) *Global Status Report on Alcohol and Health 2014.* Geneva: World Health Organization. Available at: http://www.who.int/substance_abuse/publications/global_alcohol_report/msb_gsr_2014_1.pdf?ua=1 (accessed 07/07/2015).

Wilkinson C, Allsop S, Cail D, Chikritzhs T, Daube M, Kirby G and Mattick R (2009) *Report 1. Alcohol Warning Labels: Evidence of effectiveness on risky alcohol consumption and short term outcomes.* National Drug Research Institute (Curtin University of Technology), Drug and Alcohol Office (WA), National Drug and Alcohol Research Centre (University of New South Wales) and the Public Health Advocacy Institute (Curtin University of Technology). Available at: http://www.foodstandards.govt.nz/code/applications/documents/Alcohol-warning-labels-report-1.pdf

Willis C, Lybrand S and Bellamy N (2004) Alcohol Ignition Interlock Programmes for Reducing Drink Driving Recidivism (Review). Cochrane Library. Available at: http://info.onlinelibrary.wiley.com/userfiles/ccoch/file/Safety_on_the_road/CD004168.pdf (accessed 13/07/2015).

WSTA (2013) *The Wine and Spirit Trade Association Economic Impact Assessment.* Available at: http://www.wsta.co.uk/images/budget/EY-final-ADE-report-for-WSTA.pdf (accessed 12/08/2015).

Part V

Routes to recovery

Chapter 13

Twelve-Step mutual-help organizations and facilitation interventions

John F Kelly and Brandon G Bergman

Introduction

This chapter will briefly describe the history and origins of Twelve-Step (12-Step) mutual-help organizations (TSMHOs). It will then review empirical data on the efficacy and effectiveness of mutual help organizations (MHOs); what is currently known about which individuals may or may not benefit from participation; and review the latest research about the mechanisms through which TSMHOs may confer benefit. Subsequently, there follows a review of evidence on 12-Step facilitation interventions (TSFs) and ways TSMHO participation and TSFs can be integrated in other substance use disorder treatment models and approaches.

Alcohol and other substance use disorders (SUD) are highly prevalent psychiatric conditions in most developed and many developing nations, conferring a prodigious burden of disease, disability, and premature mortality (World Health Organization, 2014). Escalation in substance-related harms during the past fifty years has been paralleled by advances in clinical science and greater availability of effective psychosocial and pharmacological treatments. While these developments in professional care have been welcome and immensely valuable, the cost of managing these, often chronic, high-volume, high-burden disorders on a purely professional basis has been economically challenging for most societies. Professional services are typically only available during weekday business hours and delivered in an acute care format, ending after a few weeks or months. The cost, rigidity, and time-limited nature of professional services, together with growing awareness of the long-term vulnerability to relapse of individuals suffering from SUD have seen the expansion of freely available community-based 12-Step mutual-help organizations such as Alcoholics Anonymous (AA) and Narcotics Anonymous (NA).

AA originated in Akron, Ohio, in 1935. As other drug epidemics emerged in the US, so have other TSMHOs based on AA's original 12-Step template. Learning from the lessons of previously influential recovery-focused MHOs in the US that had experienced strong initial success but then rapid dissolution (e.g. the Washingtonian Society, see White, 2014), all TSMHOs have an explicit policy of not affiliating with any outside organizations. They maintain a completely non-professional stance in order to focus exclusively on peer-recovery support.

In contrast, since the 1950s, many professional SUD treatment programs in the US and other countries have been incorporating AA's philosophy and practices into their own treatment models. This approach consequently became known as the "Minnesota Model," having been developed initially in the state of Minnesota (McElrath, 1997).The 12-Step orientation of professional treatment, and the practice of making referrals to TSMHOs such as AA and NA following discharge, created a 12-Step synergy that contributed to the growth of TSMHOs in the US and globally (Kelly & Yeterian, 2013). Conservative estimates place current AA membership at more than two million, in over 170 countries, meeting in over 115,000 registered weekly groups (Alcoholics Anonymous, 2014). AA's widespread adoption, acceptance, and perceived effectiveness has arguably paved the way for the emergence of other substance-focused mutual-help organizations, some of which utilize the AA model (e.g. Narcotics Anonymous, Cocaine Anonymous) and some of which have developed in opposition to it. For example, SMART Recovery and the Secular Organizations for Sobriety (SOS) provide alternatives to AA (Kelly & Yeterian, 2013). Clinicians should also educate themselves about the available alternatives to 12-Step mutual help organizations in order to be able to provide this information to clients who would prefer to attend non-12-Step MHOs.

In the US, MHOs (mostly TSMHOs) are currently the most frequently sought source of help for substance-related problems (SAMHSA, 2014). TSMHOs can serve as flexible long-term addiction recovery management resources and, from an intervention dissemination and impact perspective, appear to be readily adopted and implemented, and have evident staying power (Kelly & Yeterian, 2013). TSMHOs provide 24/7 support "on demand," notably during times of high relapse risk such as during holidays, evenings, and weekends when professional services are often unavailable. TSMHOs also strongly encourage and provide daily personal recovery monitoring and mentoring via a 12-Step "sponsor," who provides more intensive support and accountability. They also recommend that all members stay in frequent contact between formal meetings by phone or text, and most offer online meetings to increase the opportunities for recovery-specific group support at any time of the day or night.

Many people attest that these organizations are responsible for their successful recovery and/or have saved their lives. While these facts represent one kind of evidence, a lingering clinical and public health question is whether they are shown to help when subjected to more rigorous, systematic, scientific scrutiny. From a scientific standpoint it is only recently that these peer-led, recovery-focused groups, and professionally delivered treatments designed to facilitate their use (i.e. 12-Step facilitation or TSF), have undergone rigorous scientific inquiry to determine whether, and how, they may help.

Twelve-Step terminology

The evidence for TSMHOs is often confused with other evidence for TSF and the Minnesota Model "12-Step treatment." To clarify, TSMHOs are independent, community-based fellowships that provide help through a network of informal gatherings, convened at rented venues, such as churches and hospitals. TSF is the name given to professional interventions designed to facilitate active engagement in these community organizations. The Minnesota Model, "12-Step treatment," typically (but not always) refers to a professional residential treatment program in which patients are educated in depth about the AA fellowship and the 12 Steps, are given preliminary exposure to 12-Step meetings, and often work through the first five of the 12 Steps during treatment.

Because of the potential to conflate these three related resources, it is important to be mindful of terminology when reviewing research studies, as it is not always immediately apparent to which of these different entities the research pertains. Consequently, throughout this chapter, we use these terms as defined above.

TSMHO and TSF clinical research

Most of the research conducted on TSMHOs has examined the effectiveness of these groups by studying attendance rates and substance use outcomes as they naturally occur. While providing one kind of evidence regarding effectiveness, it is difficult to estimate true causal effects of TSMHO participation because people self-select into these groups, and may be somehow different to those not choosing to participate. To help overcome this self-selection bias, studies have used increasingly rigorous methods to estimate the unique and independent influence of TSMHO participation on subsequent substance use outcomes. On the other hand, true experimental, randomized controlled trials (RCTs) which would allow for a direct test of the efficacy of participation in TSMHOs, are rare. RCTs may not be the most appropriate way to study these community-based groups, since "real world" participation in MHOs is usually self-initiated, voluntary, and anonymous, except when participation is mandated by the court (Davidson et al., 1999).

Are TSMHOs effective recovery management resources?

A seminal meta-analysis of 107 individual studies of AA participation found that greater frequency of AA attendance and better drinking outcomes were modestly but significantly correlated (Emrick et al., 1993). However, the methodological quality of many of the studies was poor. This finding, together with a call from the United States Institute of Medicine for more rigorous research on AA (Institute of Medicine, 1990), legitimized serious scientific investigation into the organization (Kelly & Yeterian, 2012).

Recent studies have used strong analytic approaches to establish a true causal impact of TSMHO on SUD recovery. For example, prospective, time-lagged analyses (e.g. examining the association between TSMHO participation at one time point and outcomes at a subsequent time point) have shown that AA attendance and active involvement (including obtaining a sponsor, verbally participating in meetings, socializing with other TSMHO members outside of meetings) leads to decreased alcohol consumption and fewer alcohol-related problems. Importantly, the reverse association (decreased alcohol consumption and alcohol-related problems leading to increased participation) has not been supported, and analyses have controlled for confounds such as level of initial patient motivation, addiction severity, engagement with treatment during follow-up, and comorbid psychopathology (McKellar, Stewart, & Humphreys, 2003; Kelly et al., 2006).

Two of the more sophisticated approaches warrant special mention. First, Ye and Kaskutas (2009) used propensity score matching to create matched samples of AA attenders and non-attenders based on 21 variables associated with attendance and abstinence (e.g. prior TSMHO attendance). This study found that AA attenders were 2.2 times more likely to be abstinent at one-year follow-up. Further, when examining stratified samples of likelihood of AA attendance, those with initially lower propensity to attend AA derived greater benefit from attendance.

Second, Humphreys, Blodgett, and Wagner (2014) conducted an instrumental variables analysis using data from six randomized controlled studies of TSF. This allowed isolation of the proportion of AA attendance attributable to random assignment (approximating a bias-free estimate of attendance) by using the degree of attendance in TSF conditions minus the degree of attendance in non-TSF conditions. This study found that, with the exception of the most clinically severe and AA-experienced patients from a single trial, attendance significantly predicted abstinence at both 3- and 15-month follow ups. Regarding the latter, attending two additional AA meetings per week produced, on average, an additional 3.3 more days of abstinence per month.

Although less is known about TSMHO benefits among patients with primary drug use disorders, available evidence using longitudinal studies and controlling for a host of possible confounds, suggests that TSMHO participation, and active involvement in particular, promotes increased abstinence rates among primary drug patients as well (Kelly, Greene, & Bergman, 2014).

Taken together, longitudinal, methodologically rigorous studies indicate TSMHO participation has salutary effects on SUD outcomes and can be added to professional SUD and mental health treatment to positively affect abstinence and remission. However, despite these advances in our understanding of their impact, a noteworthy limitation is the dearth of studies on TSMHOs other than AA, and positive quality of life outcomes beyond abstinence or remission.

For whom are TSMHOs particularly helpful or not helpful?

A question often asked is whether TSMHOs are helpful for individuals with co-occurring psychiatric disorders, those taking psychotropic medications including anti-relapse medication, atheists or agnostics, women, and young people. The available empirical evidence suggests that, in general, individuals with co-occurring psychiatric illness and SUD can benefit from participation in traditional AA or NA meetings as much or more compared to their SUD-only counterparts (e.g. Timko et al., 2013). An exception to these findings concerns those with more socially impairing mental illness such as schizophrenia or severe unipolar depression (Kelly, McKellar, & Moos, 2003; Aase, Jason, & Robinson, 2008) who may be better suited for dual-diagnosis focused mutual help organizations such as Double Trouble in Recovery (Magura, 2008). Research also suggests that less religiously inclined individuals are less likely to become engaged, but those that do have outcomes as good as those more religiously inclined (Kelly et al., 2006). Despite the fact that AA's recovery program and early successes were based on all-male samples, later research has confirmed that females attend as frequently as men, become more involved, and derive as much recovery benefit as men (Kelly & Hoeppner, 2013). Young people may need a greater degree of facilitation and systematic encouragement to initially engage with TSMHOs, but those that do, derive as much benefit as their older adult counterparts (Hoeppner, Hoeppner, & Kelly, 2014). Further research has found that initial TSMHO engagement and outcomes for young people might be enhanced by counseling them to attend meetings with a greater proportion of young people. Over the long-term, however, they may benefit less from these young-person meetings, indicating exposure to 12-Step meetings with a greater proportion of older adults with more life and recovery experience may enhance recovery (Kelly, Myers, & Brown, 2005; Labbe et al., 2013).

How does TSMHO participation promote better outcomes?

In 12-Step fellowships' own literature, it is stated that members achieve recovery through a combination of factors including a "spiritual awakening," service to others, sponsorship, and working the 12 Steps (e.g. Narcotics Anonymous, 2008). The empirical literature overlaps with 12-Step theories of change in many ways, though with different emphases on how participation in TSMHOs leads to better SUD outcomes.

Increased confidence in handling risky or difficult situations without alcohol or drug use has been shown to be a partial mediator of the beneficial effects of AA participation (Forcehimes & Tonigan, 2008). Participation also appears to work by increasing motivation to abstain from alcohol and other drugs (Kelly, Myers, & Brown, 2002). Enhanced abstinence-focused coping efforts (e.g. cognitive reappraisal and stimulus control) also explain, in part, how AA works (Morgenstern et al., 1997). Despite support for these common psychological processes as mediators of TSMHO's effectiveness, affective mechanisms are less certain. For example, in two studies, Kelly and colleagues (2010a, b) found that the mediating role of reduced depression became non-significant when concurrent alcohol use was accounted for (suggesting reduced alcohol use, not depression, explains that effect) and reduced anger was not associated with AA attendance during the first year.

Socially, changes in social networks, particularly building abstinence-supportive networks, are among the most consistent mediators for the effects of TSMHO attendance and active involvement on better substance use outcomes. Explanatory models where social networks and substance use are measured concurrently have been enhanced by more recent studies showing social network changes mediate AA's benefit when the variables are time-lagged, that is where social network changes are measured after AA participation and before drinking outcomes (Bond, Kaskutas, & Weisner, 2003; Kelly et al., 2011a). These changes include both reducing pro-drinkers and increasing pro-abstainers in the social network, and AA-specific network changes appear to be particularly key. For example, among Project MATCH outpatients, attending three meetings per week versus none was associated with a 20–30% decrease in pro-drinking ties and a 15% increase in pro-abstinent ties. In turn, each pro-abstinence tie was associated with a 4% increase in abstinence days while, in contrast, each pro-drinking tie was associated with a 7% decrease in abstinence days (Kelly et al., 2011a).

While there is substantial evidence for the role of these common socio-psychological factors and processes as mediators of AA's effectiveness, support for 12-Step-specific mediators have been more mixed and studied less extensively. Although increases in subjective levels of spirituality and related constructs are often associated with AA participation, in three studies neither degree of spiritual or religious beliefs among members of 12-Step and non-12-Step MHOs (Atkins & Hawdon, 2007), purpose in life (Oakes, 2008), or having had a "spiritual awakening" (Owen et al., 2003) were significant predictors of subsequent abstinence rates. On the other hand, when a more comprehensive measure (the Religious Background and Behavior Scale) was used it was found, among those with more severe alcohol problems, that increased spirituality or religiosity did mediate AA's effects (Kelly et al., 2011b). A similar result (Tonigan, Rynes, & McCrady, 2013) was found with a separate sample using a modified version of the Religious Background and Behavior's subscale called god consciousness (meditation, thinking about God, direct experiences of God).

A further two sets of findings provide overarching conclusions from these mechanisms studies. First, in a multi-mechanism analysis that tested the effects of six purported mediators simultaneously, it was found that AA's beneficial effects on future abstinence were explained in both outpatient (less severe) and aftercare (more severe) samples through its ability to stimulate increases in pro-abstainers and decreases in pro-drinkers, as well as increases in self-efficacy to cope with high-risk social situations without drinking. Increased spirituality or religiosity was also a significant mediator, but only among the more clinically severe aftercare patients. Reduced depression and self-efficacy to cope with negative emotions were not significant mediators in either group of patients (Kelly et al., 2012).

Second, how AA and other TSMHOs work may differ across the life course. Among adolescents, for example, motivation for abstinence, but not self-efficacy or coping, mediated the effect of AA and NA participation, with active involvement a stronger predictor of increased motivation than attendance (Kelly, Myers, & Brown, 2000, 2002).

Similarly, in a study comparing adults 18–29 to those 30 and older in Project MATCH, young adults benefited as much, but in different ways, from TSMHO participation. Specifically, only reducing pro-drinkers in one's social network and increased self-efficacy to handle risky social situations mediated AA's effects in the young adult group (Hoeppner, Hoeppner, & Kelly, 2014).

Clinicians' influence on TSMHO participation

Addiction treatment providers in the US are likely to refer patients to TSMHOs, although this practice varies internationally. Also, many patients referred to TSMHOs do not attend and, like professional SUD treatment, with 50% discontinuation (Stark, 1992) and continuing care, with 75% discontinuation (McKay, 2009), many attendees ultimately discontinue TSMHO attendance (Kelly et al., 2008). However, even just one or two sessions of a well-articulated intervention to facilitate patients' TSMHO participation, through commitments to attend specific meetings, linkages with current members, and preemptively addressing barriers, can have substantial impact on ultimate participation and recovery outcomes, particularly among those with less TSMHO experience (Vederhus et al., 2014).

Twelve-Step facilitation (TSF) interventions

TSF offers manualized, replicable intervention procedures that can be delivered individually or in groups, and aims to facilitate TSMHO attendance and active involvement. TSF studies provide valuable insights into the role clinicians can play in patients' TSMHO engagement and show how TSF interventions confer benefit. Studies have shown that TSF as a stand-alone treatment can effectively increase TSMHO attendance, as well as crucial aspects of participation such as connection with a recovery-supportive social network, leading to reductions in alcohol and drug use (Project Match, 1998; Litt et al., 2009).

TSMHO and TSF integration

Empirically, TSMHO participation has been found to supplement both SUD treatment (Fiorentine & Hillhouse, 2000) and mental health services (Moos et al., 2001) in bolstering SUD remission and recovery. While critics often pit them against other evidence-based approaches such as CBT, the research suggests TSF treatments and TSMHOs can be effectively integrated with, or serve as adjuncts to, these conceptually distinct treatments.

For example, patients receiving a TSF intervention called "Making AA Easier" as an adjunct to 12-Step-based treatment-as-usual were more likely to report 30-day alcohol and drug abstinence at the 12-month follow-up than those receiving only treatment-as-usual (Kaskutas et al., 2009). Another study compared three treatments: two of these treatments were variations of TSF that consisted of two different styles of delivering TSF integrated within a CBT intervention. One was more prescriptive and directive; the other, more of a motivational interviewing client-centered style. These two TSF interventions were compared to a non-TSF evidence-based CBT-only intervention. Results showed the more directive, integrated TSF approach had superior outcomes in terms of days abstinent across 3, 6, and 12 month follow-ups compared to the other two conditions (Walitzer, Dermen, & Barrick, 2009). Also, 23% of the beneficial effects from the directive TSF approach were explained by TSMHO meeting involvement. These findings indicate that TSF interventions promote better outcomes through increased TSMHO attendance and can be effectively integrated into existing SUD treatments with ostensibly different theoretical orientations.

Anecdotally, there are several possible explanations for analogous or perhaps enhanced outcomes when approaches are integrated. First, the availability and accessibility of TSMHOs during times when relapse risk is marked and professional resources often unavailable (nights, weekends, holidays) render them valuable supplements to formal SUD and other psychiatric treatments. Second, several researchers have highlighted the conceptual overlap between TSMHOs and psychodynamic individual (increased self-awareness and social relatedness) and group therapy (via cohesiveness and instillation of hope) (e.g. Kelly, Myers Rodolico, 2008; Labbe, Slaymaker, & Kelly, 2014) as well as cognitive-behavioral therapies, challenging or modifying "stinking thinking" (Knack, 2009). In this way, TSMHOs and treatment engagement may reciprocally reinforce increased patient insight and personal growth. Third, in addition to 12-Step-specific mechanisms mobilized through Step work (e.g. increased spirituality), TSMHO participation appears to effect positive change most powerfully through facilitating adaptive social changes.

In other words, TSMHO groups appear to provide both a day-to-day relapse prevention strategy (via social support and supervision/monitoring via sponsors and other members) and a recovery-supportive milieu allowing patients to modify environmental risk through corresponding increases in pro-abstainers and decreases in pro-drinkers in their social networks. Fourth, TSMHO attendance can be conceptualized as a behavioral activation strategy or prosocial activity among behavior-focused SUD treatments, such as the Community Reinforcement Approach (Sisson & Azrin, 1989).

However, integrated interventions may not be advantageous in all cases. For example, Litt and colleagues (2009) compared a TSF-based social-network-changing intervention alone to the same intervention with contingency management added, and these were both compared to a straightforward case management condition. Over two years of follow-up the TSF intervention alone was found to increase 12-Step attendance and involvement, and led to substantially better outcomes relative to the integrated TSF/contingency management as well as to the case management conditions.

As with other treatments, the patterns of TSF impact on outcomes can be nuanced, and they may differ as a function of sample characteristics and/or change over time. For example, a TSF that was integrated with 12-Step-based treatment-as-usual for patients with cocaine and methamphetamine disorders promoted greater meeting attendance, active involvement, and better outcomes (Donovan et al., 2013). However, its beneficial effects on reduced stimulant use during the index treatment episode decayed by the first follow-up, and these muted effects persisted throughout the six-month follow-up period.

Summary and conclusions

Most modern societies provide a system of professionally delivered care intended to meet the treatment and recovery needs of those affected by addiction. In practice, however, professional treatment is often expensive and limited in quantity, scope, and duration, as well as being typically oriented toward acute stabilization following a substance-related crisis (White & McClellan, 2008). Seldom is attention paid to ensuring ongoing recovery management or to assertive linkage to systems of support that promote and manage recovery from addiction over the long-term (Kelly & White, 2011). Perhaps in tacit recognition of this somewhat disquieting reality, a variety of non-professional MHOs have emerged and proliferated over the past 80 years. MHOs generally offer no-cost opportunities for during-treatment (i.e. after-hours) as well as post-treatment support by facilitating changes in one's social network.

Research (e.g. Humphreys & Moos, 2007) has shown that these community resources can be cost-effective methods to potentiate and augment professional intervention and, for some people, may also be a sufficient substitute for professional services. It also appears that, despite the lack of professional training and contemporary scientific input, peer-led TSMHOs are able to attenuate relapse risk through successfully mobilizing the same kinds of therapeutic processes that are mobilized by formal treatments, including reducing relapse risk by facilitating (a) major changes in social networks such that exposure to alcohol- or drug-related cues is minimized, (b) the development of strategies to reinterpret and cope with stressors, and (c) increased emphasis on complete abstinence so as to avoid priming doses that might kindle craving and a return to clinically significant misuse. It does all this through facilitating social, psychological, and neurobiological changes (Kelly & Yeterian, 2013). Furthermore, the development of evidence-based TSFs provide unique opportunities to effectively help clinicians facilitate their patients' engagement in TSMHOs irrespective of their preferred clinical and theoretical skill sets.

The fact that these organizations are effective recovery management resources among participants, and are readily available free of charge and over the long term, indicates that 12-Step Mutual-Help Organizations offer great value in our overall societal approach to addiction recovery and in reducing the impact of substance-related harms.

References

Aase DM, Jason LA, & Robinson WL (2008) 12-step participation among dually-diagnosed individuals: A review of individual and contextual factors. *Clinical Psychology Review* 28(7): 1235–1248.

Alcoholics Anonymous (2014) *Estimates of AA Groups and Members as of January 1, 2014*. Available at: http://www.aa.org/assets/en_US/aa-literature/f-1-aa-at-a-glance (accessed 22/04/2015).

Atkins RG, Jr & Hawdon JE (2007) Religiosity and participation in mutual-aid support groups for addiction. *Journal of Substance Abuse Treatment* 33(3): 321–331.

Bond J, Kaskutas LA, & Weisner C (2003) The persistent influence of social networks and Alcoholics Anonymous on abstinence. *Journal of Studies on Alcohol* 64(4): 579–588.

Davidson L, Chinman M, Kloos B, Weingarten R, Stayner D, & Tebes JK (1999) Peer support among individuals with severe mental illness: A review of the evidence. *Clinical Psychology: Science and Practice* 6(2): 165–187.

Donovan DM, Daley DC, Brigham GS, Hodgkins CC, Perl HI, Garrett SB, et al. (2013) Stimulant abuser groups to engage in 12-step: A multisite trial in the National Institute on Drug Abuse Clinical Trials Network. *Journal of Substance Abuse Treatment* 44(1): 103–114.

Emrick CD, Tonigan JS, Montgomery H, & Little L (1993) Alcoholics Anonymous: What is currently known? In: McCrady BS & Miller WR (eds.) *Research on Alcoholics Anonymous: Opportunities and alternatives*. Piscataway, NJ: Rutgers Center of Alcohol Studies, 41–76.

Fiorentine R & Hillhouse MP (2000) Drug treatment and 12-step program participation: The additive effects of integrated recovery activities. *Journal of Substance Abuse Treatment* 18(1): 65–74.

Forcehimes AA & Tonigan JS (2008) Self-efficacy as a factor in abstinence from alcohol/other drug abuse: A meta-analysis. *Alcoholism Treatment Quarterly* 26(4): 480–489.

Hoeppner BB, Hoeppner SS, & Kelly JF (2014) Do young people benefit from AA as much, and in the same ways, as adults aged 30+? A moderated multiple mediation analysis. *Drug and Alcohol Dependency* 143: 181–188.

Humphreys K & Moos RH (2007) Encouraging post-treatment self-help group involvement to reduce demand for continuing care services: Two-year clinical and utilization outcomes. *Alcoholism: Clinical and Experimental Research* 31(1): 64–68.

Humphreys K, Blodgett JC, & Wagner TH (2014) Estimating the efficacy of Alcoholics Anonymous without self-selection bias: An instrumental variables re-analysis of randomized clinical trials. *Alcoholism: Clinical and Experimental Research* 38(11): 2688–2694.

Institute of Medicine (1990) *Broadening the Base of Treatment for Alcohol Problems*. Washington, DC: The National Academies Press.

Kaskutas LA, Subbaraman MS, Witbrodt J, & Zemore SE (2009) Effectiveness of making Alcoholics Anonymous easier: A group format 12-step facilitation approach. *Journal of Substance Abuse Treatment* 37: 228–239.

Kelly JF & Hoeppner BB (2013) Does Alcoholics Anonymous work differently for men and women? A moderated multiple-mediation analysis in a large clinical sample. *Drug and Alcohol Dependency* 130(1–3): 186–193.

Kelly JF & White WL (2011) Recovery management and the future of addiction treatment and recovery in the USA. In: Kelly JF & White WL (eds) *Addiction Recovery Management: Theory, research and practice*. Totowa, NJ: Humana Press, 303–316.

Kelly JF & Yeterian JD (2012) Empirical awakening: The new science on mutual help and implications for cost containment under health care reform. *Substance Abuse* 33(2): 85–91.

Kelly JF & Yeterian JD (2013) Mutual-help groups for alcohol and other substance use disorders. In: McCrady BS & Epstein EE (eds) *Addictions: A comprehensive guidebook* 2nd edn. New York: Oxford University Press.

Kelly JF, McKellar JD, & Moos R (2003) Major depression in patients with substance use disorders: Relationship to 12-Step self-help involvement and substance use outcomes. *Addiction* 98(4): 499–508.

Kelly JF, Myers MG, & Brown SA (2000) A multivariate process model of adolescent 12-Step attendance and substance use outcome following inpatient treatment. *Psychology of Addictive Behaviors* 14(4): 376–389.

Kelly JF, Myers MG, & Brown SA (2002) Do adolescents affiliate with 12-Step groups? A multivariate process model of effects. *Journal of Studies on Alcohol* 63(3): 293–304.

Kelly JF, Myers MG, & Brown SA (2005) The effects of age composition of 12-Step groups on adolescent 12-Step participation and substance use outcome. *Journal of Child & Adolescent Substance Abuse* 15(1): 63–72.

Kelly JF, Stout R, Zywiak W, & Schneider R (2006) A 3-year study of addiction mutual-help group participation following intensive outpatient treatment. *Alcoholism: Clinical and Experimental Research* 30(8): 1381–1392.

Kelly JF, Brown SA, Abrantes A, Kahler CW, & Myers M (2008) Social recovery model: An 8-year investigation of adolescent 12-step group involvement following inpatient treatment. *Alcoholism: Clinical and Experimental Research* 32: 1468–1478.

Kelly JF, Myers MG, & Rodolico J (2008) What do adolescents exposed to Alcoholics Anonymous think about 12-Step groups? *Substance Abuse* 29(2): 53–62.

Kelly JF, Stout RL, Magill M, Tonigan JS, & Pagano ME (2010a) Mechanisms of behavior change in Alcoholics Anonymous: Does Alcoholics Anonymous lead to better alcohol use outcomes by reducing depression symptoms? *Addiction* 105(4): 626–636.

Kelly JF, Stout RL, Tonigan JS, Magill M, & Pagano ME (2010b) Negative affect, relapse, and Alcoholics Anonymous (AA): Does AA work by reducing anger? *Journal of Studies on Alcohol and Drugs* 71(3): 434–444.

Kelly JF, Stout RL, Magill M, & Tonigan JS (2011a) The role of Alcoholics Anonymous in mobilizing adaptive social network changes: A prospective lagged mediational analysis. *Drug and Alcohol Dependency* 114(2–3): 119–126.

Kelly JF, Stout RL, Magill M, Tonigan JS, & Pagano ME (2011b) Spirituality in recovery: A lagged mediational analysis of Alcoholics Anonymous' principal theoretical mechanism of behavior change. *Alcoholism: Clinical and Experimental Research* 35(3): 454–463.

Kelly JF, Hoeppner B, Stout RL, & Pagano M (2012) Determining the relative importance of the mechanisms of behavior change within Alcoholics Anonymous: A multiple mediator analysis. *Addiction* 107(2): 289–299.

Kelly JF, Greene MC, & Bergman BG (2014) Do drug-dependent patients attending Alcoholics Anonymous rather than Narcotics Anonymous do as well? A prospective, lagged, matching analysis. *Alcohol and Alcoholism* 49(6): 645–653.

Knack WA (2009) Psychotherapy and Alcoholics Anonymous: An integrated approach. *Journal of Psychotherapy Integration* 19(1): 86–109.

Labbe AK, Greene C, Bergman BG, Hoeppner B, & Kelly JF (2013) The importance of age composition of 12-Step meetings as a moderating factor in the relation between young adults' 12-Step participation and abstinence. *Drug and Alcohol Dependency* 133(2): 541–547.

Labbe AK, Slaymaker V, & Kelly JF (2014) Toward enhancing 12-Step facilitation among young people: A systematic qualitative investigation of young adults' 12-Step experiences. *Substance Abuse* 35(4): 399–407.

Litt MD, Kadden RM, Kabela-Cormier E, & Petry NM (2009) Changing network support for drinking: Network support project 2-year follow-up. *Journal of Consulting and Clinical Psychology* 77(2): 229–242.

McElrath D (1997) The Minnesota Model. *Journal of Psychoactive Drugs* 29(2): 141–144.

McKay JR (2009) Continuing care research: What we've learned and where we're going. *Journal of Substance Abuse Treatment* 36(2): 131–145.

McKellar J, Stewart E, & Humphreys K (2003) Alcoholics Anonymous involvement and positive alcohol–related outcomes: Cause, consequence, or just a correlate? A prospective 2-year study of 2,319 alcohol–dependent men. *Journal of Consulting and Clinical Psychology* 71(2): 302–308.

Magura S (2008) Effectiveness of dual focus mutual aid for co-occurring substance use and mental health disorders: A review and synthesis of the "double trouble" in recovery evaluation. *Substance Use and Misuse* 43(12–13): 1904–1926.

Moos R, Schaefer J, Andrassy J, & Moos B (2001) Outpatient mental health care, self-help groups, and patients' one-year treatment outcomes. *Journal of Clinical Psychology* 57(3): 273–287.

Morgenstern J, Labouvie E, McCrady BS, Kahler CW, & Frey RM (1997) Affiliation with Alcoholics Anonymous after treatment: A study of its therapeutic effects and mechanisms of action. *Journal of Consulting and Clinical Psychology* 65(5): 768–779.

Narcotics Anonymous (2008) *Narcotics Anonymous* 6th edn. Chatsworth, CA: Narcotics Anonymous World Services.

Oakes KE (2008) Purpose in life: A mediating variable between involvement in Alcoholics Anonymous and long-term recovery. *Alcoholism Treatment Quarterly* 26(4): 450–463.

Owen PL, Slaymaker V, Tonigan JS, McCrady BS, Epstein EE, Kaskutas LA, Humphreys K, & Miller WR (2003) Participation in Alcoholics Anonymous: Intended and unintended change mechanisms. *Alcoholism: Clinical and Experimental Research* 27(3): 524–532.

Project MATCH Research Group (1998) Matching alcoholism treatments to client heterogeneity: Project MATCH three-year drinking outcomes. *Alcoholism: Clinical and Experimental Research* 22(6): 1300–1311.

SAMHSA – Substance Abuse and Mental Health Services Administration (2014) *Results from the 2013 National Survey on Drug Use and Health: Summary of National Findings*. NSDUH Series H-48, HHS Publication No. (SMA) 14-4863. Rockville, MD: Substance Abuse and Mental Health Services Administration.

Sisson RW & Azrin NH (1989) The community reinforcement approach. In: Hester RK & Miller WR (eds.) *Handbook of Alcoholism Treatment Approaches: Effective alternatives*. Elmsford, NY: Pergamon Press, 242–258.

Stark MJ (1992) Dropping out of substance abuse treatment: A clinically oriented review. *Clinical Psychology Review* 12(1): 93–116.

Timko C, Cronkite RC, McKellar J, Zemore S, & Moos RH (2013) Dually diagnosed patients' benefits of mutual-help groups and the role of social anxiety. *Journal of Substance Abuse Treatment* 44(2): 216–223.

Tonigan JS, Rynes KN, & McCrady BS (2013) Spirituality as a change mechanism in 12-Step programs: A replication, extension, and refinement. *Substance Use and Misuse* 48(12): 1161–1173.

Vederhus JK, Timko C, Kristensen Ø, Hjemdahl B, & Clausen T (2014) Motivational intervention to enhance post-detoxification 12-Step group affiliation: A randomized controlled trial. *Addiction* 109(5): 766–773.

Walitzer KS, Dermen KH, & Barrick C (2009) Facilitating involvement in Alcoholics Anonymous during out-patient treatment: A randomized clinical trial. *Addiction* 104(3): 391–401.

White WL (2014) *Slaying the Dragon: The history of addiction treatment and recovery in America* 2nd edn. Bloomington, IL: Chestnut Health Systems/Lighthouse Institute.

White WL & McClellan AT (2008) *Addiction as a Chronic Disorder*. Available at: http://californiamethadone.org/wp-content/uploads/2012/03/Addiction-as-a-Chronic-Disorder.pdf (accessed 17/12/2015).

World Health Organization (2014) *Global Status Report on Alcohol and Health – 2014*. Available at: http://apps.who.int/iris/bitstream/10665/112736/1/9789240692763_eng.pdf (accessed 20/04/2015).

Ye Y & Kaskutas LA (2009) Using propensity scores to adjust for selection bias when assessing the effectiveness of Alcoholics Anonymous in observational studies. *Drug and Alcohol Dependency* 104(1–2): 56–64.

Chapter 14

Recovery advocacy in America

William L White

The history of the addictions field in America can be seen as comprising three evolving and overlapping paradigms, with the first two preparing the way for the latter:

1 a pathology-focused paradigm
2 an intervention-focused paradigm, and
3 an emerging comprehensive recovery paradigm.

(White, 2004)

The pathology paradigm

This first paradigm was sparked in the late eighteenth century with a break from the then prevailing moral and religious frameworks for understanding and responding to chronic drunkenness. Compulsive and destructive alcohol and drug use became defined as a disease of the body and of the will, and this redefinition has been sustained, amidst considerable debate, for more than 200 years of specialized professional focus on alcohol and other drug-related (AOD) problems. An enormous body of literature exists, and continues to be generated, on the psychopharmacology and epidemiology of alcohol and drug problems, patterns of consumption, acute and chronic effects, personal and social costs, and the multiple sources of individual vulnerability. As a consequence, our knowledge of psychoactive drugs and drug addiction is impressive. And it is true that the knowledge gained within this paradigm has provided significant benefits to individuals and laid the foundation for policy, educational, and clinical responses to AOD problems.

The intervention paradigm

Attempts to resolve AOD problems by interventions at both personal and societal levels also have a long history. These attempts include addiction treatment, early intervention programs, education, and prevention efforts. In this modern era of treatment we have learned how to interrupt addiction careers. We know a lot about engagement, detoxification, problem stabilization, and recovery initiation. We know a lot about what people are like in the years before they are admitted into treatment. We know a lot about what people are like during treatment. And we know a little bit about what people are like in the months following treatment.

The knowledge and experience gained from the intervention paradigm has advanced the field and allowed hundreds of thousands of individuals to initiate and sustain recovery. At the same time it has also illuminated the limitations of our current treatment system. A study by Dennis et al. (2005), using evidence from a large and heterogeneous sample, demonstrated that both substance use and treatment careers typically continue over many years (27 and 9 years respectively) involving three to four episodes of care prior to recovery stabilization. These findings challenge models of brief treatment, short-term aftercare, and follow-up studies whose designs, until recently, extended only several months following discharge from treatment. These shortcomings have led to calls for a more recovery-sustaining model of intervention and support and more recovery-focused research and evaluation activity.

Agitation for change

While the pathology and intervention paradigms have made great contributions to the understanding and treatment of addictions, in recent years an addiction "industry" has burgeoned, so focused on understanding the pathology and its treatment that it might be characterized as viewing recovery as an afterthought. There are whole professions whose members share an extremely pessimistic view of recovery because they repeatedly see only those who fail to recover. While this characterization may seem harsh, consider also that in colleges and universities we have "addiction studies" but no "recovery studies;" we see scientific journals whose names reflect an interest in alcohol and other drugs (e.g. *Journal of Studies on Alcohol*, *Journal of Psychoactive Drugs*, *Addiction*, *Contemporary Drug Problems*), and those with an interest in professional interventions (e.g. *Journal of Substance Abuse Treatment*, *Alcoholism Treatment Quarterly*, *Addiction Science and Clinical Practice*), but we see no peer-reviewed journals focused on the scientific study of addiction recovery. We see national institutes of "alcohol abuse and alcoholism" and "drug abuse" and national centers of "substance abuse prevention" and "substance abuse treatment" but no "national institute/center of addiction recovery." We can read innumerable studies that meticulously describe who uses which psychoactive drugs and with what consequences, but see only a few recovery prevalence studies (White, 2004).

One of these recovery studies (Dawson et al., 2006) evaluated 4,422 American adults age 18 and older classified with prior-to-past year alcohol dependence, according to DSM–IV (Diagnostic and Statistical Manual of Mental Disorders, 4th Edition) criteria. They found that nearly half of these people met the criteria for full remission from their alcohol problems. Such findings as these are often overlooked or rarely acknowledged, but they confront the perception that addiction is a disease from which people do not recover (Acier, Nadeau, & Landry, 2008). In short, we see a field that knows a lot about addiction and a lot about treatment but which appears to have lost a focus on the goal and processes of long-term recovery.

Emergence of the recovery advocacy paradigm

The late 1990s saw the emergence of a new addiction recovery advocacy movement in the US. There were several reasons for this emergence at this time. In the 1970s and 1980s the rise of community-based and private addiction treatment appeared to have fulfilled many of the aspirations of recovery advocates who had encouraged and supported modern addiction treatment in America. However, there was increasing concern that the original vision of professionally guided entry into recovery had mutated into a multi-billion dollar industry that had become disengaged from grassroots communities and detached from the broader process of addiction recovery (White, 2007). Worryingly, at the same time, earlier successes in improving public perceptions and policies with regard to people with alcohol and other drug problems had deteriorated. An ill-judged "war on drugs" contributed to these people becoming restigmatized, demedicalized, and recriminalized (White & Kilbourne, 2006).

The portrayal of addiction as a medical disorder suffered by sons and daughters, mothers and fathers, and brothers and sisters was replaced by the worst racial and class stereotypes, which also linked addiction with crime, violence, and insanity. Alcoholics and addicts became not people deserving of compassion and help, but people to be feared and deserving of punishment. After decades of efforts to place alcohol and other drug problems in the medical and public health arenas, health care coverage to pay for addiction treatment was eroded and many, if not most, of the hospital treatment units in America closed. People with drug and alcohol problems began to fill the courts, jails, and prisons in unprecedented numbers. A landmark report, *Behind Bars: Substance Abuse and America's Prison Population* (Center on Addiction and Substance Abuse, 1998), revealed that four out of five of America's 1.7 million prisoners were substance-involved. And, since that time, despite growing evidence of effective strategies to reduce the prevalence and costs of substance-involved offenders, the burden of substance misuse to the nation's criminal justice system has increased. In 2005 the cost for court, incarceration, parole, and probation of adult and juvenile substance-involved offenders amounted to $74 billion. At the same time federal and state governments spent only $632 million on prevention and treatment. Of the 1.5 million inmates who met clinical diagnostic criteria for a substance use disorder in 2006, only 11.2% had received any type of professional treatment since admission. Despite the overwhelming financial and social costs of this approach to substance use in America, an updated report (Center on Addiction and Substance Abuse, 2010) indicated that, of the 2.3 million adults behind bars at that time, 1.9 million (82.6%) were substance-involved and almost two-thirds met medical criteria for an alcohol or other drug use disorder.

The rise in addiction-related stigma and the transfer of alcoholics and addicts from treatment centers to correctional centers are both deeply entwined with issues of race, gender, and social class. Between 1983 and 1997, the number of black offenders admitted to prison for drug offenses increased more than 26 times, while there was a sevenfold increase for white offenders (Pager, 2007). This was in spite of the fact that black offenders reported lower rates of drug use in the month prior to their arrest and were diagnosed with lower rates of substance use disorders than white inmates (Center on Addiction and Substance Abuse, 2010). Alleyne, in 2006, reported national statistics indicating that the number of women incarcerated had quadrupled over the previous 20 years, with 54% of the incarcerated female population being African American or Latina. Harsh drug laws, mandatory sentencing, and policing strategies focused on smaller crimes and inner city low income areas led, indirectly, to the imprisonment of large numbers of mothers, grandmothers, single breadwinners, and other women whose primary offenses prior to arrest were being poor and having a substance use problem. Once incarcerated, these women often experienced family dissolution, loss of child custody, and a severe decline in mental health. Incarceration also leaves people with a criminal record, which reduces their chances once released of obtaining gainful employment, which can lead people to resort to crime, and reinforce feelings of hopelessness to which one response is seeking an escape with alcohol and other drugs.

However, a new and increasingly powerful movement is emerging which seeks to resist the urge to punish people who have substance use problems, and at the same time shift the addiction field's kinetic ideas and slogans from the nature of the problem ("addiction is a disease") and the alleged effectiveness of its interventions ("treatment works" or "prison works") to the living proof of a permanent solution to alcohol and other drug problems ("recovery is a reality"). This movement aims to use the foundations laid from the study of the problem and its treatment to build, from a grassroots base, a fully developed nationwide recovery paradigm. This new paradigm focuses on the ecology of addiction recovery, founded on the understanding that the relationship between an individual and their social and cultural environment (their community) either promotes or inhibits the long-term resolution of severe alcohol and drug problems (White, 2009a).

A number of studies have shown that the environmental context exerts a powerful influence on drug use. Rhodes (2002) talks of both micro and macro risk environments. At a micro level, he cites environment research which has suggested the powerful influence of perceived social norms, rules, and values; the nature and structure of drug using social relationships; and the local neighbourhood and context in which substance users live. At a macro level the environmental impact includes the public and legal context, as well as economic, gender, and ethnic inequalities. Rhodes (2002) suggests shifting the unit of analysis and agent of change from the individual to the social environment. Instead of constituting individuals as solely responsible for their behaviour we need to tackle the socio-political environment in which they are situated. In a review of a range of studies as well as their own experimental work, Caprioli et al. (2007) illustrated several ways that the environment can influence the propensity to abuse drugs. Certain life experiences can make an individual more vulnerable to develop drug addiction or to relapse, whereas other types of experience may protect an individual from these risks. Environmental cues, through their association with drugs, can trigger drug-taking, even after long periods of abstinence. Also, the environment immediately surrounding drug taking can alter the subjectively rewarding effects of particular drugs and encourage greater use (Caprioli et al., 2007).

Thus, a community environment is not simply a neutral space within which the trajectories of addiction and recovery are played out, coming either to tragic or happy endings. A community is more akin to the soil in which alcohol or other drug problems develop and grow or diminish, and also within which the resolutions to such problems either thrive or fail to thrive.

Recovery capital

Recovery capital is defined as the quantity and quality of internal and external assets that can be drawn upon to initiate and sustain recovery from substance use problems (Cloud & Granfield 2008; Laudet & White, 2008). Examples of recovery capital include generally good physical and psychological health, close and supportive family and social networks, as well as educational and employment opportunities. Although substance misuse is found in all strata of society, levels of recovery capital can vary dramatically and dynamically over time, between different individuals, families, and communities. It follows that the degree to which substance use problems are experienced by people, and their ability to overcome these problems, varies widely according to their social circumstances.

Individuals with low to moderate problem severity and moderate to high recovery capital may often resolve their problems on their own, through non-professional recovery supports within their family or community, or through brief professional intervention. However, as documented above, for some people the family and community in which they live may be not only a hindrance to recovery, but an actual encouragement to alcohol or drug misuse. People in this situation, with low or negative recovery capital, who develop severe and complex problems (e.g. co-occurring substance use and mental health difficulties) can be repeatedly recycled through multiple episodes of acute biopsychosocial stabilization, and consume an inordinate quantity of treatment resources (White, 2009a).

The resolution of these severe alcohol or other drug problems can only be mediated by processes of social support, which can be particularly effective in enhancing recovery. Social support is one of the primary mechanisms of change within secular, spiritual, and religious recovery mutual aid societies such as SMART Recovery, Alcoholics Anonymous, Narcotics Anonymous, or Celebrate Recovery. However, as well as individual social support, the wider community itself needs to be targeted as part of any long-term solution to alcohol and drug problems (White, 2009a), and the ecological approach to recovery from addiction embraces strategies aimed at increasing social and cultural recovery capital at individual, local community, and national levels.

A successful transition from addiction to recovery, at an individual and community level, involves a journey from one environmental culture to another, and these different cultures comprise different values, language, symbols, roles, relationships, and rituals of daily living (White, 2008a). Those most deeply enmeshed in a culture and environment of addiction require an equal or greater level of involvement in a culture and environment of recovery to successfully escape addiction and avoid relapse. To facilitate their disengagement from one world and re-engagement with another these individuals may also need the services of a guide who is knowledgeable about both cultures. The availability of a recovery culture and cultural guides constitute a form of community recovery capital (White & Cloud, 2008).

Standing up and speaking out

It could be said that people in recovery, through their public silence, have contributed to public ignorance of, or disbelief in, recovery. For example with other health conditions, such as cancer, stigma began to diminish once a critical mass of people personally knew someone in recovery from these conditions. So this new addictions recovery advocacy movement in America was sparked once a critical mass of people in recovery from addiction felt that the guiding visions of past generations of recovery advocates had been lost and that we had a duty to stand up and speak out not just as individuals but as a community.

By speaking out, we are not referring to the kind of emotional haemophilia that is in vogue in confessional writing and television exposés. We are not talking about gushing the details of our past lives in public forums, thereby offering great drama but little in the way of personal or policy guidance. And, most importantly, we are not talking about isolated individuals doing such speaking, but about thousands of people standing in unison to speak. We are talking about the act of declaring one's status as a person in recovery in appropriate contexts and at appropriate times. We are talking about proclaiming that recovery is both possible and a living reality for millions of individuals and families. We are talking about offering living proof that people who have once been part of a problem are today part of its solution.

The new recovery advocacy movement challenges individuals and families in long-term addiction recovery to step forward, publicly announce their presence, and organize themselves as a political force. Something very magical happens when people join together as a people, a community, in recovery. This realization set the stage for a new politicized coalition of recovering people, their families, and visionary addiction treatment professionals.

During the 1990s new grassroots recovery advocacy organizations began to emerge and, at the same time, many local affiliates of the National Council on Alcoholism and Drug Dependence (NCADD), founded in 1944 by Marty

Mann, one of the first female members of Alcoholics Anonymous, sought to revive their historical mission of public education and public policy advocacy. The local grassroots recovery advocacy movement continued to expand and, in October 2001, more than 200 recovery advocates from 36 US states met under the leadership of the Alliance Project to develop a national recovery advocacy campaign which emerged as Faces and Voices of Recovery (http://www.facesandvoicesofrecovery.org/who). In September 2006, more than 40,000 individuals and 45 sponsoring organizations participated in Rally for Recovery education and celebration events. These public events have continued until the present day and in 2013 over 120,000 people turned out across the nation. At these events, people in recovery, their families, friends, and allies are encouraged to celebrate their growing visibility and to participate in civic life through education and voter registration. Events frequently combine family activities like face painting, music, and food, with advocacy activities such as opportunities to meet and speak with elected officials.

In 2011, Faces and Voices celebrated its 10th anniversary and released the first in a series of Public Policy position papers, on discrimination, criminal justice recovery advocacy, and how recovery advocates can continue to advocate for change. The recovery advocacy movement is now led at a US national level by a coalition of Faces and Voices of Recovery, the Johnson Institute, the Legal Action Center, Young People in Recovery, and NCADD. At a local level, the movement is represented by more than 125 recovery advocacy organizations and more than 8,000 self-identified core recovery advocates.

Goals of the recovery advocacy movement

The goals of the recovery advocacy movement are to:

- portray alcoholism and other drug addiction as problems for which there are viable and varied recovery solutions
- provide living role models that illustrate the diversity of recovery solutions
- counter attempts to objectify and demonize those with addiction problems
- enhance the availability, variety, and quality of local and regional treatment and recovery support services, and
- remove environmental barriers to recovery by promoting laws and social policies that reduce addiction problems and support recovery for those with these problems.

(White, 2007)

The Recovery Voices Count campaign aims to build a powerful recovery advocacy movement by supporting nonpartisan civic engagement in local, state, and national elections. The overall aim is simple: to support recovery community organizations and their communities in developing and sustaining a constituency of consequence, an organized voice of people in recovery who are educated on key issues, vote on Election Day, and hold elected officials accountable long after the polls close (see http://www.facesandvoicesofrecovery.org/action/make-recovery-voices-count).

Core values

The core values of this new generation of recovery advocacy organizations recognize:

1. the primacy of personal recovery as a platform for political advocacy
2. the need for authentic grassroots recovery representation in the development of addiction-related policies and programs
3. the importance of developing local and national recovery advocacy leadership and
4. the value of cultural diversity, including representation of diverse pathways and styles of addiction recovery.

(White, 2007)

Following from these goals and values the core messages of the movement include:

1. addiction recovery is a living reality for individuals, families, and communities (see www.recoveryiseverywhere.org)
2. there are many (religious, spiritual, secular) pathways to recovery and all are cause for celebration
3. recovery flourishes in supportive communities
4. recovery is a voluntary process, and
5. recovering and recovered people are part of the solution: recovery gives back what addiction has taken from individuals, families, and communities.

(White, 2007)

A growing number of people recovering from AOD problems are using their personal transformations as a platform to advocate social change related to the sources of, and solutions to, community-wide AOD problems. The new recovery advocacy movement in America is transforming people who have been the country's problems into instruments of social action and community service (White, 2007). There is however one crucial point to keep in mind: recovery advocacy of itself is not a personal recovery program, and it would be a mistake to believe that thrusting oneself into a high level of advocacy activities will serve as a sustaining force for personal long-term recovery from addiction (White, 2005).

Comparison with traditional recovery societies

There are crucial differences between this new recovery advocacy movement and other longer-established mutual aid and support organizations such as Alcoholics Anonymous (AA), Narcotics Anonymous (NA), or Self-Management and

Recovery Training (SMART). The latter are complementary to recovery advocacy, yet have quite distinct roles. Recovery advocacy is about giving voice to the voiceless and offering real faces as an alternative to the demonized images that have long been associated with alcohol and other drug problems. It is about building a base of power and influence for people who have been historically marginalized. It is about taking the strength of recovery communities that have long existed for mutual support and extending that power into an instrument for recovery-enhancing social change. If we think about individuals in recovery as a group with a common history, a distinct culture, and a linked destiny, then we can look beyond addiction and recovery as a personal story and begin to see a larger story of individuals becoming aware of their status as "a people" and joining together for common cause.

But, importantly, it is doing this in a way that is respectful of the autonomy and traditions of traditional recovery mutual aid fellowships. The recovery advocacy movement does not have an agenda of changing AA, NA, SMART, or other recovery mutual aid societies by involving them in political and cultural mobilization activities around the recovery issue. However, individual members from these societies are choosing, as individuals and not as representatives of such groups, to also be part of the recovery advocacy movement.

Whereas AA and other recovery mutual aid groups seek to reshape the personal story, the new recovery advocacy movement seeks to reshape the collective story. The former seeks to change the individual; the latter seeks to change the world. For example, take the issue of national or local forces that promote excessive alcohol and other drug use. These include predatory illicit drug markets, unscrupulous elements of the pharmaceutical industry, and the enormously powerful alcohol and tobacco industries. There is excessive availability of illicit drugs, unchecked and medically unwarranted medical prescribing of psychoactive drugs, and alcohol advertising aimed at young people. For recovery mutual aid fellowships such as AA or NA or SMART these are not issues to be addressed, because their focus is on initiating and sustaining recovery as a personal journey regardless of the environmental circumstances. They are not trying to change the world, only to create a way for people to recover within it. And this is understandable because recovery fellowships are at great risk of getting diverted from their primary mission when they get caught up in such controversial "outside issues" and attempt to take on the political power of the licit and illicit drug industries. For a recovery advocacy organization, however, any condition in the environment that contributes to addiction and inhibits or undermines recovery is not only relevant but a fundamental issue to be addressed.

The recovery advocacy movement is distinctive in its explicit focus on creating a public culture of recovery, and on promoting a policy environment in which addiction recovery can flourish. To that end this new movement advocates the political and cultural mobilization of communities of recovery: recovery-focused public and professional education; pro-recovery laws and social policies; a recovery-focused redesign of addiction treatment; promotion of peer-based recovery support services; support for local, state, national, and international recovery celebration events; and promotion of a recovery research agenda. This approach is based upon the understanding that AOD problems are a community problem, and the way to deal with it is to recognize this and work to improve opportunities for individuals within the community (White, Kelly, & Roth, 2012).

Core strategies

The new recovery advocacy movement has, thus far, engaged eight major strategies:

1. building strong grassroots recovery advocacy organizations and linking these into a national movement that offers opportunities for recovering people to express their collective voice and participate in community service projects
2. advocating for meaningful representation and voice at policy levels for people in recovery, and their family members, on issues that affect their lives
3. assessing needs related to the adequacy and quality of local treatment and recovery support services
4. educating the public, policymakers, and service providers about the prevalence and pathways of addiction recovery
5. expanding human and fiscal resources by encouraging philanthropic and public support for addiction treatment, recovery support services, and recovery advocacy and by cultivating volunteerism within local communities of recovery
6. creating centers that deliver non-clinical, peer-based recovery support services
7. celebrating recovery through public events (marches, rallies, concerts) that offer living testimony to the transformative power of recovery
8. supporting research that illuminates effective strategies and the processes of long-term recovery.

A paradigm shift

Evidence of a shift to a recovery paradigm includes the:

- growth and diversification of American communities of recovery
- rapidly spreading Wellbriety movement in many self-governing Native American communities throughout the United States (see www.whitebison.org)
- growth of faith-based recovery support structures, particularly within communities of color (Sanders, 2002)
- organization of recovering ex-felons into mutual support networks, (e.g. the Winners Circle)
- growth of new recovery support institutions, e.g. recovery community centers, self-managed recovery homes (see http://www.oxfordhouse.org), recovery schools (e.g. the Association of Recovery Schools), and recovery employment co-operatives (e.g. Recovery at Work in Atlanta).

The shift to the recovery paradigm is also evident at the federal level in the Access to Recovery Initiative; increased support from the National Institute on Drug Abuse (NIDA) and the National Institute on Alcohol Abuse and Alcoholism (NIAAA) for studies of long-term recovery; and the Center for Substance Abuse Treatment (CSAT) initiatives such as Recovery Community Services and Access to Recovery Programs and Recovery Month. It is evident in state initiatives pushing treatment toward a "recovery-oriented system of care" (see http://www.ct.gov/dmhas/cwp/view.asp?a=2901&q=335084). It is evident in the call from members of the research community to shift addiction treatment from serial episodes of acute intervention to models of sustained "recovery management" (McLellan et al., 2000; White, Boyle, & Loveland, 2002; White, Kurtz, & Sanders, 2006; White, 2008b). And it is evident in local experiments with peer-based models of recovery support, new recovery-focused service roles (recovery coaches, recovery support specialists), and the shift from traditional aftercare services to models of "assertive continuing care" (White & Godley, 2003; Dennis, Scott, & Funk, 2003; White, 2009b).

Recovery community organizations

Examples of grassroots developments include local and regional networks of recovery community centers. These provide the type of recovery support not available via traditional treatment or mutual help, as their focus extends beyond the individual. Recovery centers host support meetings and provide recovery coaching, but they are also linked to a wide variety of resources including recovery housing, and recovery-conducive education and employment opportunities, as well as providing a central hub for recovery-focused social networking and advocacy.

Recovery community organizations are establishing employment clearing houses and incorporating work-related support into the recovery coaching process, and two specialized employment resources are emerging. The first consists of recovery-friendly employers who have had good experiences hiring people in recovery and who remain receptive to providing employment, particularly to people in a structured recovery support process. The second comprises businesses established by people in recovery themselves who exclusively employ people in recovery. In these settings, people have the opportunity to acquire work skills, establish a recent employment history, and be supervised by other people in recovery as a step along a pathway to continued employment (White, Kelly, & Roth, 2012).

Threats to recovery advocacy

To acknowledge the achievements of the recovery advocacy movement is not to ignore significant threats, some of which are common to all social movements and some unique to the recovery advocacy movement (White, 2013).

Mobilization without mission clarity

All social movements risk mistaking methods for mission and getting frozen at an early stage of development. It is important to avoid infatuation with the growing numbers of people participating in recovery celebration events, and continually ask and answer, "Mobilization for what purpose?" Mission clarity is critical to movement maintenance.

Implosion

All social movements at both national and local levels are prone to centralized leadership, ideological closure, as well as leadership and core membership exhaustion, and these processes often spawn major schisms and mass defections. The greater the centralization of leadership, the greater is the risk of such things occurring. Strategies of leadership development, succession planning, and participatory models of decision-making are crucial preventatives and antidotes to such processes.

Colonization

All social movements risk being hijacked by more powerful forces within their environment. If the recovery advocacy movement were to morph solely into an appendage to the addiction treatment system, the movement will have failed.

Marginalization

The movement faces two major threats of marginalization into insignificance. If we cannot achieve significant influence in restructuring addiction treatment, we risk becoming disconnected from these mainstream systems. This would mean that the majority of persons seeking professional help would not have peer recovery support services integrated as part of their treatment and continuing care plans. There are also widespread initiatives to integrate addiction treatment with mental health and primary health care. There is a risk that recovery representation and core knowledge of addiction recovery could be lost within such integration initiatives, leading to a death by dilution of addiction treatment and the recovery advocacy movement. It is quite appropriate to reach out to sister movements, but great care must be taken to not lose the focus on addiction recovery.

The coming backlash

No successful social movement has avoided a cultural backlash. Such backlashes are spawned by excesses within the movement itself and by established interests who experience threat from the movement's achievements. Such backlashes are intensified when they allow full expression of dormant prejudices related to highly stigmatized issues such as addiction.

There are three potential wolves at the door seeking vulnerable points in the movement. The first is the media. The same media that extols the virtues of the newly visible recovery advocate will also lead a feeding frenzy at the first sign of fallibility. The second wolf is a sector of the addiction treatment industry. This sector includes: organizations that view addicted people as a crop to be harvested for financial profit; organizations that fear close scrutiny of addiction treatment outcomes; those that fear the demands of a mobilized recovery community; and those that fear the diminished allocation of status and resources to treatment organizations. The third wolf at the door is the grouping of the alcohol, tobacco, pharmaceutical, and illicit drug industries. Some recovery advocacy activities pose great threats to their future. Of particular concern would be: exposure of their predatory practices; support for limitations on their advertising (particularly to vulnerable populations); and support for increased taxation to offset the social costs these industries entail.

When these forces coalesce, attacks to undermine the credibility of recovery advocacy organizations and leaders could be quite personal and intense. Several steps are needed to protect our leaders and our organizations. These include:

1 rigorous adherence to best practices related to fiscal management and financial transparency
2 development of ethical guidelines and ethical decision-making models to guide recovery advocacy and peer recovery support services
3 rigorous self-evaluation and training related to how private behaviour could harm leadership and organizational credibility, and
4 making sure the "faces and voices" of this movement are diverse and constantly rotating to minimize the targeting of any core leadership.
5 Finally, when any person who has been a visible part of the movement experiences a fall from grace, whether through a recurrence of addiction or other delegitimizing behaviour, it is important that we offer that person our full support for recovery re-stabilization, as we would for all others in need.

(White, 2013)

The future of recovery advocacy

How will the transition toward a recovery-focused future differ from our past? Embracing recovery as an organizing paradigm means nesting personal recovery within the larger rubric of community recovery, and the new methods being proposed to achieve these goals constitute a revolutionary leap within the history of addiction treatment and recovery. New paradigms bring new ways of perceiving, thinking, and speaking. As we move deeper into this recovery paradigm, we will need to forge new concepts and a new language. We will need better words and concepts to:

- delineate the conceptual boundaries of recovery
- describe types of recovery, e.g. partial versus full, serial recovery, solo versus assisted, medication-assisted recovery
- evaluate recovery assets, e.g. Cloud & Granfield's (2008) concept of "recovery capital"
- chart the pathways of recovery, e.g. secular, spiritual, religious
- distinguish styles of recovery initiation, e.g. incremental versus transformational change
- depict variations in identity reconstruction, e.g. recovery-positive versus recovery-neutral identities, and
- describe variations in recovery relationships with other recovering people, e.g. acultural, bicultural, and culturally enmeshed styles (see White, 2006 for a detailed discussion of this new language).

We will all need to stretch our understanding of recovery and become multilingual as we expand the words and metaphors that reflect the growing varieties of recovery experiences in America. Only time will tell whether recovery as a new organizing paradigm will reap its potential promises or will be colonized, corrupted, and commercialized in ways that will render it one more "flavour of the month" cast into the dust bin of history. But make no mistake, the recovery movement so briefly described here does have the potential to transform addiction treatment as a system of care and to transform local community life in the US (White, 2014).

References

Acier D, Nadeau L, & Landry M (2008) Remission without treatment: a review of the literature on the problematic use of alcohol. *Annales Médico-psychologiques, revue psychiatrique* 166(9): 727–734.

Alleyne V (2006) Locked up means locked out: women, addiction and incarceration. *Women & Therapy* 29(3–4): 181–194.

American Psychiatric Association (2000) *Diagnostic and Statistical Manual of Mental Disorders: DSM-IV-TR*. Washington, DC: American Psychiatric Association.

Caprioli D, Celentano M, Paolone G, & Badiani, A (2007) Modeling the role of environment in addiction. *Progress in Neuro-Psychopharmacology and Biological Psychiatry* 31(8): 1639–1653.

Center on Addiction and Substance Abuse (1998) *Behind Bars: Substance Abuse and America's Prison Population*. New York: The National Center on Addiction and Substance Abuse, Columbia University.

Center on Addiction and Substance Abuse (2010) *Behind Bars II: Substance Abuse and America's Prison Population*. New York: The National Center on Addiction and Substance Abuse, Columbia University.

Cloud W & Granfield R (2008) Conceptualizing recovery capital: expansion of a theoretical construct. *Substance Use and Misuse* 43(12–13): 1971–1986.

Dawson DA, Grant BF, Stinson FS, Chou PS, Huang B, & Ruan WJ (2006) Recovery from DSM–IV Alcohol Dependence, United States, 2001–2002. *Alcohol Research and Health* 29(2): 131–142.

Dennis ML, Scott CK, & Funk R (2003) An experimental evaluation of recovery management checkups (RMC) for people with chronic substance use disorders. *Evaluation and Program Planning* 26(3): 339–352.

Dennis M, Scott CK, Funk R, & Foss MA (2005) The duration and correlates of addiction and treatment careers. *Journal of Substance Abuse Treatment* 28(2): S51–S62.

Laudet AB & White WL (2008) Recovery capital as prospective predictor of sustained recovery, life satisfaction, and stress among former poly-substance users. *Substance Use and Misuse* 43(1): 27–54.

McLellan, AT, Lewis DC, O'Brien CP, & Kleber HD (2000) Drug dependence, a chronic medical illness: implications for treatment, insurance, and outcomes evaluation. *Journal of the American Medical Association* 284(13): 1689–1695.

Pager D (2007) *Marked: Race, Crime, and Finding Work in an Era of Mass Incarceration*. Chicago, IL: University of Chicago Press.

Rhodes T (2002) Commentary: The "risk environment": a framework for understanding and reducing drug-related harm. *International Journal of Drug Policy* 3(2): 85–94.

Sanders M (2002) The response of African American communities to alcohol and other drug problems. *Alcoholism Treatment Quarterly* 20(3–4): 167–174.

White W (2004) Recovery: the next frontier. *Counselor* 5(1): 18–21.

White W (2005) Recovery advocacy is not a recovery program. *Recover Magazine* 5(1): 18.

White W (2006) *Let's Go Make Some History: Chronicles of the New Addiction Recovery Advocacy Movement*. Washington, DC: The Johnson Institute and Faces and Voices of Recovery, 225–288.

White W (2007) The new recovery advocacy movement in America. *Addiction* 102(5): 696–703.

White W (2008a) The culture of recovery in America: recent developments and their significance. *Counselor* 9(4): 44–51.

White W (2008b) *Recovery Management and Recovery-Oriented Systems of Care: Scientific Rationale and Promising Practices*. Pittsburgh, PA: Northeast Addiction Technology Transfer Center, Great Lakes Addiction Technology Transfer Center, Philadelphia Department of Behavioral Health & Mental Retardation Services.

White WL (2009a) The mobilization of community resources to support long-term addiction recovery. *Journal of Substance Abuse Treatment* 36(2): 146–158.

White W (2009b) *Peer-based Addiction Recovery Support: History, Theory, Practice, and Scientific Evaluation*. Chicago, IL: Great Lakes Addiction Technology Transfer Center and Philadelphia Department of Behavioral Health and Mental Retardation Services.

White WL (2013) *State of the New Recovery Advocacy Movement: Amplification of Remarks to the Association of Recovery Community Organizations at Faces and Voices of Recovery Executive Directors Leadership Academy, Dallas, Texas, November 15, 2013*. Available at: www.williamwhitepapers.com (accessed 01/04/2015).

White W (2014) Tribute to the "recovery movement." *ATTC Messenger*. Available at: http://www.attcnetwork.org/find/news/attcnews/epubs/addmsg/September2014article.asp (accessed 01/04/2015).

White W & Cloud W (2008) Recovery capital: a primer for addictions professionals. *Counselor* 9(5): 22–27.

White W & Godley M (2003) The history and future of "aftercare." *Counselor* 4(1): 19–21.

White W & Kilbourne J (2006) American women and addiction: a cultural double bind. *Counselor* 7(3): 46–51.

White W, Boyle M, & Loveland D (2002) Addiction as chronic disease: from rhetoric to clinical application. *Alcoholism Treatment Quarterly* 20(3–4): 107–130.

White WL, Kurtz E, & Sanders M (2006) *Recovery Management.* Chicago, IL: Great Lakes Addiction Technology Transfer Center, University of Illinois.

White WL, Kelly JF, & Roth JD (2012) New addiction-recovery support institutions: mobilizing support beyond professional addiction treatment and recovery mutual aid. *Journal of Groups in Addiction & Recovery* 7(2–4): 297–317.

Part VI

An integrated approach to addiction

Chapter 15

Action on Addiction

The charity

Nick Barton

A brief history

The charity Action on Addiction is the product of a merger in 2007 of three other charities: Clouds, the Chemical Dependency Centre and the former Action on Addiction. The first two were largely service providers, with one (Clouds) also having an academically linked professional training arm, while the third, from which the new entity took the name, was essentially a fundraising charity to support research commissioned from the National Addiction Centre, Institute of Psychiatry, London, of which it was a co-founder. While there was a clear pragmatic rationale for this integration, the new charity began its life as a collection of services, programmes and initiatives that were for the most part aimed at facilitating recovery from addiction, without perhaps a clearly delineated role beyond that. It may have struggled to answer simply and clearly the questions: What is this charity about? What does it exist to achieve? If it did have answers they would have been provided in relation to specific objectives such as treatment and rehabilitation, support for families and children, professional education, prevention, research and advocacy, rather than as regards the charity as a whole.

With post-merger integration, a coherent and unifying purpose began to emerge which fused the constituent parts and which can now be said to drive Action on Addiction's strategic direction. The charity's vision is of a future in which people are free from addiction and its effects; and its mission and purpose is stated in these terms: 'Action on Addiction works to find ever more effective ways of disarming addiction in individuals, families, communities and society as a whole.' But that does not of course tell you what action is taken or why this approach, in particular, has been chosen.

There are many charities working 'in' addiction but perhaps only Action on Addiction is making an attempt to work 'on' addiction. There is a story to tell about how this charity moved from enacting a role in line with the first preposition to one that has come to encompass and very deliberately to embrace the second. Action on Addiction has superseded 'a variety of actions on addiction'. But what is the distinction? Rather than limiting ourselves to addressing addiction only as it manifests in the people we actually see, the name implies we are taking on the condition as a whole in the same way that charities in other fields take on cancer, heart disease, dementia or Parkinson's. If we consider the damage wrought upon individuals, families, communities and society as a whole by addiction, it seems to us that the field requires a charity of comparable authority and purpose to those interceding with other major societal threats.

Before settling into a discussion about the action undertaken, it is important to consider what it is we are taking action on; that is to say, addiction. It would be odd indeed for the charity to take action on addiction without having arrived at some understanding of what addiction is. How else could it position itself to mount an effective challenge? How could it give focus to the cause?

Characterizing addiction

There is still considerable disagreement about what constitutes addiction, whether it can be defined once and for all, and if so how. There are myriad theories and concepts and as many beliefs and ideologies. There are different sets of criteria, and discussion continues to this day as to precisely what symptoms are required for a formal diagnosis. The debate will no doubt continue. In the meantime we need something to work with and something which is accessible to the diverse demography of our beneficiaries as well as to other interested parties.

At Action on Addiction we wanted to arrive at a way of describing addiction that could be easily understood by lay person and professional alike. After much discussion we have settled on a characterization of addiction, rather than a definition. In our view, addiction may best be understood as: an all-consuming relationship with a substance or behaviour. This is driven by a conscious or unconscious urge to change the way a person feels, which becomes self-perpetuating, and in the process results in a range of harmful consequences.

The word relationship is essential to the accessibility of the concept. Everyone has experience of a relationship of some sort and no doubt of varying quality. Everyone also has some experience of doing something or using an external agent to change the way they feel. Furthermore, we are all consumers in one way or another. Describing addiction as all-consuming conveys the totally voracious nature, dynamic and consequences of this relationship. As the addicted consumer consumes he/she is consumed, as are those around him/her also.

For us to shape a meaningful or effective approach to disarming this most destructive condition, we need to keep that characterization in mind. At Action on Addiction we use the word 'disarm' because we do not believe addiction is something that can be bludgeoned into extinction or that any of the other usual metaphors generally drawn from warfare which have been adopted by various causes are at all useful. The 'war on drugs' is a case in point. The word disarm references the inherent subtleties of martial arts, which has more to do with defusing aggressive power, deflecting it, undermining it, turning it back on itself, rather than a violent attack. We want to think more about slipping the hold of addiction and building resistance to it, rather than engaging in an unwinnable battle. The first step is to understand its power and how it operates.

In casting about for helpful analogies, the word resistance called to mind the response of an immune system to a virus. It is in the very nature of a virus to seek eternal life and to grow stronger and ever more able to resist threats to its existence. Although, as far as I know, addiction is not a virus in a biological sense it nonetheless appears to behave like one in the way, unbeknownst to its potential hosts, it takes advantage of impaired psycho-emotional immune systems. It does so in ways that are not always clear and certainly not recognized as such when addiction begins to intrude. Lack of conscious awareness certainly plays a part. We may not realize that our immune systems are not functioning as well as they should be until we have become sick. This is as true for the common cold as it is for addiction. This analogy is important because it suggests we might be able to find ways to build immunity, offering a whole new perspective to the business of prevention.

Contrasting cultures of addiction and recovery

The question of culture is important to any organization and generally has something to do with its success or failure. Organizational culture was once summed up in the neat colloquialism: 'the way we do things around here'. Addiction also has a culture all of its own. The essence of this culture is a set of corrupt values such as dependence, deceit, false promises, delusion, dishonesty, narcissism, selfishness, impatience, betrayal, paranoia, seduction, control, manipulation, grandiosity, blame, dissatisfaction, discontent, fear and loathing and destruction. The culture of recovery is, in complete contrast, a culture of honesty, altruism, trust, responsibility, patience, acceptance, humility, openness, courage and creativity.

An organization setting itself to disarm addiction must recognize the corrosive values of addiction for what they are. It must work to grow and sustain an organizational culture that lives by values aligned to those of recovery or wellbeing in order to protect itself from insidious attack from within that will undermine its mission at every possible opportunity. Addiction can become reflected in the way the organization operates. For instance, addicted people tend to invite others to treat them badly, so confirming their low opinion of themselves. An organization that understands how addiction operates in this way will resist this counterproductive invitation and treat addicted people and their families with dignity and respect while offering them services of evident and even, one might say, surprising quality.

Integrated approaches

From its launch, Action on Addiction has taken a dual approach, direct and indirect, to disarming addiction. Under the direct approach we work with and for our beneficiaries 'on the front line' (an unfortunate phrase in that it once again conjures

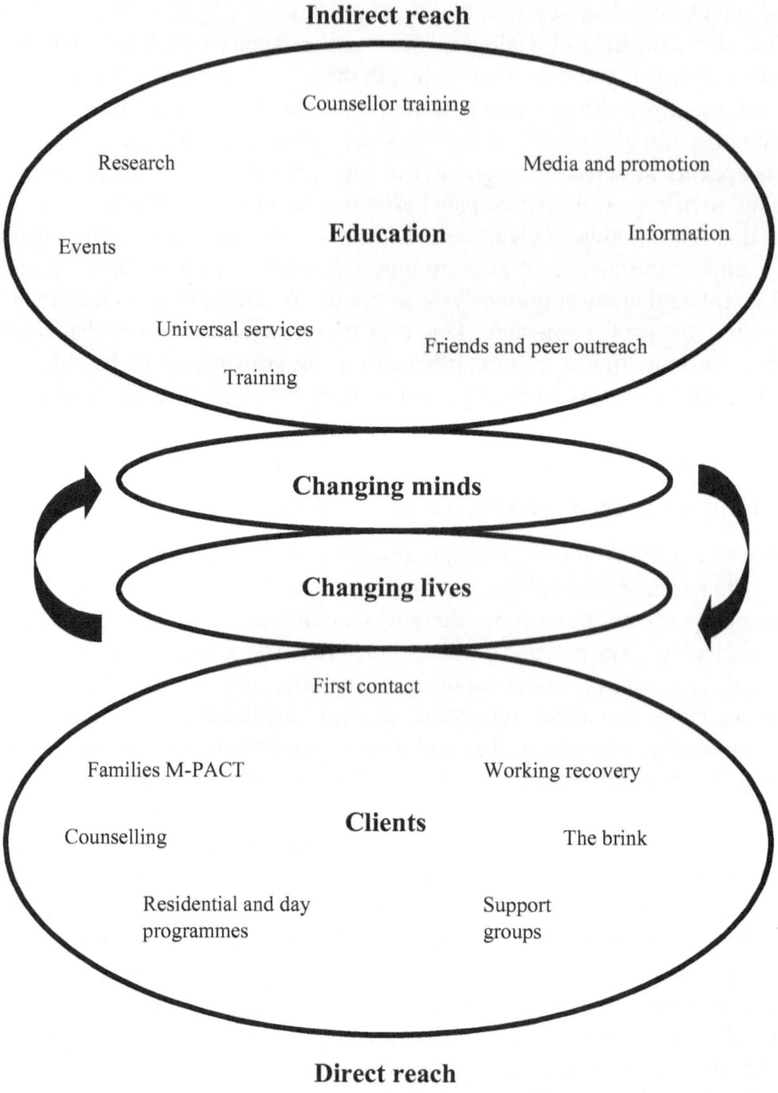

Figure 15.1 Action on Addiction: integrated approaches

up images of warfare). We see people who cross a threshold and we interact with them at a personal level in providing them a service. This may also bring benefit to others within their social sphere. Also, by training professionals to a higher standard than ever before, by commissioning research and by engaging in advocacy on behalf of our beneficiaries, we may affect the lives of a great many people whom we never meet in person.

This dual and interrelated approach has been summed up as 'changing minds' and 'changing lives'. If you succeed in one, you also help achieve the other. A person who secures recovery, for instance, may persuade sceptical observers that addicted people are not a hopeless cause and give hope to other people struggling with addiction that recovery is possible. This could be just the encouragement they need to seek help. A research project might discover a better way to help people at risk of relapse. Such an important finding could then be disseminated far and wide across the treatment field and find its way into the improvement of practice and service delivery. An individual on one of our professional education courses may well go on to enjoy a career over several decades, during which he/she will affect the lives not only of clients in their care but work colleagues and the organizations for which they go on to work. The members of families who attend an M-PACT programme may, on returning to the family home, bring with them a new approach to family life that benefits those who did not attend the programme as much as those who did. A campaign to challenge stigma may result in a better public understanding, which may in turn result in increased support for services to help people affected by addiction.

The values of Action on Addiction

Action on Addiction's stated values, which are constantly kept under review, are:

Commitment

Our commitment to our beneficiaries is at the heart of all we do and how we do it. It would be surprising if such commitment were not a given and it is easy to pay lip service but it has to be real. People unfamiliar with the organization have to see and feel this from their first contact.

Independence

We need to be free to do what is needed rather than being hidebound by controlling interests that conflict with those of our beneficiaries.

Optimism

Contrary to the oft used judgement that refers dismissively to the 'hopeless addict', change, indeed transformation, is possible, and potential can be realized. The despair of families can turn to real hope.

Art

Addiction is destructive. Recovery is necessarily creative. Disarming addiction requires imaginative responses.

Science

Disciplined in the acquisition and application of knowledge, we must build the bridge between belief and evidence to avoid wasting time and effort on activities that do not make any discernible positive difference.

Compassion

As a result of pervasive stigma, our beneficiaries commonly experience a range of attitudes from indifference to outright hostility, sometimes from the very people supposed to be caring for them. It is our job to foster empathy, and we constantly reinforce the belief that our beneficiaries are deserving.

Excellence

Always learning, always aiming to improve, and so becoming a dynamic resource to effect progress. Developing expertise will help all beneficiaries as will defining quality, not only in words but in practice. It means becoming a catalyst for change.

Obstacles to success

In reflecting upon where the field is and where it needs to be as regards progress in our mission to disarm addiction, we have identified the following obstacles:

- stigma and associated lack of public and professional understanding of addiction
- a weak evidence base and the lack of research into change processes
- best practice that is ill-defined, if at all
- interventions where available evidence is not applied
- an inadequately trained and supervised workforce
- insufficient focus on effective prevention
- systems and cultures that work against quality and effectiveness
- non-systemic approaches with a self-limiting focus on individuals.

If we successfully take up the challenge to remove these obstacles, Action on Addiction may claim to have made a major contribution to transforming the UK's response to addiction.

Many other charities provide services to individuals and, to a lesser extent, to families affected by addiction. Clearly, like Action on Addiction, they are committed to helping our shared beneficiaries and of course many do so more or less effectively. However, I think we all need to ask of ourselves the questions: What does our work add to the sum total of our knowledge and understanding of addiction? What contribution are we making to the improvement of the overall response to the condition, to advances in the field?

It appears to be particularly difficult for charities that are almost entirely funded by the state through local contracts to make such a contribution. Their lack of independence must hold them back to a degree as they concentrate almost exclusively on fulfilling the terms of the contract with the Local Authority or the National Health Service. While at Action on Addiction we recognize this as an entirely legitimate endeavour and much good may come from it, we are keen to do more and feel sure that, if we do not, addiction is likely to continue to thrive. Progress towards disarming it will be seriously limited.

Over the last couple of decades, many charities have become more and more like businesses. While there is undoubted value in drawing on business disciplines to serve the charitable purpose, such as the efficient marshalling and application of resources, we have been concerned that, in some organizations, commercial imperatives have come steadily to supersede charitable ones. All too often, it seems the beneficiaries are relegated to the role of mere commodities in the transactions of the marketplace. When charity chief executives talk more animatedly about turnover than they do of the improvements they are making to the lives of those people that their organizations were set up to serve, we should be concerned. At Action on Addiction we are absolutely clear that our bottom line is benefit, not profit. That does not prevent us from realizing that with some profit we might be able to achieve more benefit and that to do any good at all we have to be viable financially. When we are asked to identify the charity's competitors we are apt to respond that we have only one competitor and that is addiction. That is not to say that we will not compete where we feel we might be able to serve beneficiaries better than another organization in some respect.

The way forward

We want our staff to think as well as do; to learn as well as practice. While they are helping one person, we want them to consider what is being learned that might improve help provided to others, whether by us or some other organization. We were taken with the ambition of Joseph A. Califano, founder of CASA, the National Center on Addiction and Substance Abuse at Columbia University, USA, who said his objective has been '. . . to give this nation an asset with the independence to seek practical, effective ways to combat substance abuse and addiction, independent of any ideological commitment, preconception or prejudice . . . '(Califano, 2012: 2). Our aim is to develop Action on Addiction into such a national asset for the UK: a force not just for good but for better.

References

Califano JA (2012) *CASA 2011 Annual Report. Addiction: A Preventable and Treatable Disease*. National Center on Addiction and Substance Abuse at Columbia University. New York: Columbia University. Available at: http://www.casacolumbia.org/sites/default/files/files/2011-annual-report.pdf (accessed 17/04/2015).

Index